Presented to _____ Ashley Elizabeth George _____

Date _____ 10 July, in the year of our Lord 1998 _____

Occasion _____ Your Sixth Birthday _____

With Love From _____ Your Daddy! _____

2'd July, in the year of our Lord 1998

The Bible in Pictures for Little Eyes

by

KENNETH N. TAYLOR

MOODY PRESS · CHICAGO

ISBN: 0-8024-0595-9

Books by Kenneth N. Taylor

THE BIBLE IN PICTURES FOR LITTLE EYES

DEVOTIONS FOR THE CHILDREN'S HOUR

STORIES FOR THE CHILDREN'S HOUR

LIVING BIBLE *(Tyndale House Publishers)*

49 50

Printed in the United States of America

EVEN LITTLE CHILDREN can understand great truths when told to them in simple words. And when pictures are added, doubly indelible impressions are made that can last forever.

No other book has changed so many lives so remarkably as the Bible. God's Word can be a source of light to childhood's earliest pathways if carefully presented. It can be a Rock to build a life on, even when that life is very small. "Give us a child until he is five years old," some say, "and his character will be formed forever."

It is incredibly important to begin *direct* Bible training at the earliest possible age, in addition to the influences surrounding the child from earliest days in a Christ-honoring home. This book can be read to children of approximate ages 3½ to 6 with great profit. Children of that age can understand with simple trust the great doctrines of God and His dealings with mankind. With simple trust they can accept and always believe what hardened, older minds find difficult.

It is the hope of author and publisher that this book will be a means of establishing little minds in truths from which nothing that will ever happen in the years ahead can shake them, because their trust will be in the Living God and in His Son, Jesus Christ our Lord.

WHEN IT IS NIGHTTIME and the lights are out you know how dark everything gets. You can't see anything. That is how all the world once was. There were no pretty flowers; there were no trees or grass or birds. There were no children either. There was only darkness. God did not want everything to be all dark. He decided to make some people. People could not live in the darkness so God made a beautiful world full of light.

QUESTIONS:

1. *Can you see anything at night when you go to bed and the lights are out?*
2. *Did God want everything to be all dark?*

Genesis 1:2-5

7

THIS IS THE BEAUTIFUL WORLD God made. How different it is from the cold, dark picture we looked at before! Now the world is warm and bright and pleasant. The animals are playing and everyone is happy. God has made all these things and all of them are very good but there are no people anywhere. God has not made any people. All the pretty things are here but there are no people to enjoy them, so God will make some people to live here.

QUESTIONS:

1. *Can you see a lion in this picture?*
2. *Can you see any people?*
3. *Did God decide to make some people?*

Genesis 1:

THESE ARE THE PEOPLE God made. Can you see them in the picture? They are behind the flowers in the middle of the picture. Can you point to them? The man's name is Adam. The lady's name is Eve. Adam and Eve did not have a mother and father. God made Adam out of dust from the ground, and then He made Eve. God made them alive and happy and good. They love God and God loves them. In the picture you see them looking up toward God. No wonder they are so happy.

QUESTIONS:

1. *What is the man's name?*
2. *What is the lady's name?*
3. *Did Adam and Eve have a mother and father?*
4. *Who made Adam and Eve?*

Genesis 2:7-9

9

DAM AND EVE are not happy now. Do you know why they are so sad? It is because they have been bad. They did something God told them not to do. God told them they could eat anything except the fruit from one tree. God told them not to eat that one kind but they could eat all the other kinds. The tree was so pretty and the fruit on it looked so nice that Eve wanted to eat it, but God said, "No." Then Satan, who is God's enemy, told Eve to eat it even if God said not to. Eve took the fruit and ate some of it; then she gave some to Adam and he ate it too. Now God is punishing Adam and Eve. He is sending them out of the beautiful garden and they can never come back again.

QUESTIONS:

1. *Who are these two people?*
2. *Where are they going?*
3. *Why can't they stay in the garden?*

Genesis 3:8-13

10

HESE TWO MEN are Adam and Eve's children. See how big and strong they are! Once they were little children but now they have grown up. Do you see the one with the lamb? His name is Abel. It seems God had told them both to bring lambs to give to God, but only Abel is bringing a lamb. Can you see what his brother is bringing? Is he bringing a lamb? Is he obeying God? No, he is not. He is bringing some things from the garden instead of bringing a lamb. This bad brother's name is Cain. Cain got angry with Abel because Abel did what God said and brought God a lamb. And then, do you know what Cain did? He hit his brother Abel and hurt him so much that Abel died. God will punish Cain for killing Abel. Cain killed his brother Abel because he was angry at God. What a terrible thing to do!

QUESTIONS:

1. *Which of these two men is Abel?*
2. *Which is Cain?*
3. *What did God probably say to bring?*
4. *Point to the one who is obeying God.*

11 Genesis 4:8-13

THIS MAN'S NAME is Noah. Can you say his name? I am glad to say that this man loves God very much. He wants to do whatever God tells him to do. He is a good man. God has told him to build a big boat. It is so big that it takes him a long, long time to build it. Can you see the big boat he is building? See how hard he and his sons are working! They are working so hard because God has told him to build the boat and he is happy to do whatever God says. Do you know why God wants Noah to have a boat? It is because God is going to send so much water that all the ground and the houses will be covered, and if he does not have a boat he will die. The waters would go over his head and he would drown, but if he is in the boat he will be safe and dry. God is going to take care of Noah and his family and keep them safe and dry.

QUESTIONS:

1. *What is this man's name?*
2. *What is he doing?*
3. *Why is he building the big boat?*

Genesis 6:13-22

12

T LAST NOAH'S BOAT is all finished. Can you see the boat in the picture? It is away in the back, over by the sun. See how nice the boat looks! Now it is time for Noah and his family to go into the boat. God tells Noah to take a mother and daddy lion with him into the boat. He tells him to take a mother and daddy bear too. A mother and daddy of every kind of animal are going into the boat because that is what God said. In the picture you can see all the animals going into the boat. Maybe all the other people laughed at Noah for believing that God would make it rain so hard, but Noah didn't care. He believed God and got into the boat. Then God sent the rain.

QUESTIONS:

1. *Where are all the animals going?*
2. *Who told the animals to get into the boat?*
3. *Why did God want the animals in the boat?*

Genesis 7:6-17

13

FTER NOAH AND HIS FAMILY and the animal all went into the boat, God sent the rain It rained and rained, all day and all night and for many days and nights. Down and down the rain came until all the flowers and bushes were covered up with water; soon all the houses and trees and people were covered up with the water too. Noah and his family are safe in the boat where God is taking care o them. The animals are safe too. The bird you can see in the picture is a dove that was inside the boat. Noah let in go out to see if it could find a home, but now it is coming back to the boat because of the water.

QUESTIONS:

1. Where are the flowers and houses?
2. Where are Noah and his family?
3. Where are all the other people in the world?

Genesis 8:8,

OW HAPPY NOAH and his family are! They are not in the boat anymore. Now at last the water has all gone away and the ground is dry again. Now Noah and his family have come out of the boat onto the dry land. They can see the grass again and the flowers and trees. Now the little animals can run and play. Can you see what Noah is doing? He is praying to God. God is glad because Noah is praying. God says He will never again punish bad people by sending water over all the world. God put a rainbow in the clouds because of His promise. Do you see the rainbow in the picture? Have you ever seen a rainbow outside your house? Whenever you see a rainbow, remember God is telling you that He loves you.

QUESTIONS:

1. *Who are these people?*
2. *What are they doing?*
3. *What is that up there in the sky?*

Genesis 8:13-22; 9:8-17

15

O YOU SEE the high building the men are making? Why are they making this high building? They are making it because they do not like God. They want to make a high building to prove that they are very great. They think that they are greater than God! God does not like this. He will not let them make the building. He will make them talk so funny that they cannot understand each other. They will not be able to tell what their friends are saying. Then they will stop building the tall tower because they cannot talk to each other and cannot tell each other how to help. This building is called the Tower of Babel.

QUESTIONS:

1. *What are the people building?*
2. *Why are they building it?*
3. *What will God do?*

Genesis 11:1-9

16

ERE IS A PICTURE of a very important man. His name is Abram. Sometimes he is called Abraham. Abraham is a very good friend of God. God loves him and he loves God. God told him to take a long, long trip, to go far, far away and live there the rest of his life with his wife and his helpers and his camels and his sheep and his cows. Abraham said, "Yes," to God. He told God he would go wherever God wanted him to. Abraham loves God. He is God's friend.

QUESTIONS:

1. *What is this man's name?*
2. *What did God tell him to do?*
3. *Did he do what God said?*

Genesis 12:1-9

BRAHAM IS TALKING to his friend whose name is Lot. They are talking about where to live. Abraham has many sheep and so does Lot. Sheep eat grass for their breakfast and lunch and supper. There is not enough grass here for Abraham's sheep and Lot's sheep too. Abraham is saying to Lot, "There isn't enough grass here for all our sheep. Only one of us should live here. One of us should go somewhere else to live where there is more grass. You go where you want to live and I'll take my sheep and live somewhere else." Lot is telling Abraham that he wants to live where the grass is long and green and best, so that his sheep will have plenty to eat. He wants the best grass. Lot is being selfish. He wants the best things for himself. After Lot has taken his sheep and gone away, God will give the best land to Abraham. Abraham isn't selfish, so God will give him the best.

QUESTIONS:

1. *Who are these two men?*
2. *What are they talking about?*
3. *What will they decide?*
4. *What will God tell Abraham?*

18   Genesis 13:5-18

BRAHAM IS SAD. He is sad because he has no children. He needs a little boy. He talked to God about this. He asked God to give him a son. God tells Abraham to come outside with Him and look up into the sky at night and count the stars. But Abraham can't count them. There are too many to count. God says, "Abraham, I am going to give you a little boy and when he grows up he will have children and pretty soon there will be so many children that you won't be able to count them. You can't count the stars and you won't be able to count all the children and their children that I will give you." Now Abraham is happy because God will give him a little baby boy. God is glad because Abraham believed Him. Abraham knows that God will not fool him. He knows God will do just what He says.

QUESTIONS:

1. *What is Abraham looking at?*
2. *How many children did God say He would give Abraham?*
3. *Does Abraham believe God?*

Genesis 15:1-7

19

BRAHAM HAS BECOME very old. See how old he is! Sarah, his wife, is old too. They are too old to have a baby. But God promised that He would give them a little boy. Three men have come to visit Abraham. Can you see them in the picture? When Abraham saw the three men he ran to meet them even though he was so old and the afternoon was so hot. Abraham knew that the three men had come to visit him from Heaven. He asked them to come and eat with him and they did. They had a picnic under the trees. These men told Abraham that Sarah his wife was going to have a little baby. Sarah is laughing because she does not believe that God can give her a baby. But God will do just what He said. Soon God will give a baby boy to Abraham and Sarah. How happy they will be then! The baby's name will be Isaac.

QUESTIONS:

1. *Where did these three men come from?*
2. *What did the three men tell Abraham?*
3. *Why is Sarah laughing?*

Genesis 18:1-15

20

OD GAVE ABRAHAM a little baby boy just as He promised. Now in this picture you can see that the baby has grown to be a big boy. He is with his father Abraham and his father is very sorry. Do you know why the father is sad? I will tell you why. It is because God has told Abraham to bring Isaac here and to kill him. God wants to know if Abraham loves God best or loves his boy best. Abraham loves his boy very, very much, but of course he loves God the very best of all. Soon Abraham will take out his knife to kill his dear son. Then suddenly God will call to Abraham and say, "Stop, Abraham, stop! Don't do that. Don't hurt him. Look behind you!" Abraham will look and see a lamb caught in some bushes. "Kill the lamb," God will say. "Don't kill your son. I know now that you love Me." The lamb will die so that Abraham's big boy can come home again with his father. Now the father is glad.

QUESTIONS:

1. *What did God tell Abraham to do?*
2. *Why did God say this?*
3. *Who did Abraham love most, God or his dear boy?*
4. *Whom do you love best?*

Genesis 22:1-13

21

D O YOU SEE the man talking to the nice lady? Do you know what they are talking about? The man is asking the lady where her father is. He wants to talk with her father. The man has come a long way. He lives with Abraham in another country. Abraham told him to go and find a wife for his son Isaac. The man asked God to help him find the right lady. This is the lady God will give to Isaac to be his wife. The man will ask the lady and her father if she will be Isaac's wife and they will say yes. The lady's name is Rebekah. She will be Isaac's wife.

QUESTIONS:

1. *What is the man talking to the lady about?*
2. *Who sent the man to talk to the lady?*
3. *Will the lady go with him to be Isaac's wife?*

Genesis 24:10-26

HIS IS THE GIRL who said she would be Isaac's wife. Her name is Rebekah. You can see Isaac running toward her. She has come on the camels for a long, long way to be his wife. She has never seen Isaac before, and Isaac has never seen Rebekah before. They are happy because God has given them to each other. Soon God will give them two babies. They will have twins, named Jacob and Esau.

QUESTIONS:

1. *What is this girl's name?*
2. *Who is running toward her?*
3. *What will their children be named?*

Genesis 24:63-67

23

OW ISAAC HAS BECOME very old, and soo
he will die. His two baby boys hav
grown up now and one of them is knee
ing down in front of him. It is Jacob wh
is kneeling there. Jacob is not a baby now—he has b
come a big man and his father is very old. Jacob is tellin
his father a lie. His father cannot see very well becau
he is so old. He thinks it is his other boy who is kneelin
there. He does not know that it is Jacob. The fath
wants to give some nice things to his other boy, an
Jacob says that he is the other boy; so now the father w
give the nice things to Jacob. Jacob wants nice things.
will make his father very sad when he learns Jacob lied
him.

QUESTIONS:

1. *What is Jacob telling his father?*
2. *Why does Jacob tell a lie?*
3. *Who does the father think is kneeling there.*

NOW JACOB IS TAKING a long walk to another country. His father has told him to go there to find the girl who will marry him. Jacob is tired and is lying down to sleep because it is night. He is having a dream. Have you ever had a dream? Jacob dreams that he sees stairs or a ladder that is so high that it goes right up into the sky. Angels are going up and down the ladder. Then in his dream Jacob will see God standing at the top of the ladder and telling him that many wonderful things will happen to him because God loves him.

QUESTIONS:

1. *What is Jacob doing?*
2. *Where is he going?*
3. *What is his dream?*

Genesis 28:10-16

ACOB IS NOW a long, long way from home. He is in another country. He is helping a girl whose name is Rachel. She is taking care of her father's sheep. While he is talking, Jacob finds out that the girl is a friend. She invites him to come to her house. Her father will be glad to see Jacob. He will let Jacob and Rachel get married. Jacob will live in that country with Rachel. He will not go home to his father for a long time.

QUESTIONS:

1. *What is this girl's name?*
2. *Who is she talking to?*

Genesis 29:1-12

26

ACOB IS WRESTLING with an angel, but they are not trying to hurt each other. Jacob wants to win so that the angel will give him many nice things. The angel touches Jacob's leg so that he cannot use it very much, but Jacob will not stop wrestling. The angel wants to stop but Jacob won't let him. Jacob is saying, "I will not let you go unless you bless me." Then the angel says he will give him many wonderful things. Afterward Jacob knows that the angel is God.

QUESTIONS:

1. *Whom is Jacob wrestling with?*
2. *What does Jacob want?*

Genesis 32:24-30

27

OD TOLD JACOB to move to another house with his wives and children. God told Jacob to go home to his father and visit him. Here you can see them taking a long trip to their new home. The children will be glad to see their grandfather. In this picture you can see their father Jacob talking to their uncle Esau. Their father is afraid of Uncle Esau, but Uncle Esau is kissing him. A long time ago their father had been bad and had stolen something from Uncle Esau. They thought their uncle might try to hurt them because their father had done this. But their uncle is very kind. In the picture you can see him hugging their father.

QUESTIONS:

1. *Are Jacob and Esau fighting?*
2. *Why is Jacob afraid of Esau?*
3. *Where are the children going?*

Genesis 33:1-9

28

THIS BOY WITH THE PRETTY COAT is Joseph. He is talking to his father, Jacob. Jacob loves Joseph very much. Joseph is seventeen years old and is helping to take care of the sheep. His father has given him the pretty coat as a special present because he loves him so much. The little boy is Joseph's brother. His name is Benjamin.

QUESTIONS:

1. *What is the boy's name who has the pretty coat?*
2. *Who gave him the coat?*
3. *Who is the little boy?*

Genesis 37:3

OSEPH IS GOING for a long walk to find hi brothers and the sheep. His father is ask ing him to go and find them. Joseph i glad to help. He is telling his father "Good-by." He will find the brothers and the sheep. Bu the brothers aren't nice. They don't like Joseph becaus their father gave Joseph the nice coat. They are angry a Joseph. They will try to hurt him. Isn't that too bad?

QUESTIONS:

1. *Who is Joseph talking to?*
2. *What does his father want Joseph to do?*
3. *Will Joseph's brothers be glad to see him?*

Genesis 37:13-2

30

OSEPH HAS FOUND his brothers. But what is happening to him? Can you see him in the picture? He is the one without a shirt. Two men are taking him away. His bad brothers are selling him. Do you see the man paying money to one of the brothers? The man is buying Joseph. The cruel brothers are happy because they do not like Joseph. Now Joseph will be taken far away to another country. He can't go home to his dear father any more because his brothers have sold him and the men who bought him are taking him away. But God is with Joseph and it will be all right.

QUESTIONS:

1. *Which one in the picture is Joseph?*
2. *Where are they taking him?*
3. *Why is the man giving money to Joseph's brothers?*

Genesis 37:28-36

OSEPH IS IN ANOTHER COUNTRY far awa[y] from his home. But God is there with hi[m] and everybody likes Joseph very much He works hard and he always does what ever is right. The man Joseph works for likes him a lo[t] He has made Joseph his most important helper. In thi[s] picture you can see Joseph telling the other men what t[o] do.

QUESTIONS:

1. *Is Joseph at his own house?*
2. *Does everybody like Joseph?*
3. *What is Joseph doing?*

Genesis 39:1-

32

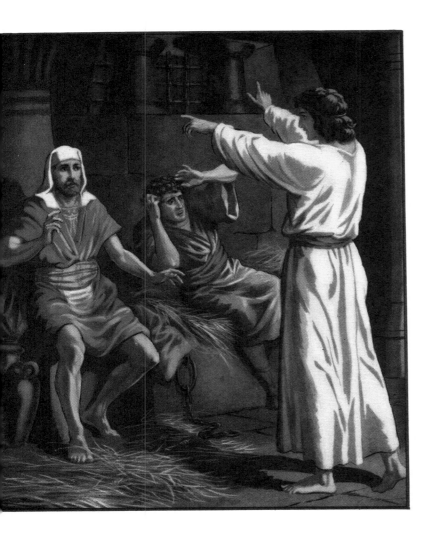

 OOR JOSEPH! He is in jail. Do you see the bars on the windows so that he cannot get out? He must stay there for a long time. He has not been bad, but someone told a lie and said that he had been bad. But God is taking care of Joseph even when he cannot get out. The other men in the jail are listening to Joseph. He tells them things that are going to happen to them. God helps Joseph know what is going to happen, and he tells the other men.

QUESTIONS:

1. *Where is Joseph?*
2. *Can he get away?*
3. *Is Joseph telling the men what is going to happen to them?*

Genesis 39:20-23

33

JOSEPH IS TALKING to the great king. Everyone is afraid of the king. He has very much money and can tell everyone else what they must do. If they do not do what he says, he will hurt them. But the king is not happy. Do you know why? It is because he had a bad dream last night. He dreamed about some cows. The cows were fat, and some other cows that were thin came and ate up the fat cows! Someone told the king that Joseph could tell about the dream and why the cows did this. Joseph was in jail but the king let him out. In this picture you can see Joseph telling the king about the dream. Joseph says that God sent the dream to the king. God wants the king to know that pretty soon there will not be enough grass for the cows and they will all get very thin and hungry. God tells Joseph about the dream, and then Joseph tells the king.

QUESTIONS:

1. *What did the king see in his bad dream?*
2. *Who is talking to the king about the dream?*
3. *Who told Joseph what the dream meant?*

Genesis 41:1-13

34

THE MAN SITTING DOWN behind the horse is Joseph. All the people are nice to him. They like Joseph. Why do all the people like him? It is because the king has made Joseph his most important helper. Now everyone must do what Joseph says, or else the king will punish them.

QUESTIONS:

1. *Who is the man everyone is looking at?*
2. *Do the people have to do what Joseph tells them?*
3. *Do you know who Joseph's best friend is?*

Genesis 41:14-16, 38-44

35

ERE IS ANOTHER PICTURE of Joseph. He is sitting on a golden chair. The other men are his brothers. Do you remember how bad his brothers were? Do you remember that they sold him? They have not seen Joseph for a long, long time. They do not know it is Joseph they are talking to. They are afraid of this man because he is so rich and so great. They have come to buy food from this man because they are hungry. These are the bad men who hurt Joseph. They sent him away to the land of Egypt. Joseph knows that they tried to hurt him. Do you think that Joseph will give them food? Yes, Joseph loves his brothers even though they were so bad, and he will give them the food they are asking him for.

QUESTIONS:

1. *Who is the man sitting down?*
2. *Who are the other men?*
3. *Why did they come?*
4. *Will Joseph give them food?*

Genesis 42:6-8

36

JOSEPH IS TELLING the bad men that he is their brother. These men thought that Joseph was dead, but he is alive and talking to them. God has made Joseph rich and strong so that he can help his brothers and his father now that they are hungry. The brothers were bad to Joseph and made him go away, but God was with Joseph all the time and took care of him. Now Joseph is taking care of his brothers. He loves them anyway, even if they were so bad. Do you know that God loves you, even when you are bad and even when He must punish you?

QUESTIONS:

1. *What is Joseph telling the men?*
2. *Did God take care of Joseph?*
3. *Will Joseph hurt his brothers because they hurt him?*

Genesis 45:1-15

37

251

HIS OLD MAN is Joseph's father, whos[e] name is Jacob. Jacob is very, very ol[d] now. He knows that God will soon tak[e] him away to Heaven. Jacob is talking t[o] Joseph, and to Joseph's two boys. He is asking God to b[e] kind to these two boys. Jacob is blessing the two boys an[d] praying to God about them. He is asking God to take car[e] of them and help them.

QUESTIONS:

1. *Who is this old man?*
2. *Where is he going to go soon?*
3. *Who is he talking to?*
4. *What is he saying to them?*

Genesis 48:9-1[0]

38

WHAT IS HAPPENING to these people in this picture? They are working very hard. One man is being whipped. A man wants him to work harder, and that is why he is whipping him. These people who are working so hard are God's people. They are called the children of Israel. Does God know what is happening to them? Yes, and God will help them. He will send a helper. In the next picture you will see who God's helper is going to be.

QUESTIONS:

    1. *What is the name of these people?*
    2. *What is happening to the man?*
    3. *Does God know about this?*
    4. *What will God do?*

Exodus 1:7-14

39

SEE THE LITTLE BABY! Why is his mother putting him in the little boat? She is putting him there because the king wants to hurt the baby. The mother is hiding him. The baby's name is Moses. When the baby Moses grows up into a big man, he will make the king of Egypt stop hurting God's people, the children of Israel. The baby will grow up and be God's helper. God is taking care of Moses by telling his mother to put him into the boat. Moses' sister will watch to see that the baby is all right.

QUESTIONS:

1. *What is the baby's name?*
2. *Why is his mother putting him into the boat?*
3. *Will the baby be God's helper when he gets to be a big man?*

Exodus 2:1-4

40

SEE WHAT IS HAPPENING to the baby Moses! Some nice ladies were walking along and saw the little boat. The lady looking at the baby is the king's daughter. She is the king's big girl. She wants to take the baby Moses home with her and take care of him. She will take the baby Moses to her house and Moses will live there with her. God is taking care of the baby Moses.

QUESTIONS:

1. *Who found the little baby?*
2. *Is God taking care of Moses?*

Exodus 2:5-10

41

OW THE BABY MOSES is a big man. He is taking care of some sheep. But God does not want Moses to take care of sheep any more. Instead He wants him to go to help God's people, the children of Israel. God wants to keep the other people from hurting His people with their whips. God is talking to Moses about this. Moses cannot see God talking to him, but he sees a bush that is on fire. The bush burns and burns but does not burn up. Can you see the fire in the picture? God is in the burning bush and talks to Moses from there. Moses is hiding his face, for he is afraid to look at God.

QUESTIONS:

1. *Where is the baby Moses now?*
2. *Who is Moses talking to?*
3. *Where is God in this picture?*

Exodus 3:1-6

42

OSES AND HIS BROTHER, AARON, are talking to the king. They tell the bad king that God wants him to let the people go and do what God says. But the king laughs at Moses and Aaron. He will not stop hurting the people. He will hurt them even more. He tells Moses and Aaron to go away and stop bothering him. Then Moses and Aaron say that God will send much trouble on the king's land, Egypt. First, all the water in the mud puddles and in the rivers will become blood. Even what is in the glasses on the tables for lunch will become bloody too. God will do this to the king to make him stop hurting His people.

QUESTIONS:

1. *Where is Moses?*
2. *Who is Aaron?*
3. *What are they telling the king?*

Exodus 5:6-19

43

HO ARE THESE PEOPLE? What are they doing? These are God's people. They are doing what God has told them to do. God said to take the blood of a lamb and put it on the sides of the doors of their houses, and on the board at the top of the door. Why did God want them to put the blood there? God is going to send an angel and in every house that does not have the blood on the door, the oldest boy will die.

QUESTIONS:

1. *What is the man putting at the side of the door?*
2. *Why is he doing this?*

Exodus 12:1-1

44

 T IS THE MIDDLE OF THE NIGHT and outside everything is all dark. In this picture everyone is crying. Do you know why? It is because the king's oldest boy has died. God's angel came and the boy died because there was no blood on the door. God said to put the blood on the door, but the king wouldn't do it. The king is sorry now that he hurt God's people. He is sorry that he did not believe God and do what God said. Now he will quickly send someone to tell Moses that he will stop hurting the children of Israel. He will tell Moses to take God's people out of his country so that God will not kill any more of his people.

QUESTIONS:

1. *Why is everyone so sad?*
2. *What will the king tell Moses now?*

Exodus 12:29-36

45

OD'S PEOPLE are going on a long trip, but they do not know where to go. Only God knows where He wants them to go. God is leading them to a good country. God has sent a big cloud that moves along in front of them. They are following the cloud. God moves the cloud and the people go wherever it goes. At night the cloud becomes fire so that the people can follow it through the darkness. That is how God tells them where to go.

QUESTIONS:

1. *How do the people know where to go?*
2. *Who makes the cloud move?*

Exodus 13:21, 22

S EE WHAT MOSES is doing now! God has told him to stand there by the water. How can all of God's people get across? The water is too deep, and they do not have any boats, and there is no bridge. How can they go across? Moses lifts up his hand, and see what happens! All of a sudden there is a path right through the water so that all of the people can walk through. God has told Moses to do this. God is taking care of His people so that they can get away from the bad king who wants to hurt them. God is very kind to His children. He is kind to you, too.

QUESTIONS:

1. *What is Moses doing?*
2. *What happens when Moses does this?*
3. *Does God love His children?*
4. *Does God love you?*

Exodus 14:21-31

47

HAT IS HAPPENING in this picture? Can you see Moses standing there? He is holding up his stick and now the water is coming to cover up the bad king and his soldiers. God pushed the water away so His people could walk through the sea on dry ground. They are safe now. Do you see them there back of Moses? The king chased after them with his soldiers but when he was right in the middle, God let the water come back and the soldiers drowned. You can see the water beginning to cover them up. But God's people are safe behind the cloud that God sent to help them.

QUESTIONS:

1. *How did God's people get through the river?*
2. *What is happening to the soldiers?*

Exodus 14:26-3

48

ERE ARE GOD'S PEOPLE out in a field. They are the children of Israel. What are they picking up from the ground? I don't think you could ever guess! They are picking up food that God has dropped down from the skies so that they can pick it up and take it home and have it for their breakfast. There are no stores to go to, to buy food, and so God has sent the food to them. God is very kind to His children. He fed His people this way every morning, and one time he sent birds that tasted like chicken for God's people to eat for supper.

QUESTIONS:

1. *What are these people doing?*
2. *Where did the food come from?*
3. *What did God send the people for supper?*

Exodus 16:2-6

49

OSES IS HITTING A ROCK with his stick. Why is he doing this? He is doing this because God told him to. God said that if he would hit the rock with his stick all of a sudden water would come out of the dry rock and there would be a river for God's people to drink from. They were thirsty and wanted to drink, and there wasn't any water, so they started crying about it. They said mean things to Moses. Moses asked God what to do. God told him to hit the rock and water would come out. Now the people have all they want to drink.

QUESTIONS:

1. *Were the people thirsty?*
2. *What does Moses have in his hand?*
3. *How did the water get there?*

Exodus 17:1-6

603

THIS IS ANOTHER PICTURE of Moses. See what he is carrying in his hands! He has two big pieces of flat stone. These stones have things written on them. God wrote on these stones and gave the stones to Moses. What does the writing say on the stones? It tells what God wants His people to do. It says to love God and obey Him. No one should ever pray to anyone but God. It says on the stones to take care of our mothers and daddies and do what they tell us to do. Another rule God gives is that we should never take anything that does not belong to us. There are ten rules, so we call these rules the Ten Commandments.

QUESTIONS:

1. *What does Moses have in his hands?*
2. *What are the ten rules called?*
3. *What is one of the rules on the stones?*

Exodus 32:15-19

51

O H, OH, OH! What are these people doing? These are the people of God, but they are praying to a baby cow. Do you see the baby cow in the picture? They have made the cow out of gold and now they are praying to it. These people are disobeying God and making God very sorry. God says we must only pray to Him. These people are praying to something else. Now God must punish these people because they are so bad. Moses is very angry because the people are doing this. He is throwing down the two stones and breaking them.

QUESTIONS:

1. *What are the people praying to?*
2. *Who is the only One we ought to pray to?*
3. *What is Moses doing?*

Exodus 32:1-6

52

THE BUILDING YOU SEE in this picture is a kind of church. It is the place where the people of Israel can come and pray to God. Moses is there talking to God. There a big cloud at the door of the church. The Lord is in the loud and He is talking to Moses. You and I cannot talk to od in a cloud. But we can talk to Him right here in this oom. And He sees us even though we cannot see Him.

QUESTIONS:

1. Where is Moses?
2. Where is God?
3. What are they doing?

Exodus 33:7-11

53

S EE ALL THE PEOPLE COMING! See wha
they have in their hands! Some of the
are bringing money and some of the
are bringing beautiful cloth and some o
them are bringing perfume. They are bringing all kinds o
things. Do you know why? It is because God has tol
them that they could bring these things and build a beau
tiful house for God to live in. They are giving these thing
to God, and then some of them will help Moses make th
beautiful house. The people are happy because they ca
give these presents to God for His house.

QUESTIONS:

1. *What are the people bringing?*
2. *Why are they bringing these presents?*

Exodus 35:4-2

54

T IS NIGHTTIME and some of the children of Israel are looking at the beautiful house they have made for God. Is the house on fire? No, it is not on fire, but there is a big cloud of fire there above the house. Do you know who is in the fiery cloud? It is God. God is watching over His house. He is taking care of all the people of Israel in the tents that you can see. Whenever the fire began to move away, then the children of Israel took their tents with them and followed the fire until it stopped. That is the way God told them where He wanted them to go when it was nighttime. In the daytime He sent a cloud for them to follow.

QUESTIONS:

1. *Is the house burning up?*
2. *Who is in the cloud?*
3. *Where do all the people live?*

Exodus 40:34-38

55

C AN YOU SEE what these men are carrying? It is a great big bunch of grapes on a pole. The grapes are so big and so heavy that the men can hardly carry them. They found the grapes far away in another country. God told them to go there. They found the grapes and brought them home for all their friends to see. God wants these people to take a long trip to that other country, where the grapes are so big and live there. But the people are afraid to go. They think the men who live in that other country will hurt them, so they are afraid. They forget that God will take care of them.

QUESTIONS:

1. What are the men carrying?
2. Where does God want His people to go?
3. Are the people afraid to do what God says?

Numbers 13:23-33

G OD TOLD HIS PEOPLE to listen to Moses, but some of them said they wouldn't obey Moses any more. God is very angry with these men. God tells everyone to get away from them, because He is going to punish them. Then all of a sudden the ground opens up and there is a big hole. They fall down into the ground, along with their houses and their friends, and everything that they own. Then the earth closes up again and they are all killed.

QUESTIONS:

1. *Did these men mind Moses?*
2. *What did God do to them?*

Numbers 16:23-35

57

CAN YOU SEE all the snakes in this picture? Do you know why they are biting the people? It is because the people have been bad again. So God has sent these fiery snakes to bite the people, and many of them are dying. These people came to Moses. They said, "We have been bad. Please ask God to take away the snakes." So Moses prayed for the people, and the Lord told him to make a brass snake and put it on a pole. Moses took a hammer and some brass and made a snake. It isn't a real snake; it isn't alive. God told Moses that anyone who looked at the snake on the pole would get well again. The people in the picture are looking at the brass snake on the pole. Now they will be all right. But if anyone won't look, he will die.

QUESTIONS:

1. *Have the people been bad again?*
2. *How is God punishing them?*
3. *What has Moses made?*
4. *What will happen to the people who don't look at the snake?*

Numbers 21:5-9

58

MAN IS RIDING ON A DONKEY and there is an angel standing in front of him with a long knife in his hand. The angel wants the man to stop because the man is going to do something bad and the angel doesn't want him to. The man doesn't see the angel at first but the donkey does. The donkey is afraid of the angel and stops. The man is angry because the donkey stops. He hits the donkey and tells it to go on. Then the Lord makes the donkey talk, and the donkey asks the man, "Why are you hitting me?" Just then the man sees the angel standing there. The man is falling down on the ground because he is so scared. This man's name is Balaam.

QUESTIONS:

1. *What was the man going to do?*
2. *Can this donkey talk?*
3. *What did it say?*
4. *Why is the man falling off his donkey?*

Numbers 22:21-34

OSES IS SITTING DOWN on the rock. He is very old man now. Soon he will go awa to die. He will go away to live with Goc He will not be with the people of Israe to take care of them any more. So now God is giving th people another leader. Now Joshua will take care of them Joshua is talking to the people and telling them what t do. Moses tells Joshua to help the people obey God.

QUESTIONS:

1. *Where is Moses going?*
2. *Who will take care of his people now instea of Moses?*

Numbers 27:18-2

60

HIS MAN IS RUNNING FAST. Do you see the other man running after him with a big knife? The first man is running into the city. He was chopping some wood with an axe and had an accident. His axe hit a man who was standing near and the man died. Then he started running to this city and the dead man's friend chased him. You can see that he is all tired out. But now he comes to the city and the other man cannot hurt him here. God made this city so that people could run there and be safe. Now he is safe.

QUESTIONS:

1. *Why is the man running?*
2. *Where is he going?*
3. *Will he be all right now that he is in the city?*
4. *Can the man with the knife hurt him now?*

Numbers 35:9-32

I N THIS PICTURE you can see one of God's people talking to his family. He is telling them about God. He wants them to know how good God is to him and how kind God is. He is teaching his children about God so that when they grow up they will always want to do whatever God says. He wants his children to love and obey God even now while they are still young. God always wants fathers and mothers to tell their little children about the Lord Jesus. That is why I am reading these good stories to you—so that you will know more about God.

QUESTIONS:

1. *What is the man telling his family?*
2. *When you become grown up, what will you tell your children?*

Deuteronomy 6:7-14

THESE PEOPLE are bringing gifts to God. They want to give them to God because they are so glad God has been kind to them. The grapes are from their own gardens. Do you see the baskets of fruits? See how many there are! They are taking the first of these fruits and are bringing them to God's house for the priest or minister to use. They will give some to poor people who do not have enough to eat.

QUESTIONS:

1. *What is in the basket?*
2. *Where is the man taking it?*
3. *Why does he want to give the grapes to God?*

Deuteronomy 26:1-11

63

 OSES IS ON A MOUNTAIN. He is standing on the top of the mountain. He is looking over to the country that God will give to the children of Israel. Moses cannot go there because once he did not obey God. God said that he would have to be punished by not getting to go to the nice country. But God will let him see the promised land. God is showing it to him now. God tells Moses to come up to this mountain so that he can look at it. In a little while Moses will die and God Himself will put Moses' body into the ground. But Moses will go to live with God while his body is there in the ground.

QUESTIONS:

1. *Where is Moses looking?*
2. *Will Moses go to the country where he is looking?*
3. *What is going to happen to Moses?*

Deuteronomy 34:1-12

I T IS NIGHT OUTSIDE. A man is climbing down from a high window. Soon another man will come down too. A lady is helping them. These two men do not live here. They live in another country. They live with Joshua and God's people. God told them to come here and see this city. The name of the city is Jericho. When these two men came to the city, the people who lived there tried to catch them, but the lady is helping them get away. God will be kind to the lady because she is helping these two men.

QUESTIONS:

1. *Do these two men live here?*
2. *Did God tell them to come?*
3. *What did the people try to do to them?*
4. *Who helped them get away?*

Joshua 2:1-15

65

GOD IS DOING A WONDERFUL THING for His children. He wants them to go across the river to the land He said He would give them. There is no bridge for them to go across, and no boat, and the water is too deep to wade. But God makes a way for them to go across. See how the water is standing up like a wall! Now there is a path through the bottom of the river for the people to walk on. The ground is dry beneath their feet. Look at the priests walking ahead of the people of Israel. God is making the water stand up instead of getting the people all wet.

QUESTIONS:

1. *How did the people get across the river?*
2. *What is happening to the water?*
3. *Who fixed the river so the people could walk across the bottom of it?*

Joshua 3:13-17

OD'S PEOPLE are walking around the big city called Jericho. God has told His people to walk around it every day. They have already walked around it once yesterday. They have walked around it once every day this week. Today God told them to walk around it seven times instead of once. Now the people are yelling very loudly and the priests are blowing their trumpets. The high walls are falling down, and now all of God's people can walk right into the city. The people in the city built high walls to keep them out, but God is knocking down the walls. This is the city where the lady lives who helped the two men climb down the wall. The people of Israel do not hurt this lady when they go into the city because she was kind to them.

QUESTIONS:

1. *What are the people doing?*
2. *What is happening to the walls?*

Joshua 6:1-20

67

DO YOU KNOW who this man is? He is Joshua the leader of God's people. God's people are having a great fight with some other people. In the picture you can see all the men fighting. The sun is beginning to go down and it will soon be dark. Joshua and God's people will not be able to see to fight. In this picture Joshua is talking to God about the sun. He is asking God to keep the sun from going down. He wants it to stay where it is so that it won't get dark for a long time. God is listening to Joshua's prayer. There will be no night at all on this day. It does not get dark because God is keeping the sun up there in the sky. God listens to Joshua and doesn't let the night time come.

QUESTIONS:

1. *Does Joshua want it to become dark?*
2. *What does Joshua ask God to do with the sun?*

Joshua 10:6-14

68

WHY ARE THE MEN drinking water? Some of them are putting their mouths into the water and drinking like dogs. Others are putting the water into their hands. They will drink out of their hands. Can you tell which ones will drink from their hands? God told Gideon to tell the men to drink the water. He told Gideon to choose the men who drink out of their hands. Gideon will take these men with him to fight with the people who don't like God. He will send all the other men home. God only wants a few men to go. There will not be enough men, so God will help them. God will help them and they will win.

QUESTIONS:

1. *Does God want Gideon to take lots and lots of people with him to fight?*
2. *What are the men doing?*
3. *Which ones does Gideon ask to go with him?*

Judges 7:2-7

69

THIS IS A PICTURE OF SAMSON. Samson is th strongest man who ever lived. He is stron because God made him that way an helped him. God said that as long as h did not cut his hair he would be strong. Do you see hi long hair? Here is a picture of Samson and some heav doors. They are the doors to keep people from going i and out of the walls of that city he is looking at. Th doors were shut, and Samson wanted to go out. He di not have the key, so he went out anyway and just took th doors along with him! What a strong man Samson is!

QUESTIONS:

1. *What is the man's name?*
2. *Did he have the keys to the door?*
3. *How did he get out?*

Judges 16:

THE STRONG MAN, SAMSON, has chains on his feet. Can you see the chains? How did they get there? I will tell you. One night when he was asleep some men cut off his long hair. Then Samson wasn't strong any more. The men put chains on him and made him blind by hurting his eyes. But now Samson's hair has grown long again and he is stronger. He asked the men to let him stand by the two posts that held up the house. He is pulling the house down and Samson and the people will all die.

QUESTIONS:

1. *What did the men do to Samson's hair?*
2. *How did Samson get the chains on his feet?*
3. *What happened after Samson's hair grew out again?*

Judges 16:18-30

71

HIS DEAR MOTHER is going away. Now she will live somewhere else in another country far away. She is saying good-by to Ruth. But Ruth doesn't want her to go all by herself. Ruth wants to go with her and take care of her. Ruth is kind and good.

QUESTIONS:

1. *Is Ruth kind and good?*
2. *Will she go away from the mother?*
3. *Does she want to take care of her?*

Ruth 1:8-18

72

THIS IS A PICTURE of Ruth. Do you remember how kind she was to her mother? Now she is working hard to get food for both of them to eat. Do you see the wheat in Ruth's hands? She will use it to make bread to eat.

QUESTIONS:

1. *Who is this lady?*
2. *What does she have in her hands?*
3: *What will she do with it?*

Ruth 2:5-17

73

ANNAH IS PRAYING. She is praying because she does not have a baby, and she wants one very badly. She and her husband have come to the church to pray and to give gifts to God. The minister sees her praying. He tells her that God will answer her prayer. God will send her a little baby because of her prayer.

QUESTIONS:

1. *Why was Hannah praying?*
2. *What does the minister tell her?*

I Samuel 1:9-19

74

257

GOD GAVE HANNAH a little baby boy. You can see him in the picture. The little boy's name is Samuel. Samuel was a tiny baby but he grew and grew and now he is not a baby any more. Hannah wants to give her little boy to God. She has brought him to the church to be a helper to the minister whose name is Eli. The little boy Samuel is talking to Eli. Samuel's mother will go home now and Samuel will not see her very much. He will live with Eli and be God's helper.

QUESTIONS:

1. What is this little boy's name?
2. Who will Samuel stay with now?
3. What will he do?

I Samuel 2:18, 19

75

 T IS NIGHTTIME and Samuel has been asleep. Now he is awake. Now he is awake and listening to someone talking. He hears someone calling, "Samuel! Samuel!" The little boy thinks that Eli is calling him from the next room. He runs quickly to Eli and says, "Here I am, you called me." But Eli says, "No. I didn't call you." "Who called me, then?" Samuel wants to know. Eli tells him that God was talking to him. Samuel will listen to what God says, and do it.

QUESTIONS:

1. *Was Eli calling Samuel?*
2. *Who was calling him?*
3. *What is Samuel going to do?*

I Samuel 3:1-10

76

ELI IS SITTING ON A ROCK while a man is telling him what has happened. God's people have been fighting with some bad men called the Philistines. The man is telling Eli that God's people are all running away, and that Eli's two sons have been killed. Now Eli is very sad. The man tells him that God has let the Philistines win the fight. Eli falls off the rock he is sitting on, and he is hurt so badly that he dies.

QUESTIONS:

1. *What is the man telling Eli?*
2. *Is he telling him happy things?*
3. *What happens to Eli when he hears about it?*

I Samuel 4:5-18

77

THE LITTLE BOY SAMUEL is now an old, old man. Samuel is pouring oil on the head of a young man whose name is Saul. God has chosen Saul to be king over His people Israel. See how tall and strong Saul is! See how he is kneeling there in front of Samuel! Samuel is pouring some oil on Saul's head because Saul is going to be king. It looks like he will make a good king for all of God's people to obey. But do you know something that is very sad? I will tell you what it is. Saul's heart has sin in it. That means that Saul will do wrong things.

QUESTIONS:

1. *What is the name of the young man?*
2. *Is he good?*
3. *Why is Samuel pouring oil on his head?*

I Samuel 9:15-27

78

THIS FINE YOUNG MAN is David. He takes care of sheep. When a lion came to catch David's sheep, David killed the lion. Can you see the lion lying there under his ee? David is strong and good and God is going to let m be the king over His people. God wants Samuel to ur oil on David's head now, so that David will know at he is going to be the king.

QUESTIONS:

1. *What is the name of this young man?*
2. *Does he take care of sheep?*
3. *Will he become king?*

I Samuel 16:1-13

 GIANT HAS COME to fight against God's people. The giant's name is Goliath. All the men of Israel have run away from him. They are afraid to fight him because he is so big but David is not afraid. David knows that God will help him. David does not have a gun but he has a slingshot. Do you see it in his hand? He takes some stones and uses his slingshot to throw a stone at the giant. The stone hits the giant in the head and the great Goliath falls over dead.

QUESTIONS:

1. *What is the giant's name?*
2. *What does David hit him with?*
3. *Why are all the other people afraid of Goliath?*

I Samuel 17:38-50

80

DAVID AND JONATHAN are talking together. They are good friends and like to talk to each other. Jonathan is King Saul's son. He is a prince. But Jonathan will never be the king because God has told David to be king. Does this make Jonathan sad and angry? No, Jonathan loves David and he is glad that David is going to be the king. Do you see David and Jonathan talking together in the picture?

QUESTIONS:

1. *What are the names of these two men?*
2. *What is the name of the one who is going to be the king?*

I Samuel 20:4-17

81

THE MAN WHO IS ASLEEP is King Saul. He has been chasing David. He wants to catch him so that he can hurt him and kill him. Saul does not like David. He knows that God is going to make David king instead of him. Saul wants to keep on being king but God won't let him. David and a friend with a spear find King Saul sleeping. David's friend wants to kill King Saul with the sharp spear. But David is good and he won't let his friend hurt King Saul. David knows God would not like this. David only wants to do whatever God tells him. David obeys God.

QUESTIONS:

1. *Can you see King Saul?*
2. *What is he doing?*
3. *Can you see David in the picture?*
4. *What is he doing?*

I Samuel 24:1-12

82

NOW SAUL IS DEAD. David is the new king. The old man is pouring oil on his head. He is doing this to make David a king because that is what God said. Now everyone must mind King David. God told David a long time ago that some day he would be king and now he is.

QUESTIONS:

1. *Who is the king now?*
2. *Did David know he was going to be king?*
3. *What is the old man doing to David.*

II Samuel 2:1-4

83

AVID IS BRINGING HOME the golden Ark. I
anyone looked into the Ark he would die
The Ark belongs to God. David is happ
that the Ark is coming. He is walking
along in front of it playing on his golden harp. Everyon
is happy. God is coming to live with them.

QUESTIONS:

1. *Is David happy?*
2. *What happens to people who open the golde*
   box?

II Samuel 6:12-1

84

HIS IS King David when he was a boy. In the Bible there are many songs that David wrote. In this picture you can see him playing and singing. The music is very pretty and the words are nice because they tell how much he loves God. Some of the words he wrote are:

"The Lord is my Shepherd,
I shall not want.
He maketh me to lie down in green pastures.
He leadeth me beside the still waters."

QUESTIONS:

1. *What is the name of this man?*
2. *What is he doing?*
3. *Where are some of his songs written down?*

Psalm 23

HE MAN WITH THE CROWN on his head
King David. God has sent Nathan th
prophet to talk to him. See how he
pointing his finger at King David and ho
David is afraid. David has done a very bad thing and Go
saw him do it. God sent Nathan the prophet to tell Davi
that God is going to punish him. David is sorry that h
has been so bad and asks God to forgive him. God fo
gives David, but he will have much trouble because o
the bad thing he has done.

QUESTIONS:

1. *Which of these men is King David?*
2. *Has David been good or bad?*
3. *Who sent the other man to talk to Kin*
   David?
4. *Did God punish David for being bad?*

II Samuel 12:1-1

86

HIS MAN who is getting caught up there in the tree is Absalom. Absalom is David's son. He is a prince because his father is the king. Absalom doesn't want his father to be king anymore because he wants to be king instead. God does not like this. God wants David to still be king. Now look at Absalom. He is caught in the tree. His mule is running away. He has been riding on the mule but now he will hang there by his hair because it has gotten all tangled up in the tree and he cannot get down. Soon some men will come who do not like Absalom. He will not be able to get away from them and they will kill him. Now Absalom cannot be the king. God does not want him to be king.

QUESTIONS:

1. *What is happening to Absalom?*
2. *Can he be king?*
3. *Does God want Absalom to be king?*

II Samuel 18:9-18

ING SOLOMON is telling two ladies what to do. They have come to ask him what to do with the little baby. Each of the ladies says that the baby is hers. One of them is telling a lie. Which one is it? God tells Solomon how to find out. He says to cut the baby in half and give half of it to each of the ladies. Then the baby's mother says, "No, no, let the other lady have the baby. Don't cut it in half." Then Solomon knows the lady who doesn't want the baby hurt must be the baby's mother. Solomon gives the baby to his mother. God made Solomon very wise.

QUESTIONS:

1. Does the baby's mother want him to be hurt?
2. Who made Solomon wise?

I Kings 3:16-28

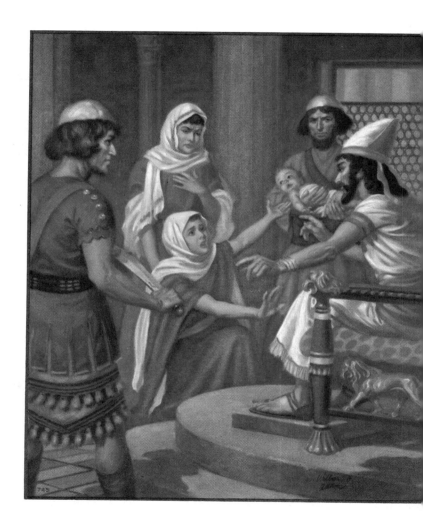

ING SOLOMON built this new house. Do you know who he made it for? It is God's house. It took a long time to build it because it is so nice. Many men have cut down trees and made them into boards and other men cut big rocks and worked very hard. Solomon is glad because he could make this beautiful house for God to live in.

QUESTIONS:

1. *Whose house is this?*
2. *Is Solomon glad?*

I Kings 6:11-14

89

SOLOMON IS STANDING in front of God's house. See all of the people who have come to have a big party because they are so glad that God's house has been built! Now it is all finished and Solomon is praying. He is standing there with his hands raised before Heaven talking to God. He is thanking God for being so kind to him and to his people and to his father, David. He is asking God to take care of them and help them all the time. God is listening. God says He will take care of the people as long as they do what He tells them.

QUESTIONS:

1. Why have all the people come to God's house?
2. What is Solomon doing?
3. Is God listening?
4. What does God say?

I Kings 8:22-29

90

WHAT A SAD THING is happening! Solomon, the great king God loves, is bad. He is praying to someone else. He is praying to that thing sitting there. A man made it and it is not even alive. It is called an idol. Solomon is praying to it. It cannot hear Solomon's prayer because it is not alive. God in Heaven is watching Solomon. He is very angry about this. God says that now Solomon must be punished. Poor Solomon! Why did he do such a wrong thing? I wish he had remembered to love God and had never prayed to the idol.

QUESTIONS:

1. *Is Solomon praying to God?*
2. *Where is God?*
3. *Will God punish Solomon?*

I Kings 11:1-10

91

HIS MAN IS ELIJAH. He is a great friend of God's. Elijah is good but other people tried to hurt him. Elijah asked God to stop it from raining for a long, long time. God listened to Elijah and stopped all the rain. Now the king is angry at Elijah for asking God to do this. Elijah is afraid of the king and runs away and is sitting here by a little river. There is no food here for him and no stores where he can buy it so God is sending him some. The birds are bringing food to him. God is taking care of his friend Elijah.

QUESTIONS:

1. *What did Elijah ask God to do to the rain?*
2. *Why is he hiding?*
3. *How is Elijah getting food?*

I Kings 17:1-7

92

T

HIS LITTLE BOY was out playing. Then he began to feel sick. After a while his mother put him into his bed but he didn't get any better. Then the little boy died. His mother asked Elijah to make him alive again. Elijah could not make the little boy alive unless God told him to. Elijah asked God to make the little boy alive and all better again. In this picture you can see what happened when Elijah prayed. The little boy is all right and Elijah is giving him to his happy mother.

QUESTIONS:

1. What happened to the little boy?
2. Who did the boy's mother ask to help?
3. What is happening in the picture?

I Kings 17:17-24

93

IN THIS PICTURE you can see Elijah praying to God. He is asking God to send fire from Heaven to light the big sticks he has piled on the stones. Do you see the stones and the sticks? Suddenly a great flame of fire comes sweeping down from the sky. God sends the fire because Elijah asked Him to. The fire is burning the sticks. How frightened and surprised God's enemies are as they watch. They did not know that God would answer Elijah's prayer. But Elijah is not surprised. He knew that God would hear him. Now all the people know that the Lord is the only God.

QUESTIONS:

1. *Where is the fire coming from?*
2. *Did God hear Elijah's prayer?*

I Kings 18:20-39

94

ELIJAH IS GOING UP to Heaven. His friend Elisha is watching on the ground. They were walking along together when all of a sudden this chariot of fire came down from Heaven and took Elijah up to God. Elisha sees him go. He is picking up Elijah's coat. Now Elisha will not be able to talk to Elijah any more but he can still talk to God. God is with Elisha and talks to him and makes him strong.

QUESTIONS:

1. *Who is in the fiery chariot?*
2. *Where is he going?*
3. *What is the name of the man who is picking up the coat?*

II Kings 2:1-14

95

D O YOU SEE THIS LADY and her two boys? She must pay some money to a man to-morrow, or the man will take her two boys away from her. He will make them come and live in his house and work hard. Elisha tells her to get all the jars and pans that she can find. He tells her to take the little jar of oil she has in her hand and pour it out into the other jars. She keeps pouring it out but her little jar never gets empty! The oil in it fills all the big jars. See how many big jars she has already filled up. She will sell the oil and get enough money to pay the man so that she can keep her children. God never let the little jar get empty.

QUESTIONS:

1. *Why was the lady sad?*
2. *What did Elisha tell her to do?*
3. *Why doesn't the little jar get empty?*

II Kings 4:1-7

THIS LADY IS WAVING GOOD-BY to her husband. He is going away. He is sick. The girl sitting there told her about God and about God's friend Elisha. The girl said that Elisha could make the sick man well again. He is going away to find Elisha and to ask Elisha to make him well. Elisha will ask God to help and then the man will be well again. It was nice for the little girl to tell the man and the lady about God. The man did not know about God until the little girl told him.

QUESTIONS:

1. *What did the little girl tell the man and the lady?*
2. *Where is the man going?*

II Kings 5:1-14

97

HIS IS THE MAN we saw in the last picture when he was going away. He came to ask Elisha to make him well again. Elisha said he should go down to the Jordan River and wash in it seven times and then he would be well. At first the man didn't want to do that. He thought it was a funny way to get well. But soon he went to the river. One, two, three, four, five, six, seven times he dipped into the water and then he was well again. Now he is bringing presents for Elisha to pay for making him well, but Elisha says, "No." Elisha doesn't want his money.

QUESTIONS:

1. *Who is this man who is standing up?*
2. *What does Elisha tell him to do?*
3. *Does Elisha want his money?*

II Kings 5:9-16

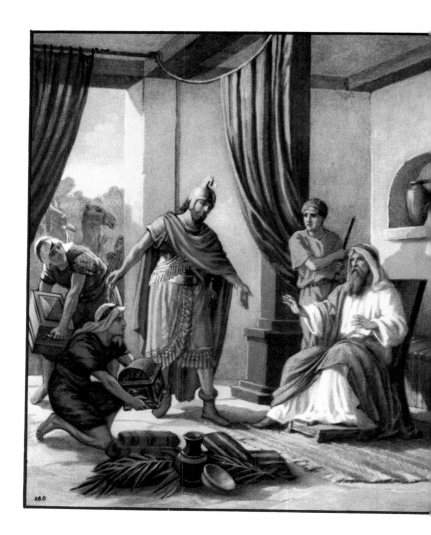

98

ELISHA IS SITTING on top of his house. He is watching some angels up in the sky. They have come to help him and the boy who is there with him. Some bad people want to hurt Elisha so God sends these helpers. They won't let anybody hurt Elisha and his friend.

QUESTIONS:

1. *What is happening in this picture?*
2. *Can we always see the angels?*
3. *Are there any angels here in this room?*

II Kings 6:13-17

99

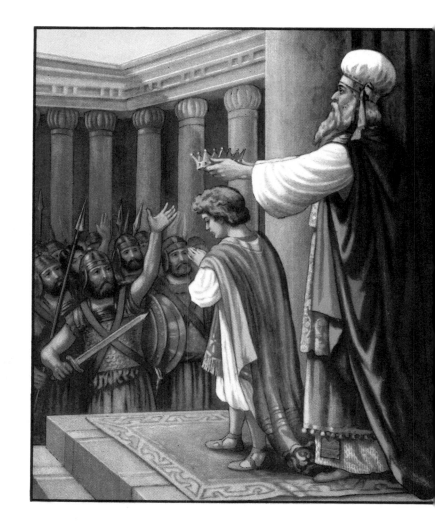

THIS LITTLE BOY is seven years old but he is already the king over God's people. God has said that everyone must obey him. He has helpers so that he will know what to do. The little boy's name is Jehoash and he loves God very much. The people are happy because he is their king. When he grows older he will notice that God's house needs to be fixed up and he will fix it. I am sorry to say that when he becomes a big man he won't love God so much. Then he will pray to idols. What a sad thing to happen! When you get big I hope that you will only love God and pray to Him. The little boy in the picture will be very sad after he forgets about God.

QUESTIONS:

1. *How old is the little king?*
2. *Will he still love God when he grows up?*
3. *How old are you?*
4. *Do you want to love God?*

II Kings 11:1-12

100

ING HEZEKIAH IS CRYING OUT TO GOD for help. He got a letter in the mail from a man who said that he was going to bring a lot of soldiers to catch him. King Hezekiah is very sad and doesn't know what to do. So he comes to God's house to pray and to ask God about it. He is saying, "O Lord, save me and my people! Show everyone how strong You are and that You are our God." God hears King Hezekiah praying. He will send a man soon to tell him that God will help. God will answer Hezekiah's prayer and take care of him.

QUESTIONS:

1. *Why is the king sad?*
2. *Who is he talking to?*
3. *Does God hear King Hezekiah?*

II Kings 19:1-20

101

HE MAN SITTING ON THE CHAIR is another of God's kings. His name is Josiah. He became king when he was just a little boy eight years old. Now he is grown up into a big man. See how surprised he looks! Someone is showing him a Book that he has found in God's house. It is part of the Bible. The king has never seen the Bible before and did not know what God wanted. Now he will begin to do whatever God says because he has found God's Book and can read it.

QUESTIONS:

1. *Why is the king surprised?*
2. *Where did the man find God's Book?*
3. *Do you have a Book that tells what God says?*
4. *What is the name of the Book?*

II Chronicles 34:18-21

102

THESE PEOPLE ARE ALL CRYING because they have done such bad things. The man who is talking to them is Ezra. He is one of God's friends so he knows what God wants them to do. Do you know what they have done? These men have married ladies who do not know about God. These ladies want God's people to pray to sticks and stones instead of to God. This is very wrong. Ezra tells the men how bad it is for them to marry ladies who don't love God. God does not want them to marry ladies who do not love Him. Now these men are sorry for what they have done. We should never marry anybody who does not love the Lord Jesus.

QUESTIONS:

1. *What did these men do?*
2. *Can you guess what Ezra is reading to the men?*

Ezra 10:1-12

103

HE MAN IN THIS PICTURE, who doesn't hav[e] any shirt on, is named Job. He was ver[y] rich. He had many sheep and cows. The[n] he lost all his money and animals. No[w] Job is very sick and sad. Satan has taken away all of h[is] cows and camels and all of his boys and girls so that h[e] doesn't have anything left. Now he is very, very poo[r.] Job is sorry but he does not blame God. He says, "Go[d,] You are good and I love You no matter what happens t[o] me."

QUESTIONS:

1. *What is this man's name?*
2. *What happened to all of his cows?*
3. *Does Job still love God?*

Job 1:1-[?]

104

HAVE YOU SEEN THIS MAN BEFORE? Yes, this is Job, the man who became so poor and sick, and now he is all right again. God has given him more than he had before. He has more cows and more sheep and more money. Job knows that God is good. Job loves God and God loves Job. Do you love God like Job did? Will you do what God says even if God gives you no presents? I hope you will always love God more and more because God loves you so much.

QUESTIONS:

1. *What is the name of this man?*
2. *Has God made him rich again?*

Job 42:10-17

THIS IS A MAN whose name is Isaiah. G[od] sent him to tell the people what th[ey] should do. He is called a prophet. C[an] you say "prophet"? The people are b[ad] and God sends him to tell them to stop. He says that [if] they don't, God will hurt their country, and wreck the[ir] cities, and burn up their houses. God is sorry when H[is] people sin and do wrong things. God sends Isaiah [to] help them stop doing what is bad.

QUESTIONS:

1. *What is this man's name?*
2. *What did he tell the people?*

Isaia[h]

106

OOK AT THE LITTLE CHILD. Do you see all the animals that are with him? He is touching the cow. A big lion is standing quietly beside him. The lion does not hurt him. Do you see the little lamb, and the black wolf behind the lamb? The wolf does not eat the lamb or hurt it. Some day God will make everything happy. He will make cats and dogs like each other instead of chasing each other. The children will not quarrel and nothing will hurt them. God will make everything want to be kind and gentle.

QUESTIONS:

1. *Will the lion hurt the little child?*
2. *What is God going to do some day to the cats and dogs?*

Isaiah 11:1-10

107

THIS MAN IS JEREMIAH. Can you say "Je
emiah"? He is one of God's friends. Go
has sent him to tell the people to be goo
The people do not like Jeremiah to te
them this. They want to be bad so they have tied Jer
miah's hands together. They will put him in a room an
lock the door so Jeremiah cannot get away. He must :
there all day. People go by laughing at him and makir
fun of him. Poor Jeremiah! But God is with him and Go
will punish the people who do this to His friend.

QUESTIONS:

1. *What has happened to Jeremiah's hands?*
2. *Is Jeremiah God's friend?*
3. *Will God help Jeremiah?*

Jeremiah 20:1

108

ERE IS ANOTHER PICTURE of Jeremiah. Do you remember seeing him in the last picture? Jeremiah is talking to another man who is writing down all the things that Jeremiah tells him to. God is talking to Jeremiah and telling him what to say to the man, and the man is writing it down. He is writing down what God says. He is writing part of the Bible. The Bible is what God says and wants us to know. When the man has finished writing the Book he will read it to all the people, so they will know what God wants them to do.

QUESTIONS:

1. *What is Jeremiah doing?*
2. *Who is telling Jeremiah what to say?*
3. *What is the man doing who is sitting down?*

Jeremiah 36:1-4

109

I N THE LAST PICTURE do you remember how Jeremiah listened to God and told a man what to write? When it was all written down, God said to take it to the king so he would know what God said. The king read some of it. It said for him to be good and to stop doing bad things. The king is very angry. He does not want to mind God. Oh, oh, do you see what a terrible thing he is doing? He is throwing God's letter into the fire. He is burning it up. He does not want to have God's letter. Oh, how much God will have to punish this king because he will not listen to God or mind Him!

QUESTIONS:

1. *Who is this man?*
2. *What is he doing?*
3. *What will happen to the king because he is doing this?*

Jeremiah 36:19-24

110

HERE IS A SAD PICTURE. It is a picture of God's people being taken away to another country. They are going away from their homes. They want to go home but they can't. The people who are taking them away do not like them and will hurt them and kill some of them. See how sorry the people are! Do you know why this has happened? It is because they are God's people and they are bad, and God is going to punish them. They have prayed to sticks and rocks and the sun instead of praying to God. Instead of spanking them, God takes them away to another country where they don't want to go. In the picture you can see them going away.

QUESTIONS:

1. *Are the people going home?*
2. *Why is this happening?*

Jeremiah 39:1-10

111

THIS MAN'S NAME IS JONAH. He is running awa[y] from God. God has told him to go to a bi[g] city and tell the people there to stop bein[g] bad. Jonah does not want to go. He doe[s] not want to tell the people what God said. So now he [is] running away instead of doing what God told him to. H[e] is getting on a ship to sail far, far away to another countr[y]. He thinks God will not find him there. But nobody ca[n] run away from God. Jonah should know that. You kno[w] it, don't you?

QUESTIONS:

1. *Where is Jonah going?*
2. *Is he obeying God?*
3. *What did God want Jonah to do?*

Jonah 1:1-[4]

112

HO IS THIS MAN swimming in the water? It is Jonah. He was in that boat and a big storm came along. All the men in the boat prayed to God to help them. They asked God to keep their boat from sinking. Then Jonah told them to throw him into the water and the storm would go away. He said he was running away from God and that God had sent the storm to punish him. The men were sad, but they did what Jonah said and threw him out of the boat into the water and now the storm is going away. Jonah is in the water but God won't let him die. He has sent a great fish to swallow Jonah without hurting him. Do you see the fish? After three days this fish will swim over to the beach with Jonah inside and spit Jonah out onto the sand. After that Jonah will do whatever God tells him to.

QUESTIONS:

1. *Why is Jonah in the water?*
2. *What is the fish going to do?*
3. *How long will Jonah be inside the fish?*

Jonah 1:3-17

113

ERE IS ANOTHER PICTURE of Jonah, the man who ran away from God and was swallowed by a big fish. After the fish had spit him out onto the dry ground, God spoke again to Jonah and told him to go to the city of Nineveh and to preach to the people there. "Jonah," God said, "tell the people who live in Nineveh that they have been bad and I will need to punish them next month." Here in this picture you can see Jonah doing what God told him to. He is telling all the people what God said. The people are listening. They are sorry and afraid. Now they will stop doing bad things because they know God will punish them if they keep on doing them. Now God will not need to punish these people because they are listening to Jonah. Aren't you glad that Jonah did not try to run away again?

QUESTIONS:

1. *What is Jonah telling the people?*
2. *What are the people doing?*
3. *Will God need to punish these people now?*

114

Jonah 3:1-10

N OW I AM GOING TO TELL you a very wonderful story about a boy named Daniel. The king has sent some very good food for Daniel to eat, but Daniel won't eat it. In the picture you can see him telling the servants to take the food away. Shall I tell you why? Daniel doesn't want to eat the good food because the king doesn't believe in God. The king prays to sticks and stones and idols. When the king asks the blessing at the table, he doesn't ask God to bless the food. Instead the king prays to sticks and stones and ugly idols and asks them to bless it. Daniel doesn't want to eat that kind of food, even if it is cake and candy and ice cream. Daniel wants God to be happy, more than he wants to eat. Daniel would rather have oatmeal or soup from God than to have cake from the bad king.

QUESTIONS:

1. Who is this man?
2. What is happening in this picture?

Daniel 1:3-17

HE KING HAS MANY FRIENDS with him eating lots of good food. But do you see something very strange in this picture? Can you see where Daniel is pointing? Do you see the hand on the wall writing strange letters? No one is there, only a hand. Where does the hand come from? It must be an angel's hand, or perhaps the hand of God that is writing these letters. The king does not know what they mean. Daniel is pointing to the letters and reading them to the king. Daniel tells the king that God is angry and that the king can't be the king any more. God won't let him.

QUESTIONS:

1. *Whose hand is writing the letters on the wall?*
2. *Who is telling the king what the letters mean?*

Daniel 5:1-17

116

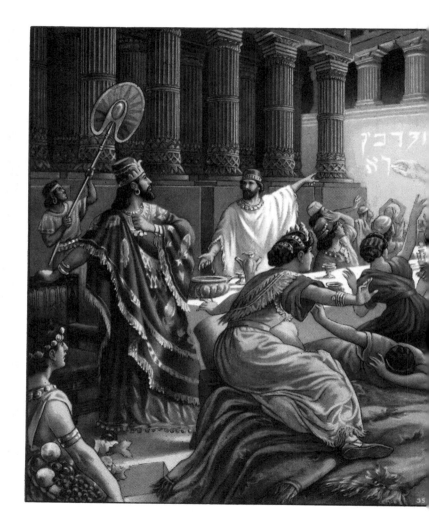

DANIEL IS PRAYING. That is good because God is hearing his prayer and will do what Daniel asks. But do you see the men hiding outside Daniel's door? What are they doing there? They are listening to Daniel. They want to know whether he is praying to God. They say that Daniel must not pray to God. They will hurt him if he does. Daniel knows the men are there listening but he does not care. He prays to God anyway. He would rather pray to God even if the men hurt him.

QUESTIONS:

1. *What is Daniel doing?*
2. *What are the men doing?*

Daniel 6:1-9

117

HE MEN HAVE PUT DANIEL in with all of these lions. Why did they do this? It is because Daniel was praying to God. The men did not want him to pray so they put him by these lions. They thought the lions would eat Daniel up. Are the lions hurting him? No, God has sent His angel to take care of him. The angel will keep the lions' mouths shut so that they cannot hurt Daniel. He prays to God and God is taking care of him.

QUESTIONS:

1. *Why is Daniel there with the lions?*
2. *Will the lions hurt him?*

Daniel 6:10-23

I T IS NIGHTTIME and these men are out in the fields taking care of their sheep. They chase the bears away so that they will not eat the sheep. Can you see their sheep? But now what is happening? Who are these angels who have come? What are they saying? They are telling these men that God's Son has been born that night. He is a little baby. The angels are glad and the men are glad. They go quickly to the place where the baby is, so that they can see Him.

QUESTIONS:

1. *Why are the men outside at night?*
2. *What are the angels telling them?*
3. *What do they decide to do?*

Luke 2:1-15

119

HE MEN WHO WERE TAKING CARE of the sheep have come to find God's Son. The angel told them where to find Him and now they have come to see the baby Jesus. There is the baby and His mother. The mother's name is Mary. God is the baby's Father. The men who were taking care of the sheep will tell many people what the angel said about the baby Jesus.

QUESTIONS:

1. *Who is this baby?*
2. *Who is the baby's Father?*
3. *What is His mother's name?*

Luke 2:16-18

120

WHO ARE THESE MEN? They are riding on camels. Have you ever seen a camel? Where are the men going in such a hurry? They are going to find God's Son. God has told them that His Son is going to be born. They are bringing many gifts to give Him. They know where to go because God has sent a star for them to follow. The star will take them to the baby Jesus.

QUESTIONS:

1. *Where are the men going?*
2. *How do they know where to go?*
3. *What is the name of God's Son?*

Matthew 2:1-9

121

THE MEN WHO WERE ON THE CAMELS have come a long way from another country. Now they have found the little baby they were looking for. They know that the baby is God's Son. They have brought many gifts to give Him. Mary, His mother, is holding Jesus while they worship Him and thank God. God is kind to these men to let them see His Son, Jesus.

QUESTIONS:

1. *Are the men giving presents to the baby Jesus?*
2. *Can you see one of the camels?*

Matthew 2:10, 11

CAN YOU SEE THE OLD MAN in the picture who is holding the baby? He has waited all his life to see God's baby Son. The old man has asked Mary if he can hold Jesus. He has never been so happy in all his life before, because now at last Jesus is born and he can hold Him in his arms. He knows that Jesus will take care of God's people. The name of the lady standing behind him is Anna. God has told her, too, that this baby is His Son and she is very, very happy.

QUESTIONS:

1. *Why are the man and the lady so happy?*
2. *Is Jesus God's Son?*

Luke 2:25-38

123

HIS IS ANOTHER PICTURE of Jesus. He ha
become a big boy now. In this picture w
see the big men He is talking to. Thes
old men are preachers and teachers. Th
boy Jesus is listening to them and asking them question
These men cannot understand how a boy can know s
much about God. They do not know that this boy is God
Son. This is Jesus.

QUESTIONS:

1. Who is this boy?
2. Why are the men surprised?
3. Why does the boy know so much about God

Luke 2:40-5

HIS IS ANOTHER PICTURE of Jesus. Now He is a man. Another man whose name is John is pointing up to God and praying. John will baptize Jesus. Jesus is glad because God wants John to do this. As soon as Jesus is baptized He will hear a voice from the sky saying, "This is my Son and I love Him. Listen to what He tells you to do." Do you know where the voice will come from? It will be God talking to Jesus and the other people who are watching him. God wants everyone to know that this is His Son.

QUESTIONS:

1. *What is John doing to Jesus?*
2. *Where will the voice come from?*
3. *What will the voice say?*

Matthew 3:13-17

125

**J**ESUS HAS GONE FAR AWAY. There are no other people here to help Him or to make Him happy. He is alone. He has not eaten anything for breakfast, or lunch, or supper. He did not eat anything yesterday or the day before that. He has not eaten anything for forty days. Soon Satan, God's enemy, will come and try to get Jesus to do something bad but Jesus will not listen to bad Satan. Jesus is God's Son and He is good. He has never done anything bad at all. He will never listen to Satan. Jesus listens only to God His Father and does only what God says.

QUESTIONS:

1. *Why is Jesus hungry?*
2. *Will He ever do anything bad?*
3. *Who will try to get Jesus to be bad?*

Matthew 4:1-11

126

ESUS ASKS TWELVE MEN to be His special friends. These men are called His disciples. They go with Jesus wherever He goes and help Him in all His work. These men are happy because Jesus has asked them to help Him. Some of the names of these men are Peter, John, James, Thomas, and Andrew. These twelve men are Jesus' helpers.

QUESTIONS:

1. *Who are these men?*
2. *Will they help Jesus?*
3. *Do you know any of their names?*

Mark 3:13-19

127

NE DAY JESUS was at a big dinner where a lady was getting married. After a while they needed more grape juice for the people to drink. They ask Jesus what to do. Jesus tells them to fill up six big jars of water and tells them to take them to the man. And do you know what? It wasn't water any more. It was better than they had ever tasted. Jesus can do things like that because He is God.

QUESTIONS:

1. *What did the people ask Jesus to do?*
2. *What did Jesus tell them to do with the big jars?*
3. *Can Jesus help us when we need Him?*

John 2:1-11

ESUS IS MAKING SOME MEN go out of the church. They didn't come to church to love God and pray. No, they are doing things there that God does not want them to do. They are selling things to get a lot of money and be rich. They don't love God and don't want to pray. Jesus has a whip in His hand and the men are afraid of Him. He tells them to take all of those things away. He says that they are in His Father's house and they must not do things like that when they are there.

QUESTIONS:

1. *What does Jesus have in His hand?*
2. *What does Jesus want these men to do?*

John 2:13-17

129

D O YOU SEE JESUS standing there? He to[ld] Peter to throw his fishing net in the wate[r]. Peter did not think that there would b[e] any fish but he did what Jesus told hi[m] to do, and now just see how many fish there are! Pet[er] minded Jesus and now Peter has all these fish. Can yo[u] see all the fish? There are almost too many to count. Pet[er] and his friends don't know what to do with all of them[.] They have so many in their boat that it is almost sinkin[g.] They give some to the men in the other boat and it [is] almost sinking too. Where did all these fish come from[?]

QUESTIONS:

1. Who told Peter to catch the fish?
2. Can you count how many fish there are, [or]
are there too many?

Luke 5:1-1[1]

130

WHAT IS HAPPENING HERE? Look at the men at the top of the picture. They brought their friend to Jesus. They have taken away part of the roof of the house and put im down right in front of Jesus where He will be sure o see him. The man could not walk and was lying on his ed. Can you see his bed? They brought him to Jesus beause they want him to walk again. Jesus tells the man o get well and now he is standing up. He has already earned to walk. Jesus makes him well right away.

QUESTIONS:

1. *How did the men get their friend down to Jesus?*
2. *Could the man walk before?*
3. *What did Jesus do?*

Luke 5:17-26

131

IT IS NIGHTTIME and Jesus is talking to a man whose name is Nicodemus. Can you say, "Nicodemus"? He is a good man but he does not know that Jesus is God's Son and he doesn't know very much about God. Jesus is telling him about God. He is telling him how to get to Heaven. He says, "Nicodemus, you cannot get there by yourself but God will take you there if you believe in Me. God loves you, Nicodemus." Jesus died so that Nicodemus could go to Heaven. Jesus died so that you and I can go to Heaven if we love Him.

QUESTIONS:

1. *What is this man's name?*
2. *Did he know God?*
3. *Why did Jesus have to die?*

John 3:1-5, 14-18

THIS MAN IS GLAD because his little boy feels all better again. Yesterday he was so sick that he didn't want to run and play. He only wanted to be there in his bed. His father was sad. He went to see Jesus. He asked Jesus to come and make the little boy well. Jesus said that He would help. He told the father to go home and the little boy would be all right. Jesus is far away but He makes the little boy well again.

QUESTIONS:

1. *Was the little boy sick?*
2. *Is he sick now?*
3. *Where is Jesus?*

John 4:46-54

133

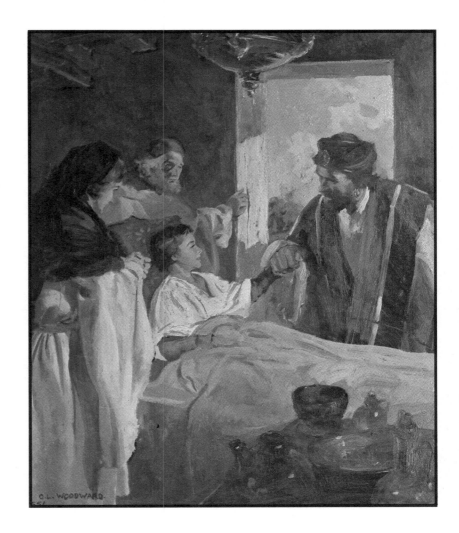

ESUS IS TALKING TO THE PEOPLE. See how many of them there are! They want to hear what Jesus says. They know Jesus is their Friend and they want to mind Him. He is telling the people to be kind and good. He tells them not to quarrel. Some of these people will love Jesus always and some of them will go away from Him and not want Him to be their Friend any more. Isn't that too bad? If Jesus is not their Friend, then God will not let them come to Heaven. Jesus wants to be your Friend too.

QUESTIONS:

1. *Who is talking to the people?*
2. *Is Jesus your Friend?*

Matthew 5:1-1

ESUS TOLD A STORY about two men who built houses. One of them built his house on the sand. He was a foolish man. It rained and rained and all of the sand washed away and the house fell down. The other man built his house upon a rock. Even though it rains the rock will not wash away. He is a wise man because he built his house upon a rock.

QUESTIONS:

1. *Was it a good idea to build a house on the sand?*
2. *What happened to that house?*
3. *When it rained did the house on the rock fall down?*

Matthew 7:24-29

135

ESUS IS HELPING A MAN SIT UP. The ma[n] was dead and his mother was sad. Jesu[s] saw the mother crying. He went over t[o] see the man lying on the bed. The ma[n] could not move. He was dead. Jesus tells him to be aliv[e] again. When Jesus says that, all of a sudden the man be[-] gins to move. He opens his eyes and sees Jesus and h[e] sees his mother too. The man and his mother are glad an[d] Jesus is glad too.

QUESTIONS:

1. Was the man dead?
2. What did Jesus tell him to do?
3. Then what happened?

Luke 7:11-1[ ]

136

JESUS AND HIS FRIENDS are in a boat. It is at night. There is a great storm. The wind is blowing. It is raining hard. The friends are afraid the ship will sink and they will all be drowned. Is Jesus afraid? No, He isn't. No, because He knows His God will take care of them. Jesus is standing up and holding up His hands and now the storm is going away. Jesus tells the storm to stop and it goes.

QUESTIONS:

1. *Is Jesus afraid?*
2. *What is He doing?*
3. *What will happen to the storm?*

Matthew 8:23-27

137

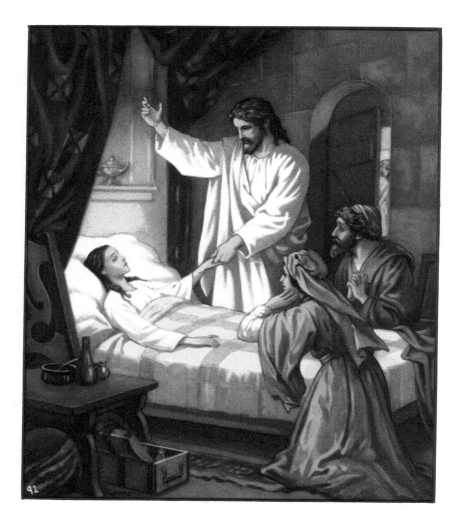

THIS LITTLE GIRL is twelve years old. Sh[e] was very sick and her father went to fin[d] Jesus. He asked Jesus to come and mak[e] his little girl well again. The docto[r] couldn't get her better, but he knows Jesus can. Jesu[s] comes and takes the little girl's hand and says, "Get u[p] little girl." Right away she will sit up and get out of be[d] and start to play and be all right again. The little girl die[d] but Jesus is bringing her back to life. He will give her [to] her mother and father. That is why they are so surprise[d] and happy.

QUESTIONS:

1. *Why are the mother and father so happy?*
2. *How did Jesus make the little girl well?*

Mark 5:22-[

138

ESUS IS TALKING here with a man who cannot see Him. The man is blind. His eyes are hurt so that he cannot see anything at all. Close your eyes now and you can tell what it is like to be blind. Everything is dark. Someone told this man Jesus was coming. The man heard Jesus coming. Then he cried out very loudly, "Jesus, please help me. Please make my eyes well so that I can see." Jesus touches his eyes and says, "Be open." And right away his eyes are all right and he can see. Isn't Jesus a wonderful Friend?

QUESTIONS:

1. *Could the man see Jesus?*
2. *What did Jesus say to make his eyes open?*

Matthew 9:27-31

139

THIS POOR MAN lying on the ground w: going on a trip, and all of a sudden som men came and took away his money an some of his clothes and hurt him and ra away. They left him lying there on the road. Some peop he knew came walking by but they wouldn't stop to he him. They just looked at him and went on. Then a ma he didn't like came along and stopped. You can see hir in the picture helping the poor man who is hurt. He pouring some medicine on some places and soon he w: lift him up and put him on his donkey and take him to hotel. Jesus wants us to be kind to everyone, even peop who hit us or don't like us.

QUESTIONS:

1. *Why is the man lying there?*
2. *What is the other man doing?*

Luke 10:30-

140

ARY IS SITTING DOWN listening while Jesus is talking to her. He is telling her many things that she needs to know. Do you see the other lady, the one who is standing up? Her name is Martha. She is Mary's sister. She is getting supper ready. Martha is working very hard and wants Mary to help her instead of talking to Jesus. Martha asks Jesus to make Mary help her get the supper. But Jesus says, "No, let Mary sit here and listen, because that is even more important than getting supper." Did you know that it is more important to listen to Jesus than it is to eat?

QUESTIONS:

1. *Who are these two ladies?*
2. *What does the one standing up want the other one to do?*
3. *Did Jesus say that Mary should keep on listening to Him?*

Luke 10:38-42

141

ESUS IS ANGRY with these men. He is talking to them while they are eating their dinners. He is angry because they say that they love God and they really don't. They say that they want to obey God, but they are telling lies because they want to do things their own way instead of the way God says. They give money to God but they do not love Him. They go to God's house but they do not love God. That is why Jesus is angry. He wants them to love God. He does not want their money unless they love Him.

QUESTIONS:

1. *Why is Jesus angry with these men?*
2. *Do these men love God?*
3. *Do they give money to God?*
4. *Does God want their money if they do not love Him?*

Luke 11:37-44

142

THIS MAN IS A RICH FARMER. He has lots of money. He is looking at his barns. Do you see his men putting hay into the barns? But this man does not love God. He loves his money and his farm more than he loves God. He has so much money and food that he doesn't know where to put it so he is going to build a bigger barn. But tonight God will let this rich man die so he will not wake up tomorrow morning. He can't use all his food in the barn any more because he will die tonight and never come back. God will take him away. The man is bad because he loves his farm but doesn't love God.

QUESTIONS:

1. *Does this man have lots of things?*
2. *Does this man love God?*

Luke 12:16-21

143

ESUS IS TALKING to His friends. Do you see the pretty flower He is pointing to? Jesus is telling them to look at the flowers. The flowers don't work hard to cook their suppers, do they? No, flowers don't need to cook and work hard, because God takes care of them. They don't need fine clothes, because God has made them grow with their beautiful clothes right on them. Jesus is telling His friends that God takes care of the flowers and He will take care of them too if they ask Him, and do whatever He says.

QUESTIONS:

1. *What is Jesus showing the disciples?*
2. *Will God take care of you?*

Luke 12:27-32

144

THIS MAN IS PLANTING SEEDS. He is carrying them in his bag over his shoulder. He throws the little seeds out on the ground. He wants them to grow and become soft green grass. He wants them to become big plants. Oh, look, do you see the birds behind him? They are eating up some of the seeds. Those seeds will not grow because the birds are taking them away. Some of the seed is falling down on the rocks and thorns. Can you see the thorns? The seeds cannot grow there very well. But some of the seeds fall on good ground and will grow up and become big plants.

QUESTIONS:

1. *Will the seed grow on the rock?*
2. *Where will the seed grow best?*

Matthew 13:3-8

145

OOK AT ALL THESE PEOPLE. See how man[y] there are? They are all hungry. They hav[e] not had any lunch and now it is time fo[r] supper and they don't have anything t[o] eat. One boy brought his lunch so he will not be hungry. He would be glad to give his lunch to all the people bu[t] do you think that would be enough for them to eat? No[,] of course not. The boy is giving his lunch to Jesus. Jesu[s] will break the bread in pieces and give the pieces to Hi[s] helpers, and do you know what will happen then? Jesu[s] will make the bread grow so that there will be enough fo[r] everyone.

QUESTIONS:

1. *What is the boy doing with his lunch?*
2. *What will Jesus do with it?*

Matthew 14:15-2[0]

146

WHAT IS HAPPENING in this picture? There is water with a boat in it and there are some men in the boat. Do you see Jesus in the picture? Is He swimming in the water? No, He is walking on top of it. Can you walk on top of water in your bathtub? No, of course not. But Jesus made the water. He can stand on it if He wants to. One of the men in the boat is Peter. When Peter sees Jesus on the water he wants to walk on it too. Peter will step out on the water and start to walk toward Jesus. Then he will become frightened and begin to sink, and Jesus will come and save him.

QUESTIONS:

1. *Can Jesus walk on top of the water?*
2. *Will Peter walk part of the way on top of the water?*
3. *When Peter gets scared, then what will happen?*

Matthew 14:22-33

147

ESUS IS TALKING to Peter and James and John. They are up on a high mountain. No one else is there. All of a sudden Jesus' clothes begin to shine and become brighter and brighter, and whiter than snow. Peter and James and John are frightened. Then all of a sudden they see two other men standing there talking to Jesus. You can see them there in the picture. These two men are Moses and Elijah who lived long ago. They have come down from Heaven to talk to Jesus. They are talking about how some bad men are going to take Jesus and hurt Him and kill Him. Soon Moses and Elijah will go away again and a bright cloud will come over above where Jesus is standing. God's voice will talk out of the cloud and say, "Jesus is My Son, listen to Him."

QUESTIONS:

1. *What color did Jesus' clothes become?*
2. *Who came to talk with Jesus?*
3. *What did the voice in the cloud say?*

Matthew 17:1-9

148

LAZARUS IS JESUS' FRIEND. One day Lazarus got sick and died. Jesus wasn't there to make him well again. The friends of Lazarus took his body and put it in the hole in the big rock and covered the hole so that no one could go in or out. When Jesus came he told the men to roll away the stone, and Jesus prayed and asked God to make Lazarus alive. Now can you see what is happening in this picture? Lazarus is coming out again. He was dead but now he is alive. Do you know why? It is because Jesus is here.

QUESTIONS:

1. *Did Jesus make the man alive?*
2. *Are the people glad that Jesus came?*

John 11:1-45

149

ESUS LOVES LITTLE CHILDREN. In this picture He is holding some of them on His lap and talking to them. Once Jesus' friends tried to send the children away. They thought that Jesus didn't want children around Him. Jesus talked to the disciples and told them never to say things like that. He wants the children to be with Him. He says, "Let the little children come to Me. Do not send them away because I love them and want them with Me."

QUESTIONS:

1. *What is Jesus holding in His arms?*
2. *Does Jesus love little children?*
3. *Are you a little child?*
4. *Does Jesus love you?*

Matthew 19:13-15

150

JESUS IS CRYING. He is looking at the old city of Jerusalem. There are many people in this city where He is looking. They do not love Jesus or His Father. They do not know that Jesus is God's Son. Jesus knows that some day a great army will come and knock down their city. If these people would only believe in Jesus then these terrible things would not happen to them. Jesus loves them and wants to help them, but they do not love Jesus and that is why He is crying.

QUESTIONS:

1. *What is Jesus looking at?*
2. *Why is He crying?*

Luke 13:31-35

151

HE MAN IN THE PICTURE has lost one of hi[s] sheep. It ran away and fell down an[d] couldn't get back up again. The littl[e] sheep is lost and crying and helpless. Th[e] man went to find him and finally he is there picking it up[.] He will take it home and get it all warm again and get i[t] something to eat. The man in the picture is good becaus[e] he takes care of the sheep. Jesus is like that man. Jesu[s] wants to take care of us when we get lost. Jesus loves yo[u] very much. You can be one of His little lambs.

QUESTIONS:

1. *How did the little sheep get there?*
2. *What is the man doing?*

Luke 15:3-[7]

152

HIS LADY IS PUTTING PERFUME on Jesus' feet and then wiping it off with her hair. The perfume has cost a lot of money. The men sitting at the table with Jesus are telling Him that the lady shouldn't do this but Jesus is glad. He wants her to use the perfume because she is doing it to tell Jesus, "Thank You." Jesus has been kind to her. She has done many bad things but Jesus will forgive her. Jesus will die for her sins. She is glad that He is so kind and so she has put the perfume on His feet to tell Him, "Thank You." Jesus died for you, too. Have you told Him, "Thank You"?

QUESTIONS:

1. *Where did the lady put the perfume?*
2. *Was Jesus glad?*
3. *Have you ever told Jesus, "Thank You," for what He has done for you?*
4. *Shall we thank Him now?*

John 12:1-7

THIS BOY IS GOING AWAY from home. He [is] saying good-by to his father. Now [he] will jump on his horse and ride away. H[is] father is sorry because he doesn't wa[nt] the boy to go away. But the boy thinks it will be mo[re] fun away from home. He asks his father to give him [a] lot of money and now he will go away. Are you sorry th[at] the boy is so bad? He should have stayed at home an[d] worked and helped his father instead of going away.

QUESTIONS:

1. *Did the boy want to stay home or go away?*
2. *Is the father happy or sad?*

Luke 15:11-1[8]

154

N THIS PICTURE you can see the boy who went away from his house even when his father didn't want him to. Now he has come back home again. He is sitting in a big chair and his father is very happy. After he went away he began to get very hungry and so he decided to come home again. His father is glad to see him. He didn't know if his father would want him to come back, but you can see how happy the father is to see him again. When the father saw him he ran and welcomed him and is telling him how glad he is.

QUESTIONS:

1. *Did the father let the boy come home?*
2. *Is the boy happy?*
3. *Is the father happy?*

Luke 15:20-24

155

O YOU SEE THESE MEN who are walking away from Jesus? They were lepers. That means that they were very sick. Everyone was afraid to go near them because they were so sick. People who touched them might get sick too. When they saw Jesus they called to Him and said, "Jesus, help us. Please help us." Jesus saw them and heard them calling. He wanted to help them and He made all of them well. He healed them all but only one of them came back to tell Him, "Thank You." This man is so glad he is well again that he falls down in front of Jesus. All the others forgot to tell Jesus, "Thank You."

QUESTIONS:

1. *Were all these men sick?*
2. *Who healed them?*
3. *What is the man in the picture doing?*
4. *Have you thanked Jesus because He is your Friend?*

Luke 17:11-19

156

HY IS THIS MAN LYING HERE so still? It is because he is dead. His father owns that land but some other people are growing grapes there. His father sent his son to get his money for the grapes, but the people wouldn't give the money to him. Instead they hurt him and killed him and threw him out on the ground where you can see him lying. What do you think the father will do when he hears about this? He will see to it that these men are killed because of the terrible thing they have done to his son.

QUESTIONS:

1. *Who owns this house?*
2. *What did the man's father send him to get?*
3. *What did the people do?*

Matthew 21:33-41

157

JESUS was in God's house watching the people putting money into a box. They were giving this money to God. In the picture you can see a lady who doesn't have very much money. She has brought a few pennies. That is all the money she has, and she is giving it all to God. When she puts this in she will not have any more money left at all. She is giving God everything that she has. Jesus is glad because the lady loves God so much. He doesn't think the rich men standing there have given very much at all. They have put in lots and lots of money but they are still rich and have lots more money left for themselves at home. Jesus says the poor woman's few pennies are better than all the money from the rich people who don't love Him.

QUESTIONS:

1. *Did the rich men put in a lot of money?*
2. *How much does the poor lady have left after she puts in her money?*

Mark 12:41-44

EVERYONE IS HAPPY because Jesus has come to visit them. He has come to the city of Jerusalem. All the people think he has come to Jerusalem to be their king. They want Jesus to be king because He is so kind to them and can help them. See how some people are putting their coats on the ground for Jesus to ride over. Others are cutting down branches from the trees and making a path for Him. The people shout and thank God because they think Jesus will help them all be rich and have lots of money and other things that they don't have now. They do not know that Jesus will soon be killed.

QUESTIONS:

1. *Are the people happy?*
2. *What are they putting down on the road for Jesus to ride over?*
3. *Why are they doing this?*

John 12:12-19

159

ERE IN THIS PICTURE you can see Jesus talk
ing to some of His friends. He is tellin
them about what is going to happen t
Him. He is pointing up to Heaven, tellin
them that soon He will go there to be with God, Hi
Father. Jesus says that some day all His friends will com
to Heaven too and live there with Him always.

QUESTIONS:

1. Where is Jesus pointing?
2. What is He telling His friends?

Luke 22:14-2

160

HIS MAN HAS MADE a great dinner and is ready to eat it. Can you see the man pointing to the food on the table? But who is coming to eat it? The man asked many of his rich friends to come and have dinner with him but they wouldn't. They didn't know what a wonderful dinner it was going to be so they said they had other things to do and couldn't come. Then the man invited the poor people who were sick and crippled and blind. Do you see them coming? They are glad to come and eat. Soon the table will be full of people. The man is glad because of his new friends but he is sorry because of those who would not come. Jesus wants you to come and live with Him some day. Will you be glad to come?

QUESTIONS:

1. *Who did the man invite at first to come and eat the good dinner?*
2. *Did the people he asked first want to come?*
3. *Who finally came to the dinner?*
4. *Does Jesus want you to come to Him?*

Matthew 22:1-14

SOME MEN ARE ASKING Jesus a question. They want to know what is the most important rule for them to obey. Can you think what that rule would be? Would it be to eat nicely? Or would it be not going across the street alone? No. These things are very important and you should eat nicely and must be careful about cars or you will get into trouble. But there is something even more important that we should do. Jesus tells these men what it is. He says that the greatest thing for them to do is to always love God. Do you love God? Do you do whatever He says? What are some things God wants you to do?

QUESTIONS:

1. *What is the most important rule to obey?*
2. *What are some things God wants you to do?*
3. *Do you love God by doing what He says?*

Matthew 22:35-40

162

WHAT IS HAPPENING IN this picture? Jesus has a loaf of bread in His hand. He is breaking it into pieces. He will give these pieces to His disciples who are sitting here at the supper table. Jesus will tell them to eat the bread. He says that the bread is His body. Jesus is telling His disciples that He must soon die. He died for you. He died for me. We have done bad things that God must punish. But Jesus asked to be punished for you. God punished Jesus instead of you. Jesus didn't do anything bad but God punished Him. Do you know why?

QUESTIONS:

1. *What does Jesus have in His hand?*
2. *Who will eat the bread?*
3. *What is going to happen to Jesus?*

Luke 22:14-20

163

ESUS IS TALKING to His disciples. He is tell
ing them what is going to happen to Him
Some men are going to take Him and kil
Him but Jesus tells them not to be afraid
He says that God will take care of them. Jesus tells them
that He will go away to His Father, away up in Heaven
When He gets there He will get places ready for them t
come to live. He is getting a place ready for you to liv
in Heaven too, if you love Jesus.

QUESTIONS:

1. *What is Jesus telling them?*
2. *Where is Jesus now?*

John 14:1-1

164

ESUS IS PRAYING all alone. He is in a garden and it is night. He is talking to His Father in Heaven. Jesus is very, very sad because He knows what will happen to Him soon. He knows that some men will come to get Him and take Him away and nail Him to a cross so that He will die. He will die on the cross so that God will not need to punish you and me for the bad things we have done. Jesus is sad because He does not want to die. He doesn't need to, either. He could ask God to send the angels to take care of Him but He will let the men kill Him. Jesus is glad to die for you.

QUESTIONS:

1. *Is Jesus happy or sad?*
2. *What is going to happen to Him?*

Luke 22:39-48

165

D ID YOU EVER HEAR about a man named Judas Iscariot? Judas pretended that he was one of Jesus' friends. Some bad men said they would give Judas money if he would help them catch Jesus. In this picture Judas is bringing them to where Jesus is. It is night. They are bringing torches. Do you see the torches in their hands, giving light? They don't have flashlights and so they use these torches instead. Is Jesus going to run away from them? No, Jesus is standing, waiting. He could go away if He wanted to, but He will let them take Him.

QUESTIONS:

1. *What is the name of the man leading these bad people to Jesus?*
2. *Why doesn't Jesus run away?*

Luke 22:47-54

166

PETER IS ONE of Jesus' friends and disciples. He is getting warm by being near the fire with some other people. Peter looks angry. The lady is pointing at him but he is telling this lady, "No." Why is he saying that? This lady has asked Peter if Jesus is his Friend. Peter tells her, "No." He says that he doesn't know Jesus at all. What a bad thing to say. Peter is telling a lie because he is afraid the other people there will hurt him if they know he is Jesus' friend. Soon he will look up and see Jesus looking at him and then he will cry because he has done such a bad thing.

QUESTIONS:

1. *Was Peter a friend of Jesus?*
2. *What did Peter tell the girl?*

John 18:10-27

167

 OW THE PEOPLE HAVE TAKEN JESUS to
man whose name was Pilate. Pilate ca
let them kill Jesus or else make them le
Jesus go. He is talking to the people and
telling them that he thinks he ought to let Jesus go. He
says Jesus is good. He tells them that Jesus hasn't don
anything bad at all. See how angry the people are! They
want Pilate to let them kill Jesus. They are shouting a
Pilate and Pilate is afraid of them. Soon he will decide
to give Jesus to the men so that they can kill Him.

QUESTIONS:

1. *What is this man's name?*
2. *What do the people want Pilate to do?*
3. *What will Pilate do?*

John 19:1-16

168

HE BAD MEN have taken Jesus up the hill and have nailed His hands and His feet on these big pieces of wood so that He will die after a while. Can you think what it would be like if you were hanging there with nails through your hands? Oh, what a terrible thing they are doing to Jesus! Do you know why Jesus was nailed there? It is because He loves you and me. You and I have done bad things and God should punish us. But God doesn't want to do that because He loves us. God sent His dear Son Jesus who wanted to be punished for us. In this picture you can see Jesus being punished for your sins by dying there on the cross. That is how much Jesus loves you. He died for you.

QUESTIONS:

1. *What are in Jesus' hands?*
2. *Why did Jesus let them kill Him?*
3. *Does Jesus love you?*

John 19:16-24

169

 ESUS IS DEAD. His body is all wrapped
in a white cloth. His friends are putting
His body into a great hole in the rock.
Soon they will leave Him there all alone.
They do not think they will ever see Jesus again. They
will go away and leave Him here because He is dead.
How sad they are! They do not know that soon He will become
alive again and come out of the place where they
are putting Him. Jesus is dead but God is going to bring
Him back to life.

QUESTIONS:

1. *Where are they putting Jesus' body?*
2. *Will His body stay there in the hole?*

John 19:40-

170

 HESE THREE LADIES are Jesus' friends. They have come to His grave to put some sweet perfume on the clothes He was wrapped up in after He died. They thought this would be a nice thing to do even though Jesus was dead and couldn't smell the perfume. Then they would sadly go away and leave Jesus there and never see Him again. But what is happening? An angel is inside the grave where Jesus was. The angel tells them Jesus isn't there! Jesus is alive and has gone away! Jesus was dead, but God made Him alive again! Jesus said this would happen, but no one believed Him. Now His friends know that whatever Jesus says is always true. He says that He will make all His friends alive again after they are dead. He will take them up to Heaven to be with Him always and always. Are you one of Jesus' friends? Aren't you glad that Jesus is alive?

QUESTIONS:

1. *Who are these three ladies?*
2. *Who is talking to them?*
3. *What is he telling them?*

Mark 16:1-8

171

T LAST some of Jesus' friends are meeti[ng] Him again. They are very surprise[d] They thought Jesus was dead. They did[n't] know that Jesus was alive again. They a[re] walking along and they see somebody standing there, a[nd] it is Jesus! How surprised and happy they are. They kn[ow] now that Jesus is God's Son and they bow down at H[is] feet. Jesus is saying, "Don't be afraid. Go and tell M[y] other friends to go to a certain place and I will meet the[m] there."

QUESTIONS:

1. *Who are these ladies talking to?*
2. *Why are they surprised and happy?*

John 20:11[-]

172

DO YOU SEE THESE TWO MEN running as fast as they can? One of them is Peter and the other one is John. Peter is the older man and John is younger. Why are they running so fast? It is because the women have told them that Jesus is not in the grave but is alive again. Peter and John can hardly believe what the women have told them and they are going to see for themselves. They do not understand how Jesus could be alive and not in the hole in the rock. What an exciting morning this was when Jesus came back to life again!

QUESTIONS:

1. *Who are these two men?*
2. *Where are they going?*
3. *What will they find out?*

John 20:1-5

ETER AND JOHN ran right into the place where Jesus had been buried. In the picture you can see Peter inside, looking for Jesus. Is Jesus there? No, the cloth that was wrapped around Jesus is lying there, but Jesus has come out and gone away. He is alive again and isn't in the grave. Peter is surprised. John is surprised too. John is standing outside looking in. Finally they know that Jesus is not dead any more.

QUESTIONS:

1. Which man is Peter?
2. Where is Jesus?

John 20:6-10

174

HREE MEN ARE WALKING along a road. Two of them are going to their home. When the third man came along and asked them why they were so sad, they said it was because Jesus was dead. The third man began to tell them more about Jesus and why He had to die. He told them that Jesus died for their sins. The two men are asking this third man to come and eat with them. While they were eating, all of a sudden they realized that the third man was Jesus. They had been talking to Jesus and didn't know it! As soon as they knew this, suddenly Jesus disappeared and wasn't eating there with them anymore. He had gone away.

QUESTION:

1. Who is the third man?

Luke 24:13-32

THE DISCIPLES WERE TALKING together when all of a sudden Jesus was standing there with them. He hadn't knocked or come in at the door. He was just there! He must have come right through the walls because Jesus can do anything. His disciples were scared but Jesus says, "Don't be afraid. I am Jesus." In this picture you can see Him showing His friends the holes in His hands and His feet, so that they will know that this is really their very own Jesus who was nailed to the big pieces of wood and died. Now He is alive again and they are seeing Him. Pretty soon He will eat some fish with them and some honey, so that they will know that He is really alive and is not just a ghost.

QUESTIONS:

1. *Who is the man talking to the disciples?*
2. *Did He open the door and come in?*

Luke 24:33-48

176

ONE DAY WHILE JESUS was talking with His disciples out on a hill, all of a sudden He began to go up into the air. Do you see the cloud? When Jesus goes into the cloud, they will not see Him anymore. Do you know where He is going? He is going to Heaven to live again with God His Father. When Jesus has gone away, two angels will come and talk with Jesus' friends and tell them that Jesus will come back again some day. Some day Jesus is going to come and take all His friends to Heaven. Are you one of Jesus' friends?

QUESTIONS:

1. *Where is Jesus going?*
2. *Will He come back again?*

Acts 1:9-11

177

ONE DAY WHILE JESUS' FRIENDS were praying together, there came a noise that sounded like a big wind coming from the sky, and the noise was all around them in the house, although they couldn't feel any wind. Do you see what is on the men's heads? It looks like tongues made of fire on each of them. Why is this happening? It is because God the Holy Spirit is coming down upon these men. After a while the tongues of fire will go away but the Holy Spirit will stay in their hearts. The Holy Spirit will help them and tell them many things and make them very strong. Jesus sent the Holy Spirit to comfort and help them.

QUESTIONS:

1. *What is on the men's heads?*
2. *Who is coming into these men?*
3. *Who sent the Holy Spirit to them?*

Acts 2;1-4

PETER IS TALKING to all of these other people who don't know about Jesus yet. He is telling them that Jesus wants to be their friend and their Saviour. They have come from all over the world. Peter is telling them about how Jesus died and came back to life. These people come from a different country, but Peter is talking to them in their own language. God is helping Peter and the other disciples to talk in whatever language they need to tell people about Jesus. When these people hear about Jesus dying for them they are sad and ask what they should do. Peter told them to believe on the Lord Jesus and be baptized. And many of them did.

QUESTIONS:

1. *What is Peter telling these people?*
2. *Do they decide to love Jesus?*

Acts 2:4-8, 14-21

179

PETER AND JOHN have come to God's house to pray. A man is sitting there who can't walk. Something is the matter with his legs. He was that way when he was a tiny baby and he has never been able to walk. That is why he is sitting there near God's house asking people to give him money to buy food. When he sees Peter and John he asks them to give him some money. Peter says he doesn't have any, but he can give him something else that is a lot better. He says, "Get up and walk. Jesus will make you well." In the picture you can see the man beginning to get up. He will walk and run. He will give thanks to God.

QUESTIONS:

1. *Could this man walk before Peter talked to him?*
2. *Where is Jesus?*
3. *Did Jesus help Peter make the man walk?*

Acts 3:1-11

180

PETER IS TALKING to the bad men who killed Jesus. They don't like Peter and would like to kill him. They are angry because Peter made the man walk, who was sitting on the steps of the church. In the picture you can see the man standing there with Peter. Peter tells them that Jesus made the man well again. They are telling Peter not to talk about Jesus anymore and Peter isn't obeying them. Peter obeys God, but not these men, so he will keep on telling how kind and wonderful Jesus is.

QUESTIONS:

1. *Do the bad people want Peter to talk about Jesus?*
2. *Will Peter stop talking about Jesus?*

Acts 4:5-21

181

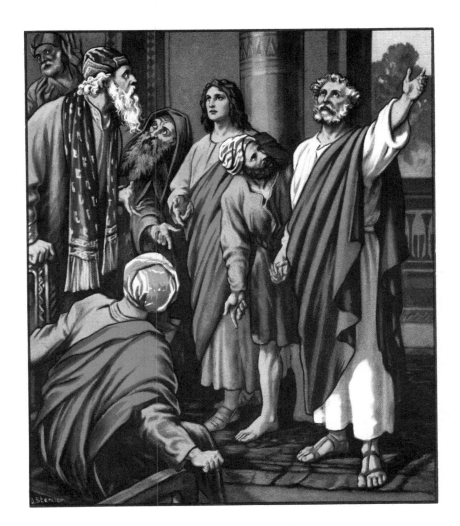

HE MAN LYING DOWN on the floor is dead. The man standing up is Peter. Peter was sitting there and the man came in and told him a lie. As soon as he told the lie he suddenly fell down and died. God punished Ananias because he told a lie. Soon the people will carry him outside and make a hole and put him in it and cover him up.

QUESTIONS:

1. Why is the man there on the floor?
2. Did he tell a lie to God?

Acts 5:1-11

675

ETER IS IN JAIL. The bad people who killed Jesus have put him there. The doors and windows are all locked so that he can't get out. He has been there all night. Here in this picture you can see Peter lying there in jail when all of a sudden an angel comes. The angel is waking Peter up and telling him to come with him. The angel will unlock the doors of the jail. The angel doesn't have a key but he will open the doors anyway. When he is safely out he will tell Peter to go and tell more people about Jesus. God sent His angel to help Peter.

QUESTIONS:

1. *Does the angel have a key to the door?*
2. *What did the angel tell Peter to do?*

Acts 12:1-17

H, WHAT IS HAPPENING to this man? He is kneeling down and praying while the bad men are killing him with big stones. Is he crying? No. He is praying and asking God not to hurt these men even though they are hurting him. These men are angry because Stephen told them about Jesus. They don't want to hear about Jesus and so they decided to kill Stephen. Stephen is happy because he sees Jesus up there in Heaven. In a little while he will go there and be with Jesus.

QUESTIONS:

1. *What is the man's name?*
2. *Why are these men throwing big stones at him?*

Acts 6:8-15; 7:54-60

184

THE MAN SITTING in the chariot and reading the Book wants to know more about God. He is reading part of the Bible. He has stopped the horses and is talking to Philip. Philip is one of Jesus' disciples. The Holy Spirit told him to run over to the chariot and start talking to the man. He is telling the man what the Bible means. He is telling him about Jesus. Soon the man sitting in the chariot will be a Christian.

QUESTIONS:

1. *What is the man's name who is standing there?*
2. *Who is he talking about?*
3. *Will the other man become a Christian?*

Acts 8:26-40

185

HIS MAN'S NAME IS PAUL. He doesn't li[ke]
Christians. He would like to kill all [of]
them or put them in jail. He is walkin[g]
down the road trying to find some Chri[s-]
tians to hurt. He thinks that all Christians are bad. H[e]
does not know that Jesus is God's Son. Paul thinks Go[d]
likes him to hurt Christians. But soon God will tell Pa[ul]
to love Jesus and His people. Then Paul won't hurt the[m]
any more.

QUESTIONS:

1. *What is this man's name?*
2. *Why does he hurt the Christians?*

Acts 9:1,

ERE IS ANOTHER PICTURE of Paul. While he was walking down the road all of a sudden Jesus started talking to him from Heaven. He is telling Paul not to hurt the Christians anymore. He is saying, "Paul, you too must become one of My friends. I am Jesus, and you must stop hurting Me and you must leave My people alone." Paul is very surprised and afraid, and is asking Jesus what He wants him to do. Jesus tells him and now Paul will always do whatever Jesus says.

QUESTIONS:

1. *Who is talking to Paul?*
2. *Does Paul decide to love Jesus?*

Acts 9:3-19

HO IS THIS MAN in the basket? It is Paul. H[is] friends are helping him to get away. Pa[ul] has been telling everyone about his ne[w] Friend Jesus and how much he loves Hi[m.] Paul doesn't hurt God's children anymore. The peop[le] who don't like God try to catch Paul, so his friends a[re] helping him to run away. Paul is God's friend now and h[e] loves Jesus.

QUESTIONS:

1. Who is the man in the basket?
2. Why is he running away?

Acts 9:22-[25]

188

AUL AND SILAS are in jail but they don't care very much because they know that God loves them. They don't care what happens to them so they have been singing. All of a sudden a great earthquake shakes the jail and all of the doors swing open and the chains fall off their hands and feet so that they can run away. But they are not trying to run away. They are staying there and talking to the man who is supposed to keep them in jail. He is kneeling there asking them what to do. They are telling him to believe on Jesus and he will be saved.

QUESTIONS:

1. *Where are Paul and Silas?*
2. *Who are they talking to?*
3. *What did they tell the man to do?*

Acts 16:22-34

189

AUL IS ON A BOAT and there is a great storm. Do you see the waves and how the ship is sinking? But God took care of Paul and all the people who were with him and none of them were hurt. They came through the water and got to the shore all right. Paul is standing there telling God, "Thank You," for taking care of them. God loves Paul, and God loves you.

QUESTIONS:

    1. *Did the ship sink?*
    2. *Were the people saved?*
    3. *Does God love you?*

Acts 27:14-44

Sweet Sound of Bird Song

a novel by Anne Wilensky

and cartoons by Billy Stampone

Published by Haiku Helen Press

Written, edited, and published by Anne Pyne

Drawings on front and back cover and inside
book by Bill Pyne aka Billy Stampone

cover designed by Helen Kritzler aka Haiku
Helen

ISBN
978-0-9840976-7-8
0-9840976-7-8

Contact information: Willard Kraft
(520) 465-0999
5152 East 8th Street, Tucson, AZ 85711

First edition
Printed in the United States of America.

Welcome

I send you our beautiful Arizona sunshine, our
flawless blue skies.
Let every day come up roses for you
Love, Anne

Boy sees girl needs help with bike

She gets back on bike after he fixes it for her.

Thank you

I thank everyone. I have been helped in infinite ways by all of you, in Tucson, in NYC, and on my internet forums.

Thank you to my wonderful husband Bill Pyne who got me to be a writer (all the cartoons and drawings are by him).

And thank you to my good friend Helen Kritzler who helps me with my books and does the covers for all of them.

And thank you to my angels

Driving Lessons (the second half of this book) is about a brand new chapter in my life.
I am being helped by angels. I want to thank them here
Bill Kraft, and Sharon, and Frank Grijalva
Also Jack Schiro and Danny.
God bless you always, and thank you for everything.
Your neighbor and friend, Anne

Sweet Sound of Bird Song is a book in two parts

Part One is Moving to Tucson and Summer 2010

Bill is a wonderful helpmeet

Part 2 is Driving Lessons

Jim laughs up his sleeve while teaching Anne to drive

Moving to Tucson

Anne buys a house

I called my realtor, Gene, yesterday to ask about finding a house for my friend Cora in the neighborhood she lives (where she is so happy and comfortable) and where the mortgage is the same as her rent. Gene said he will try but it is not so easy.

I hadn't talked to Gene since before Jan and Harry bought their house with him, so it is some years since I have talked to Gene. It was nice hearing his voice on the phone. Gene and I are very fond of each other. He is a warm wonderful being.

And it is very intimate, the person who was your realtor, who did all the arrangements for the house you are living in. I know his wife Sue too and like her a lot. It was my first year in Tucson and she took me to two tupperware parties.

I met Gene because my first summer in the apartments a young woman had just moved there with her parents. She was walking around trying to make friends. No one would talk to her so I did.

I was lying under a tree with my dog Clio on a leash, reading *A Course In Miracles,* when Sheila came over to be friends. She invited me to a church social that evening and gave me the flyer for it.

After I agreed to go, her father showed up at my apartment and said I don't have to go, that his daughter has mental problems.

I said "I like Sheila and I want to go."

So the arrangement was made that Sheila's mom would drive us and drive us home. Which back then made no sense to me. I had so recently moved from New York City that I was used to walking everywhere. I thought Sheila and I would just walk the mile to where it was and walk the mile home.

However that did not go over with Sheila's parents who insisted it was not safe. Which is the most absurd thing in the world.

Nothing could be safer than the neighborhood our apartments were in Tucson. Sheila was 20 years old and they treated her like a child. And because I was her friend I got to be treated like a child too.

I don't think Sheila had mental problems, I think the problem was them treating her like a child constantly. There was no reason Sheila and I could not go to the social at the pastor's house on our own. Instead we were both treated like 4 year olds going to a birthday party.

Before we went Sheila explained we each had to bring something. So we walked over to the Circle K together, which was just across the parking lot. And she bought a big bag of popcorn and I bought a big bag of pretzels and potato chips

And then an hour later, at about 6 pm, her mother drove us over there in her car.

I don't remember the sequence of events now. I think first we all watched a Christian video. I hated the video and closed my eyes and put my fingers in my ears till it was over.

I was reading *A Course In Miracles* then, and the story of the video was the opposite of what I was learning in *A Course In Miracles*. In the video a young man sets out to help people and he winds up murdered for his efforts, he gets killed.

It was the opposite message from *A Course in Miracles* which is purely love and forgiveness. The video was just death and sacrifice.

Then we played a Christian board game. I liked the game because I like board games. You pick a card and answer the question. The card I got asked me when I started Sunday School. Which made me burst out laughing.

They said "why are you laughing?"

I said "I am Jewish, I never went to Sunday School."

Then we played some version of Charades which was not religious. I remember everyone guessing kinds of trucks, they were so very well versed in automobiles and trucks, which I knew nothing about.

And then everyone sat and schmoozed and ate.

And I walked outside to a table in the backyard to be in the night air and be myself. The people were all very nice but they were all close from their church, and I was still upset by the video.

While I was sitting out there by myself, a man came out to join me. I guess he came to convert me. He sat down next to me and said he has a store of Christian videos and he is the one who brought the video we saw tonight.

I didn't tell him I hated the video.

He said "here is my card, you can rent a video here anytime."

I didn't even look at the card. But he said "it says Freedom Realty because I also sell real estate."

He made a shame face and said "you have to earn a living, but at least it is not selling liquor." He seemed proud that he rented and sold Christian videos and ashamed that he also sold real estate.

And then he said "any time you want me to explain the Bible to you, I will be glad to do it."

I had just started to read *A Course In Miracles* and was excited out of my mind about it.

"Guess what!" I told him, "Jesus Christ wrote a new book, it is called *A Course In Miracles*."

He was polite enough to let me finish my spiel. Altho now I realize he probably thought I was cuckoo, and responded with "the Bible is good enough for me," and he went back inside.

That is how I met Gene. I politely put his card in my pocket and forgot all about it.

But that Sunday my friend Leah from the neighborhood called and said "I want to swim in your apartment complex swimming pool."

So I brought my dog Clio, let her run around the deck. I didn't have a real bathing suit then. I wore shorts and top. And Leah and I played in the water while Clio ran around the deck.

But Sunday is the day, I didn't realize it, when the manager of the apartments would show everyone around who was looking for an apartment. She had a fit about Clio running around the deck. And when I got out of the water she said "Get yourself a proper bathing suit!"

The appealing thing about the apartments is when I would come back from walking Clio (in the inferno summer heat) I used to just jump in the pool in my shorts and top, and Clio would hang out with me on the deck.

Now it meant I would have to return to my apartment, which was so heavily air conditioned I would not want to go swimming afterwards. And I could not have my Clio with me, and the joy of it was having Clio with me.

It meant a very appealing thing about living here was taken away from me.

Plus I didn't like being yelled at in that abrupt manner. I had liked Phyllis very much, the manager of our apartments, but now I was shy of her.

I lied on my bed. I was upset. And talked it all over with my Higher Self. The very first thing my Higher Self said is "You misunderstood what happened with Phyllis. She brought you a message from Heaven, now is the time to buy a house."

"How can I buy a house, I have no money?" I said to my Higher Self.

"Remember the man at the church social who gave you his business card for the Christian videos. Remember how he told you he also sold real estate.

"Find the card and call him and tell him you want to buy a house and your father pays the rent on the apartment, $330 a month, so you want a house where the mortgage is $330 a month. Do it right now!"

So I found the business card in the pocket of the jeans I had worn that night, got it out, went to the telephone.

I asked for Gene. She said she is his wife, Sue.

I said "can Gene find me a house where the mortgage is $330, what I pay in rent now?"

And she said "no problem, Gene will call you back."

Then one minute later he did call me back. He too said "no problem."

"Where do you want to live?" he asked me.

I said "I want to stay in this neighborhood, it is starting to become familiar to me."

"No problem!" he said

"Where do you want to live?" I asked Bill.

He said "on Glen Street."

"No problem," Gene said.

And the next day he took me and Bill to 3 houses. One on Glen Street the street Bill had chosen. It was a very nice brick house, with a backyard of grass and a very nice ramada built in backyard and the mortgage was $300.

But I preferred the other house, which was run down and falling down, because the tree in the backyard was the same as the tree right out my window in New York, the acacia tree.

When I told Gene my choice he said "I will have to talk to your father." It was clear from Gene's face that the Glen Street house was totally superior.

"It is a superior house?" I asked.

"Totally superior!" he said.

It really was a quality house. So I said OK, and took a deep breath and decided to call my mother.

The next morning when Bill rushed me out of the bathroom so he could take his shower and go to work, after he left I called Gene and said "Can I have a house with 2 bathrooms. I have been rushed out of the bathroom for 20 years so my husband could go to work."

That was during the era when I liked to take a long bath in the morning, wash my hair, and chit-chat with my Higher Self in the bath.

I had a lot of stress in my life and discovered that combination really helped me, long hot bath, wash my hair, and long chit-chat with my Higher Self.

When I asked Gene for a house with a second bathroom, he said "remember you said you want the mortgage to only be $330, you can't have a second bathroom for that mortgage."

"OK" I said, "I am going to call my mother now, wish me luck."

My dad was in the hospital then. My mother was so stressed. When I called and said I wanted to buy a house she went out of her mind with joy. She was a girl who really really wanted to hear some good news.

She had grown up in houses in Rochester and both her parents were into buying and selling houses her whole life. She had always wanted to buy a house but my dad had vetoed it. He had grown up in an apartment in New York and was used to that convenience of the landlord doing everything for him, and he didn't have to do anything.

I told her about the house we had found and how I just called the realtor to ask for second bathroom because Bill has rushed me out of the bathroom for 20 years to go to work.

And she said "I would like you to have that second bathroom and I would like you to have a porch, call your realtor and tell him we can do better."

And she wrote a letter saying I can have a house for up to $75 thousand and I took the letter over to Gene who read it very carefully and made a xerox copy of it.

And the next day he took me and Bill to look at 6 houses and this is the one I chose.

And an hour after we got home I called Gene and said "this is the house I want to buy."

I called my mother and said "I found the house I

want."

She said "I'm sure it is a pretty house but I am not going to pay any money till your cousin Pete approves it because it might be house which will fall down."

So I called my cousin Pete who asked me what kind of roof does it have.

I called Gene. Gene said "it has a flat roof."

My cousin Pete said "I won't approve a flat roof, they develop problems."

So I called Gene, he said "nearly all the houses in Tucson have a flat roof."

So I had my neighbor come over and look at it. He is also an expert on houses. He said "it won't fall down and it won't burn down."

But he found a lot of problems with it. I decided to ignore what he said.

I didn't know what to do when Pete said he would not approve the house because it has a flat roof.

So my Higher Self said "Call your father, he is back home from the hospital and ask him what to do, he doesn't know anything about houses, so he is the perfect one to help you."

I said "Daddy, mommy said I could have a house but

she would not let me have any house till cousin Pete approves it. And the house I found has a flat roof and Pete said he won't approve a house with a flat roof."

My father said "I don't know anything at all about houses, but mommy doesn't know anything about roofs, just don't tell her about it."

So I called Gene and told him the whole story. He said "an independent inspector which you will pay for will inspect the whole house and write a report. Tell your mother that. And tell her we will send her a copy of the report."

So I called my mother back. I said "Pete is too busy to look at the house (that was true) but the realtor said we pay for the inspector to inspect it, and he will send you a copy of the report."

So my mother said "perfect!" and gave me the earnest money.

The inspector discovered the pipes are very old and could go at any moment. But my Higher Self said "it could be 20 years before they go, ignore it!"

Everything the inspector turned on, went on.

Altho when I moved into the house I did discover everything was broken. Luckily I did not discover it till I moved into the house.

I guess my mother was satisfied when I told her "my neighbor said it won't burn down or fall down," and believed that.

So I called my father. I said "the house costs $76 thousand."

He said "offer 70,000 for it."

He authorized me buying the house.

So I walked right over to Gene's store with my dog and said "my father said I can have it and should offer 70."

Gene said "the lady will come down to 73."

So I said "Done!"

And I bought the house.

Turning Tucson Intimate

The Mass Awakening for our planet is just one year away now. I feel like we are in the last chapter of the old world, then the first chapter of the new world will begin.

In a way it is similar to my last days in New York before I moved to Tucson. The end to my New York City sojourn.

But that all happened so quickly. I decided to move to Tucson totally out of the blue and a month later we walked into our new Tucson apartment.

And I was in shock the whole time that I had decided to make this move and there was a lot to accomplish when you have to do it all in a month.

So I did not have the leisure in time or mind to say "this is my last month in New York, I want to do the things I can only do while I am here."

Instead all I did was prepare for the move and kept to my regular routine— walk my dog Clio in the morning and in the evening, and whoever I bumped into on the street that is who I bumped into.

I bumped into Marjorie on the street the last few mornings so we talked and talked about it.

And the morning before I left I bumped into Victor's big brother, Joey, so we talked about it. I don't remember anyone else I bumped into during that final few days. I just know that Marjorie and Joey were the only people I said "I am moving to Tucson."

Altho I do remember going to the pet food store on 5th Street to try to buy a little water attachment for Clio's pet carrier for the airplane. The Arab owner was sitting outside his store and even tho he saw me he did not stop sitting there quietly.

And finally, it was a long time I was waiting (I realize now he is a Muslim and he was doing his prayers) finally I said something, what I needed.

And he said "for you I will stop" and he went in to look for it.

And I remember all the love he expressed for me and all the love I felt for him.

"I am moving to Tucson," I told him.

"It is a big loss," he said.

I knew I was leaving behind a lot of love when I decided to move to Tucson.

I had not known he loved me till he said "it is a big loss" and I felt such love for him. I was so touched the owner of my pet food store loved me.

On my next to last day I walked with my friend Marjorie to withdraw the money I had in the savings bank. I had bumped into her on the street while I had Clio. I said I would write to her and she was so happy.

She said she had had a boyfriend who collected snakes and he moved to Phoenix and so she used to get letters from Arizona and now she will get letters from Arizona again from me.

She walked with me to 8th Street and 4th Avenue and would go no further even tho my bank was only across the street.

She said "I don't leave the neighborhood."

I thought it is only across the street and the last time she will ever see me. But I completely understood. I was like that myself about leaving the neighborhood.

And that is the last time I saw Marjorie, she would not take one foot off the curb.

And I continued on, just me and Clio. Bill had quit his job at NYU a few months before, that is why it was so easy for us to make the move, he was no longer at NYU. And when he had hunted and hunted for another job he had not been hired.

But I guess he had not collected his final paycheck. So first I went to the building at NYU, right across the street, where they give you the paycheck.

I must have asked someone on line "we are moving to Tucson, is this the right place to pick up my husband's paycheck?"

They said yes but every single person on line said "I am jealous you are moving to Tucson."

I thought "they don't have to be jealous, if they want Tucson they can have it too. They can do the same thing we did. Moving is easy, just making the decision is hard."

Then I walked across the street and withdrew my savings of $200 and then came home. And informed my neighbor Carmine I was moving to Tucson on Sunday.

"What about your furniture?" he said

"I will leave it behind" I said.

When he got back from the saloon later in the afternoon he said "write it down where you are moving."

He had tried to tell his friends in the saloon where I was moving and had not remembered Tucson Arizona. I knew Carmine cannot read or write so I wrote it down for him to show them.

Leaving Carmine was the most emotional for me. I used to buy him his vodka and Pall Malls each morning when I walked the dog.

And when he got back from the saloon in the late afternoon he would call from the bottom of the steps "Annie I am home!"

And I would instantly make him a pot of fresh coffee. He liked a giant mug of coffee and a fried egg sandwich on toast, so I would make both and bring it down to his apartment.

Carmine and I were very close and I liked taking care of him.

The first night in my new apartment in Tucson while I was taking a long bath to calm down, I kept hearing thru the walls Carmine calling "Annie I am home!"

And I put my face in the water and cried and cried. I missed my neighbors so much I couldn't believe I had moved away from them.

But of course I had wanted to escape from New York City for a very long time and never thought I would succeed in it. It still seemed like a tremendous miracle I had succeeded.

Understandably it took me a long time to be happy in Tucson. I was very shy in a place where no one knew me and I didn't know anyone. I had left a place where everyone knew me and I knew everyone and everyone loved me and I loved everyone.

It wasn't till Valentine's Day of the following year, we had been in Tucson 14 months, that I realized if I wanted to have love in Tucson the way was to give love.

And so when we went to the library that morning I gave so much love to the librarian and she gave love in return.

And then we went to Carl Juniors and I gave so much love to the girl who got my order and she gave me so such love in return. We had a really nice and interesting conversation and filled with love too.

And then I guess I was home free. I had figured out how to be happy in Tucson, just give love to everyone I encountered ..... and that would turn Tucson intimate and friendly and loving for me which it did....

Skipper Sleeping
Bill loves drawing Skipper

Letting my hair down

In my dream before I awoke this morning Franny and my aunt Celia were having conversation. It was intellectual conversation. Celia is the youngest of my father's siblings. She is 12 years younger than my father, and 13 years younger than Esther, the eldest.

Franny is Celia's Tucson friend, a few years younger than she. Franny was also my first friend when I moved to Tucson. Because she found the apartment for her friend Celia's niece, me. And lived in the same apartment complex, and befriended me when we first arrived.

When I first decided to move to Tucson, I called my cousin Pete and asked him to find me an apartment which accepted dogs. My aunt Celia was in Tucson, her son Pete was in Tucson, and the youngest of her 4 children, Bobby. Her other two children were living in California.

I chose Pete, because when my dad was driving my aunt Esther and me back to Manhattan after a family gathering at his house, my dad and his sister gossiped in the front seat. All their concern was about their baby sister in Tucson. When she no longer had a husband, they took over worrying about her and being in charge of her.

It was the '60s, and they were very concerned about Celia's report that her son Pete was now living with the Jesus Freaks.

My dad said "but they have a good record of getting kids off drugs."

And my aunt Esther said "but we don't know Pete is

on drugs."

I was so young myself then that I had no judgment about my cousin Pete in Tucson living with the Jesus Freaks. I merely thought it was interesting.

But by the time I decided to leave NYC and move to Tucson, Jesus was a big part of my life. And it made me feel close to my cousin Pete in Tucson that he believed in Jesus, which is why I chose him to call and ask for help.

I confided that to Pete after I had been in Tucson for several months, I told him why I chose him to call and ask for help. There was a long silence and finally he said, "that was an embarrassing episode in my life and I don't believe in Jesus."

So much for having so much in common. But I guess it served its purpose. I needed to feel close to someone to ask for help.

It had made me feel close to Pete. And Pete had delivered help. He had found me an apartment in apartment complex called Willow Brook which accepted dogs, and which was the price I wanted to pay, $300 a month. But it fell thru because dog could not weigh over 33 pounds and Clio weighed 37 pounds. But I was immensely encouraged.

Then I got phone call from Celia saying Pete had tried and not succeeded so he had turned the job over to her, and she had consulted apartment finders. "It is not easy to find apartment in Tucson which accepts dogs."

Then I got the phone call the apartment had been found. I had asked for one bedroom for $300. I was sure I could not afford bigger apt. But Celia had found 2 bedroom for $330.

"Great! take it!" I said. "Drive right over! Put down the money and take it! I will send you money order for it." And that is the apartment we moved into two weeks later.

It turned out Celia had been visiting her friend Franny and said to Franny "what I really want for my niece is an apartment like yours, Franny."

So Franny said "let's go over to management and see if they have any."

And sure enough they had the two bedroom for $330. And when Celia called me, I said "grab it! drive over now and put the money down!" And Celia drove over and put the money down. And when she got back home she said "the apartment is yours."

And I said "great!"

We had already started packing up all our stuff in

boxes, but we now had an address to send them to.

And when we walked into our new Tucson apartment in the middle of the night two weeks later there was a note from Franny with a jar of salsa as a gift. The note gave helpful hints and welcomed us.

Unfortunately Franny had forgotten how old-fashioned NYC is. We shivered at night in the Tucson apartment for a whole month before Franny showed us how to turn on the heat.

Back in NYC at around 5 o'clock on cold winter nights, you would hear the reassuring gurgle of the steam in the radiator. It meant the landlord had turned on the furnace.

And at 5 pm in Tucson, when Sun went down and it turned ice cold, I listened for that reassuring gurgle but it never came.

I had no idea there was a dial, which you could set at any temperature you want, and be as toasty warm as you wanted to be, and didn't have to wait for the landlord to decide to give you heat.

Franny had walked with me a few mornings when I walked my dog. She was the only person I knew in Tucson, I was grateful to have her as a friend. Franny told me all about herself, and I did learn a lot about Franny's life as a result, altho I could not absorb any of it at the time.

She did say one very practical thing tho. She pointed to the mountains which were always in view, and said "that is north." After that I stopped worrying I would get lost when I took my dog out in the morning, I knew I could always orient myself from the mountains.

When we were here 3 months we ran into troubles. And when Franny passed by, instead of hiding my troubles, I confided all of them to her.

And a very remarkable thing happened. Because I had let down my hair, Franny let down her hair, we became very close. Before that I had been her best friend's niece in her eyes, and she had been my aunt's friend in my eyes. For both of us the other was an extension of Celia.

I confided all my troubles and the barrier came down.

The wonderful thing about that conversation with Franny at the table was how much we laughed about all our troubles.

I said "come in Franny sit down, I'll make us a cup of coffee."

And as soon as I poured the coffee, she said "Where's Bill?"

I said "Bill got drunk on his night job, and passed out,

they didn't know he was passed out from drinking, they called ambulance and took him to the hospital.

"Then Bill got home and for 3 days he raged at me 'Call up your family and have them find you an apartment in New York City, we're going back.'

"And I refused, finally the neighbors called the cops on Bill. The cops took him to jail last night.

"This morning, Ron from apt. A4 and I went to the Pima County jail and picked Bill up when he was released.

"Then Ron told Bill about the Lark, a treatment center for free. Ron told Bill it is very nice there and they all have a lot of fun. So Bill said 'OK I'm willing to go.'

"So Ron drove him there, he will be there for two weeks. So that is why I am alone, and you can sit at kitchen table and we can talk to our heart's content."

And I cracked up at everything I said. I laughed uproariously at every step of the misadventure, and especially laughed at the point when Bill was hauled off to jail.

Of course none of this was funny while it was happening, the whole thing from beginning to end had been one long nightmare.

But confiding it to sweet Franny across the table, and

laughing my head off about it, was the sweetest experience in the world. I was girl who needed a friend. And Franny was willing to be my friend.

Obviously this changed the entire atmosphere between me and Franny. Instead of being the impressive niece, which is how Celia had billed me to her friend, of her impressive friend Celia, I was just a girl with problems up the bezum.

My husband had just been taken off to jail the night before. I had spent the morning hanging out at Pima County jail waiting for him to be released. He had gotten drunk on his first Tucson job, passed out and taken to hospital. I was alone friendless and broke in Tucson.

Franny and I drank coffee and laughed and laughed and laughed. We let our hair down about everything.

Then Bill, surprisingly walked in the door. I guess he didn't like Lark, he didn't find it so much fun. And Franny left. And phase two of our Tucson life began.

Bill said everyone at Lark was just like him, and one thing he learned from listening to them all, is Tucson is a place where it is very easy to start your own business.

And that afternoon he and Ron started their business as handyman. And when Ron did not want to keep doing it, Bill started his own business as yard worker, which he did successfully and full-time until he started art school.

Becoming an artist was Bill's dream, and he decided to follow his dream. As Grant Lewi, my favorite astrologer, wrote, "One moves to New York to fulfill a dream, and one leaves New York to fulfill a greater dream."

It's true. Bill loves doing his art and is a wonderful artist. He finally found the thing which made him happy.

Drawing Bill did of me during his first year in art school

20 years later…

Summer 2010

Boy pumps up tire for girl

Bill is good at making me happy

July 25th 2010

The girls in the beauty parlor..

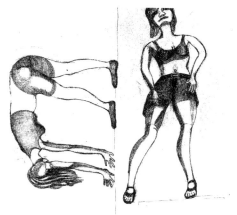

I spent the whole summer up in the air

I woke up in a better mood today thank God. I woke up, opened my eyes, looked out window, saw a luminous damp cloud and thought "I'm in a good mood."

I was so happy I didn't wake up in the bad mood I did yesterday and the day before. The bad mood did not stick around all day, by noon it no longer had me in its grip, it had dissipated. But I experienced it as an obstacle to my joy. It was like a bully in my mind, I just wanted it to leave.

I see now I did the best I could do. A bully was sitting on me, but I went over to Facebook, clicked on the art, copied the pictures which were my favorites and posted them on my blog diary. To have something to say with them I even wrote a squib.

Interestingly enough posting those 3 pictures with a squib I wrote was the first thing which harmonized me, it made me feel good. Everything else I had done was finger in the dike, what I was doing to try to feel good.

But actually posting the 3 pics and my teeny blog entry— when it was done and up there, I liked it. It made me feel good. I found it pretty and attractive to look at it. It soothed me. I was so rattled by my bad mood.

My day got better as it wore on. Altho swimming was not a tremendous success. It was Saturday and overcrowded. Bill and I did not get a lane, we hung out in children's area. I swam a little.

It wasn't so bad because all week we had gotten a lane and had such nice swims. And because I thought "many of those swimming now, the reason there is no lane for me, they don't swim on the weekdays, they just come on weekend."

I mean I was glad for their happiness. I didn't care so much that I didn't get what I wanted because I was glad they got what they wanted. It was easy to be so generous because we had so much of a good thing all week.

Many times we had lucked out. We had heard thunder and I had called Jerry. "Should I come?" I asked him, "I heard thunder."

He said "I'm not closing the pool Anne, nothing is happening, come on over for your swim."

"Great" I said "great."

Bill and I were so happy to have long wonderful swim when we thought we wouldn't have any. All the way over Bill said "we might get lucky and get 20 minutes." But we got the whole shmear.

That's why neither of us were greedy yesterday, we thought we were lucky to be in the water. Our monsoon season had brought no rain, no storms. Nada. All it does is rumble occasionally which scares the dog. And if it happens right before our swim we are in suspense if we will get our swim.

Which has worked out fine because each time we have had swim, we have been so grateful. There is no taking a swim for granted during monsoon season. During monsoons getting your swim is called "got lucky."

So even tho all we could do was swim in circles in the children's area, I was just glad to be in the water, and looking forward to our activity after the water. We were out of soda and Bill had said we would go to Frys supermarket for soda and the other things we wanted.

I was glad because the beauty salon is in that shopping center. They sell a shampoo I like and my bottle was almost empty. They also sell that expensive leave-in conditioner I put in my hair before I swim believing it will save my hair from making dreadlocks.

I was out of it and wanted to buy more. The girls who work there always give me a big discount on all these beauty supplies I buy (shampoos and conditioners, creams to put on after my swim) because the day I published my first book *Ruthie Has a New Love*, which was just about a year ago, I had a satchel of them with me to give away to people and offered them to the girls in the beauty parlor.

And to my surprise while I was consulting with one of the girls about the shampoo and conditioner and chatting it up a little, the other girl sat herself down in the chair you sit in when you get your hair cut and began reading the book, she just opened it up and began reading it.

41

And at the point where I was thanking the girl for giving me such a big discount on everything, the girl reading my book said "who is Ruthie?"

I said "Ruthie is my friend."

She said "is this real?"

"Yes" I said, "it is real."

And then she went back to reading the book.

I found it very gratifying someone was reading my book and seemed to like it. I got excited, very excited.

It turned out they all liked my book, I had given each of them a copy. So when I published my second book at Christmas (*Girl Blog from Tucson*) I couldn't wait to bring it to them.

But it was a very odd winter. Jerry's pool was chilly and overcrowded (they had closed so many city pools to save on heat bills) and ice cold showers. So I just joined the Y.

For 4 months I did not step into Jerry's pool but one day when we arrived at the Y (Bill never swam at the Y, he went to weight room, just me swam) when we arrived they said "the pool is closed because the water is cloudy."

So we turned around and went to Jerry's pool and by a miracle I had a whole bunch of copies of my new book in car. I brought copies for all the lifeguards.

And when we shopped at Frys afterward, I brought copies for the girls in the beauty parlor. I thought "if they love the Ruthie book they will love this one, it is so much fun."

But when I went back few months later they said "we started it." (That can mean read a few pages, put it down and never get back to it.) I wasn't too disappointed because I was so touched they loved the Ruthie book, that was the book of my heart.

I guess I have not been back for a long time. When I walked in yesterday they asked me "Is there going to be another book?"

I almost went thru the roof with joy because I have spent the past 4 days being driven crazy by the new book I am publishing (*MORE Girl Blog from Tucson*).

The book is really good-to-go but each time I find a little thing to fix, I try to fix it, but I just don't have enough experience with formatting for publishing, I seem to louse up a bigger thing.

I have now spent the past 4 days trying to un-louse up the things I have loused up.

I guess none of this would matter if I thought people will love the book but I am tremendously shy about this book. Instead of thinking of the people I will give it to, "they will love it," as I did with the last one, I keep thinking of all the people I won't give it to "they won't like it."

"I won't give it to the lifeguards," I think, "they won't like it."

"I won't give it to the girls in the beauty parlor they won't like it."

"I won't give it to the girls who work at the post office they won't like it."

"I won't give it to the swimmers they won't like it."

I couldn't think of anyone I knew who would like it. So you can imagine what it was like for me when they asked "do you have another book?" I was thrilled out of my mind.

"YES" I said, "I have a new book, I am going to publish it next week, but it's not fun like my last book." I didn't want them to be disappointed.

"We don't care" they said, "we want it."

"You want it anyway?" I asked.

"Yes we want it."

I could have kissed the ground in gratitude, it was an answer to a prayer, they wanted my new book. I couldn't believe my ears, I went into total joy.

And they gave me big discount on all my shampoos and conditioners. It was like being giving overflowing gifts in every department. They wanted my book, I was so happy with all my new shampoo and conditioners and creams, I got my first author's perk, they sold it to me at wholesale price.

I thought to myself "I wonder if the girls in the beauty parlor are fans of my writing." I was so overjoyed to have fans.

I put the heavy bag of the stuff I had bought in backseat of car and walked over to Frys to meet Bill.

He had already gotten most of the stuff I wanted, a lot of soda, gallon of milk, box of corn flakes. He forgot half-and-half so I bought two bottles of that.

Then I went over to frozen food and bought 7 chicken pot pies, one for each day of the week. And then I went to check-out.

I was still sailing on air because of what the girls in beauty parlor said, plus I was glad we bought soda and milk and cereal and chicken pot pies, and I was glad it was not the huge shopping I always did in the past. Everything was going my way. O I got candy too, a lot of candy.

It was nice driving home. I was so excited about the encouragement I got in beauty parlor about my new book, someone wanted to read it! I loved all the things I had bought there. And I liked my little supermarket shopping too. I felt like I was laden with gifts.

When I was in that lousy mood all morning which I could not shake, I had actually thought "today could be a wonderful day, how do I know?"

It was nice to say that to myself but secretly I thought it was pie in the sky. I couldn't see any way it could turn into a wonderful day made out of treats. I was whistling in the dark. It was like believing in Santa Claus, it was a fairy tale. But that is exactly what did happen… I got a lovely miracle. I am so happy…

August 5

LOL a stupidity unbelievable (mine)

I woke up in a good mood this morning. I wish I could describe the good mood because it was unusual. It was sort of "I'm back." As if I had strayed off, I don't know for how long? a month? two months? But it was an unusual stray. Everything felt very odd the whole time and I had all kinds of adventures.

And then to my surprise I woke up this morning and my first feeling was of having come back. The oddness and the stray were over. I guess there was a nice sense of solidity.

I then proceeded to have a very normal and nice day. But I now see being back to normal has surprises too, mine took place while waiting on line at the post office.

The proof copy of my book (the first proof copy, I am

now waiting for a second one) had arrived last Tuesday. I had ordered 2 copies so I could send one to Ruthie in New York so she could read it on the airplane on way home. I knew she was returning home the following Tuesday.

So last Tuesday I had Bill take me to post office to send it to Ruthie by 2 day rate, and I took her address in NYC with me. I hadn't known that they all had to be out of that apartment on Saturday. But still that gave the book about 5 days to reach her.

When she relocated to the Bronx for the last few days of her stay, the book had not arrived. I was sure it would arrive on Monday and had been strategizing in my mind how she could pick it up.

Instead the book was returned to me, it was in my mailbox yesterday. So I took it to post office today to send it by 2 day priority rate to Ruthie, she was now home back in San Diego.

While I was waiting on line, I had left the book in its envelope because I wanted to show the postman I had paid the 2 day rate and wondered if he would forward it to Ruthie in San Diego.

But while I was waiting on line, the woman behind me was helping me write out the new envelope for 2 day priority mail. And she looked at the one I had sent to NYC which had been returned to me and said "You left out her address. That is why it was returned to you."

"That's impossible" I said.

But I looked closely at the address I had written for Ruthie in New York. I had written her name clearly, her apartment number clearly, and New York, New York and the ZIP code clearly.

I had forgotten to put in her street address. The building she was staying at was at 340 East 44th Street. But all I had written was Ruth Lakin, apartment 14K, NYC 10017.

There is no way they could have delivered the book. They had to return it to sender. And in tiny letters I saw something printed below "undeliverable."

I was completely stunned I had done that.

A tremendous amount of effort had actually gone into arranging that book arrive to Ruthie before she left New York so she could read it on the plane. If someone had bet me I would make that mistake, leave out the address, I would have bet a million dollars I couldn't make that mistake.

I have been a secretary my whole life and I am a good

secretary. Sure I make mistakes all the time, but nothing at level of forgetting to put in the address. I've forgotten to put in apartment numbers, but that is as far as it goes.

And to say I made the mistake because I was in a hurry and chatting it up with Michelle, the postmistress, while I was doing it all, doesn't wash with me.

Because I've done things in a rush while chatting it up with Michelle the postmistress, a million times before.

And I've never forgotten to put in an address. I would say it's an impossibility except it happened. I saw it with my own two eyes.

Maybe I was so focused on putting in the apartment number. After all the apartment had been rented for just a few months. Ruthie's name would not be on any mailbox.

But just because I concentrated to remember to put in the apartment number and made sure I did that in big clear letters and numbers still doesn't explain how I could leave off the whole street address.

I could give a million reasons why I did, and yet none of them wash with me. I can be a good secretary with both hands tied behind my back.

I never had to give my full mind to a minor secretarial chore like addressing an envelope or in this case a small package.

I was so stunned I did that I told the woman and the whole post office what an idiot I am and "I can't believe I could be this stupid!"

For the first time Bill had come into the post office with me to sit on the bench instead of waiting in the car. He wanted to be in the air conditioning instead of out in the hot sun.

I probably went on for 10 minutes about how stupid I was. I was so stunned by it. As I said to the lady, "It's like setting a record. How would I ever beat this level of stupidity. It is record-setting stupidity. It is a whole exponent beyond any stupid thing I have ever done before."

I am talking about secretarial things here. As for my life, that is another story. I have had a lifetime of stupidity. Consistent stupidity has been my hallmark. Nothing would surprise me there. In fact I would be stunned to look back at my life and discover there was any time I was not totally stupid.

Usually the fact that I am so good at secretary things gives me a layer of confidence. To have done a mind boggling screw-up made me insecure. I got in the car with Bill to go home and discovered I had zero confidence in myself at all. No confidence about anything.

I lied down on bed, ate my hot dog from the 7/11, and my donut, and drank my soda and turned on the tv. And watched second half of a news program. I was still stunned.

It's not so much that I berated myself, it was that my whole mind was spell-bound by my mind boggling stupidity. It seemed impossible to think about anything else. It was tidal wave in my mind.

And then after an hour of that, I just thought "there has to be a reason for it, things like this don't just happen, it has to have some purpose."

What the purpose was, I had no idea. It is good I thought of that, because I just don't think I could have functioned in any way if I felt the potential was there to be mind-boggling stupid at the drop of the hat. You simply can't function if you have zero confidence in yourself.

I wasn't just saying that to myself, that there had to be a reason this happened, to comfort myself, it actually seemed more logical than out of nowhere I had fallen into bottomless stupidity. In any case, after that I was willing to try functioning again. I no longer felt doomed to be a dumb-dumb.

Post script, I wonder what Bill thought about his wife telling the whole post office what an idiot she is. No wonder he sat at end of bench pretending he did not know me. And left the instant I finished mailing the new package to Ruthie. He didn't want anyone to see him walk out with me.

I'm lucky he didn't leave me behind, in the unclaimed wife department of the post office.

At the post office

My Labor Day Weekend

Friday

We go to JC Penney

It is beautiful early September morning. We are having a beautiful September. Every morning the sparrows are all in the tree right out my window. I love it. They play in tree, they sit in tree, they fly around the tree, they change their spot, they occupy the tree. Mainly they perch in it, but there is a lot of flitting from branch to branch.

Obviously they love this tree, they are always in it and I love it they are the view right outside my window.

Yesterday was an interesting and nice day. Hahaha it was hotter than hell in the morning which infuriated Bill more than it did me.

Of course he is right. It is first week of September it's not fair it be hotter than hell, we should be done with the hotter than hell weather.

He wasn't seriously mad about it, just felt he should editorialize about it in our open convertible on way to pool.

He remarked on it almost all the way, and I think again on the way home.

"It's as hot as June" he said. "It's just like June, it's as if June came back."

The theme of all his remarks was the heat is back. I didn't mind him editorializing about the weather, I just wasn't into it myself. I am sure I was hot in the car but for some reason I wasn't into noticing it.

I actually found both things pleasant, big heat while driving in car and Bill's running commentary about it. It seemed appropriate he was talking about the weather, we were in it.

The public pools were all closed yesterday for Furlough Day. This is some new thing the city does to save money. One Friday a month it gives all city workers an unpaid day off. So we went to the Y.

I was restless during my swim because when I tried to make coffee yesterday morning, when it came out bitter the first time I thought the problem was the coffee. So I threw it out, made a second pot with a gourmet coffee and that was acrid too.

So I wanted to buy a new coffee maker, I figured the one I had was plotzing

I had seen on tv that JC Penney was having their 80 percent off summer Labor Day sale Friday and Saturday so I said to Bill "Let's go to JC Penney after the Y. You want to buy Bermuda shorts, now they will be on big sale."

He was very happy about that. He wears Bermuda shorts year round now and for a whole year he has been wanting new ones, the ones he has been wearing are threadbare.

"And I will get myself new coffeemaker while you get your shorts."

It is so rare that he was willing to go shopping with

me. Usually when I want to go to mall for something he lets out huge groan when I tell him.

Then a flurry of protests, he puts up every obstacle he can think of. Seeing how much he doesn't want to do it rains on my parade.

So you see why it was so pleasant for me yesterday morning when I said "JC Penney, coffeemaker, summer sale on men's shorts," and he was enthusiastic and happy and looking forward to it.

Hahaha he was actually looking forward to taking me to the mall instead of pulling teeth.

It changed it all to a pleasant adventure and my whole time in swim pool I was looking forward to it and restless to get out and start my shopping adventure.

He let me off in front of JC Penney because it was so hot and I headed to the Home Department first. Altho I looked at the nighties on sale when I first got off the escalator to downstairs. They had some cute ones and they were 80 percent off and I put them over my arm and went to look for coffeemakers.

They had one on sale in a big box. And I said to her "how can I carry it?" and she put it in a huge black net bag JC Penney has available for shoppers to use while they are in the store.

It wasn't heavy, just huge and cumbersome, and I stuffed the nighties in there too and took the escalator upstairs.

When I then went to women's clothes on sale I found two little blouses, and got out my 4 nighties and looked at everything. I looked at the other blouses I had taken off the rack for consideration and decided to just keep two of the little blouses. And hung everything else back on the rack, the 4 nighties and the 3 other blouses.

And walked thru pocketbooks. They had a pretty little red change purse on sale, and a cute little quilted pocketbook so I added them.

A coffeemaker isn't fun, the 2 blouses did nothing for me, but I loved the crimson change purse and pretty blue pocketbook. It was fun having two items I actually liked.

And I headed to cashier's desk in men's department to pay for them and called out to Bill. He was still looking at all the men's clothes on sale. He had found 4 pairs of shorts on a great sale, they were very nice and he was overjoyed, but they didn't have the pocket T shirts he wanted.

He was actually still contentedly looking for more

things he wanted when I found him.

So I said "let me pay for everything and you go get the car, take the top down and bring it outside."

Bill was right outside when I got out with top down, and did not mind it had taken me 10 minutes at cashier's desk. He was very happy about his purchases and said he would wear a pair of his new shorts to the game tonight.

It was a pleasant ride home, that is when he said how June is back, "it is just like June." June is our hottest month in Tucson usually.

And I went in to watch TV and he went on his computer. He likes to play chess with the computer. And I guess an hour or two later the huge thunder arrived, my dog was terrified, and then the big rain arrived.

Bill was so happy about the storm, "it will cool everything down."

I guess yesterday was really the story of how Bill was happy about everything. He was happy we went to the Y (and he took me early) because when we go to the Y he goes to the weight room, he doesn't swim. And he seems to always be glad when he accomplishes lifting weights.

He was overjoyed with his purchases at JC Penney and he commented on it all afternoon. "I would have to wait a whole year for these shorts which were $35 to come down in price again."

He was very happy about the storm. The plan had been for him to go to his friend Jim's house to watch the first Wildcats game of the season on TV with Jim and then they would both go to the high school game.

But because Beanie was so terrorized by the thunder he called Jim and said "I will watch the game here at home, and you pick me up when the high school game starts, we will go together."

On the way to the Y in the morning he said maybe he will buy a new Wildcats hat if it is on sale.

"But if we lose tonight" he said, "I will be so upset I will throw the hat out the window."

That's how I found out how much it meant to him that we win.

So of course I was happy when I overheard him call Jim at half-time and say how far ahead the Cats are. And "come over now and we will go to the high school game."

The storm had knocked out the internet but only for an hour. When it knocked out the internet Bill stopped playing chess on the computer, it wouldn't reload, and sat and read in his chair until his game came on.

By the time he called his friend Jim at half time internet was back on. I was on my computer and I heard him.

I was happy internet was back on because there was nothing on TV I liked watching. And I emailed and went on Facebook. And fed my doggie his favorite treat, liverwurst, to make it up to him for scaredy during the storm.

And all the cats arrived for their food too. I filled up 3 bowls of their crunchies. I guess they had come into the house during the huge downpour. Most of them live outside now, I only see them on the patio when they come to eat.

It was so unusual seeing them come out from places in house. They are all Priscilla's kittens altho bigger than she is now. They were born in this house and even tho they run away from me and Bill, they all like Beanie, and do feel at home here, it is their nursery.

When nothing was happening on Facebook and there were no incoming emails I went in to lie down, watch TV and read a mystery. And Bill came home. He looked happy.

I asked him how the Cats had done, he said "they won big." He was overjoyed and said "I want to play chess with the computer." Which he did till 3 am.

I waited till the storm was over to put up the dishes and even washed part of the old coffeemaker. "Maybe now it will work" I thought. The foot of my bed was soaked from the rain but I didn't care...

And I watched old sitcoms and read my mystery till I fell asleep.

It was a perfect day. Bill was so happy about his new shorts and his team won.

And Beanie was so happy with his liverwurst treat after the storm, and I loved seeing all the cats at their crunchy bowl eating their crunchies.

Sunday of Labor Day weekend

Sparrows, my mom, and being...

It is September, the month my mom came into the world, and ninety years later, last September, she left the world and returned to Heaven, again in September, a week or two after her birthday.

And now it is a year later. I understand now why many religions observe this one year mark. Because it is one year now and I can feel the difference. There is a peace about it all. I don't know how to describe the peace.

It's as if for a whole year I was keyed up about it, maybe caught in the drama of it. Perhaps it was shock too, as if I had been shocked. Whatever it is, now at the year mark there is peace and relaxation.

And I can only describe it as a lovely acceptance, or a

sweet acceptance, a sweetening. Something deep within me relaxes. And there is a beautiful calm.

I really can't describe it because there is perspective in there. I never experienced perspective before in this sensual way. It's like looking at the horizon over a vast ocean. All the peace and calm the vast ocean gives you as you look at the horizon off in the distance.

And how attractive it all is, the horizon, the sky, and the vast ocean. It's like that in your mind as if you are calmly looking out at distance.

I have no idea why a year after a traumatic thing like your mom going to Heaven should be absorbed this way, turn into all this peace and calm, and looking out at horizon. And deep peace in your solar plexus.

I guess everything about mothers is a mystery to me. Such a deep relationship, yet overlaid with personality for so many years. All the tumult of clash of personality. And because she embodied the world for me for so long.

Maybe that is what the one year mark is, she is completely out of the world. World and personality have evaporated from her. What is left is the peace and the love. Which is maybe what it all started with.

Maybe that is where this odd contentment comes

from. She is restored to what she was at my beginning, glowing beautiful source of my contentment, all my peace and love.

How odd it is felt all thru my body, the way it started at my birth and how new it makes everything, that all that be restored again. That everything which is not that, has been lifted off, and returned back to the simplicity of love.

All the tumult gone, all the noise gone, it is very quiet. It is an inner experience of the heart. And oddly enough matches very well with this beautiful early morning in early September with sparrows on the branch in tree right out my window.

Because of the quietness of both. And because they are both outside the world in their own way.

The sparrows are just in their own sparrow world, happy birdies enjoying the morning, not making a sound, flitting from tree to earth and back to tree, just having a happy experience of being.

And I experience my mom's being in my heart too. Without all the dramas and the stories, it is a world of being. Sparrows being, my mom being. Being in the being world. It is nice breather.

The sparrow is walking to the very edge of the

branch, it is so cute. And now they all jumped down to the low-lying thin branch right out my window.

They are close to me now. I can see them so well. They are on the swinging branch, just one long thin twig with leaves coming off from it.

I bet sparrows don't weigh much but that twig branch is so light when they alight on it, it swings. Maybe they find that fun. It swings when they take off and it swings when they alight.

I guess that is why I see this tree as their playground. The first thing little children do on arriving at playground is go on the swings. Kids love to swing and so do sparrows.

I am still intrigued that this one year mark brings all this odd contentment. I hadn't realized how much huge drama was associated with my mom when she was in the world, the idea of her in my mind was always a huge drama. Her leaving was huge drama.

All the drama halted now. The perfect peace in my heart now when I think of my mother.

It's funny knowing that is what it is like for so many in the world, nearly my whole generation. The place in their heart which is their mother, which is a big place in your heart, is perfect peace.

They may not be aware of it because peace is so quiet. They may not notice this quietness in their heart, but it is there, a very deep rich peace in the middle of their heart. And a contentment about life. Our moms have turned into peace, which must be their true natural state.

O the sparrow is looking at me, or if not looking at me, looking around, he keeps swiveling his head from side to side. He is looking.

How interesting the sparrow keeps looking. His friend landed near him but my sparrow keeps looking, swiveling his head from side to side, looking.

It's all a bit like everything being tied up with a bow. The sparrows, mom, even back into long ago past memories (I am remembering my sweet dog Clio boarding the airplane with us to move to Tucson).

The bow of course is the 4 sparrows on my thin little branch now. Just as the bluebirds tied the bow on Cinderella's dress, these wonderful sparrows are tying my whole life up with a bow. I like it.

O what a sight! Now 5 sparrows on one branch all together, with two or three above, and one sticking out on branch at side.

I wonder how long my peaceful heart will last. But it sure is nice right now. It is my mother's gift to me. That is how it must work.

A year goes by and they fill our hearts with peace. 7 little sparrows sitting in a tree. One for you and one for me. It's just odd knowing this layer of peace is in everyone's heart. That is our mother's gift to us. They fill our hearts with peace.

And no matter what happens now, no matter how much full-force the world and its dramas return into my life I will remember this moment because it is there underneath everything.

All the quiet contentment peace our mothers gave us. Their gift to us.

Anne's Labor Day

I put the groceries in the wrong car

Out of it..

I am glad Labor Day Weekend is over.

Saturday and Sunday were normal weekend but Monday was Labor Day. Pools again were shut and instead of Monday bringing start of new week and start of new energy, it was just a weird hot sultry day which lasted forever.

O well it is over and under our belt now. Today is a fresh day, it is start of fresh week and thank god the blue sky is back, it is fresher outlook out my window.

Where all those clouds came from yesterday I have no idea. All they did was confuse everything, yesterday was a story of trying to make headway thru confusion.

And I did some very odd confused things in the early morning. Bill's friend Jim took me to the Racquet Club where he is a member at 8 am. (That is the club I used to belong to.)

I actually had nice swim and jacuzzi and shower and then went to Pro Shop for their Labor Day Sale. To my joy the skirt I didn't buy at their sale on Christmas and which I could not buy when I changed my mind a week later because it was already boxed up, was back on the table, and they had even lowered the price.

I had loved the skirt on Christmas but even on sale I did not want to pay that much money. But after wanting the skirt all these long months I decided I would pay that much money.

So it was a treat they lowered the price. Hahaha it was still a lot of money for a skirt but I thought I got a bargain because it was half the huge money it was on sale for at

Christmas. So I bought another skirt too, it was pricey also but affordable.

I was so happy with my purchases I gushed about them to the girl who sold them to me, then gushed about them to Pam and everyone at the desk.

And then Jim and I took off to go home. And when we were driving two miles Jim got call on his cellphone.

"Who could that possibly be!" Jim said. And it turned out my friend Pam who works at the desk, who I had gushed and gushed to about the skirt, called to say the girl from the Pro Shop came out to report that I had forgotten to take my skirts. I have to come back and get them.

I said to Jim "maybe I am an idiot."

He said "You can't be an idiot you just wrote and published 3 books, an idiot could not do that."

And I let him talk me out of the idea that I was an idiot.

But then we went grocery shopping at Frys. We both did huge shopping. Usually when I do grocery shopping Bill waits on bench for me. When I emerge from check-out with my shopping cart full, he wheels it to car for me and puts all the groceries in car.

Of course I didn't expect Jim to do that for me. In fact I wanted to bend over backwards so he would not have to wait for me.

He is driving some car I never saw before. It is an old car that looks a bit like a station wagon. I don't know where he got it, I will have to ask him.

When his sports car totally plotzed we lent him our 2nd hand Chrysler and for a year he was driving that which made it easy to recognize his car since it was our own car.

I wheeled my cart to what I was sure was his car, but for some reason when I looked inside it didn't seem like it was his. So I thought "wrong car" and then a few cars down, that one looked like his. I couldn't figure out how to get to back seat so I loaded all the huge groceries in the drivers seat and went to look for Jim.

He was coming out of Frys, I guess he had gone to look for me as I had gone to look for him. "I put all the groceries in the car" I said and headed towards the car.

"That's not where it is" he said, and he headed in other direction. My groceries were not there.

"You put them in wrong car" he said.

"Yes I did" and headed in the direction of the car where I had put them.

Very luckily just as I was approaching it a man was

standing there and said "are these your groceries you put in my car?"

"Yes" I said.

He had already moved them all to the back of his car and was on his way to Frys to ask them to say on loudspeaker about groceries in wrong car.

I thanked him a lot and put them in a cart to wheel to Jim's car and Jim asked him "why didn't you just drive off with them?"

And he told Jim "because I thought they could have been someone's last money, that they spent on the groceries, I wasn't going to take them, I wanted to return them."

Jim fit them in the back seat of his car and we began to drive home again. The first thing Jim said was "let's reconsider the question of whether you are an idiot."

He had spent all the way from Racquet Club to Frys reassuring me I was not an idiot because I had left behind the skirt I had waited all year to buy.

But he sang a different tune all the way home from Frys. "Don't worry I won't tell Bill" he said. And "you must be on some great drugs, the stuff I have is nothing like that."

For half the trip he insisted I must be high on something and whatever it is he wants it. And he said the instant he gets home he will smoke a joint in honor of me (lol to recognize the totally stoned thing I had done in the Frys parking lot.)

But of course I hadn't been stoned, I had been totally straight, I am just an idiot.

I didn't see why it had to be kept a secret from Bill, I thought he would just get a laugh out of it. But when I decided to tell him about it in mid-afternoon before he left for the movies, when he was playing chess on the computer, he didn't have a laugh about it.

He said "this is an upsetting story, I don't want to hear it."

"I only did it because I didn't want to impose on Jim, I didn't want to make him wait, I bent over backwards for him."

"Well you shouldn't have done that. You should have waited for him in Frys and gone to his car with him."

It was the longest afternoon in the history of Christendom. Jim and I got back to my driveway at 10 am. Bill didn't want to come out in his pajamas and get the groceries, I had to force him. But I didn't want to take a chance of forgetting something in Jim's car.

I had my purse, my swim bag, and my two new skirts in another bag, plus those huge bags of groceries, and my wet swim suit.

I wanted it all to make it back into the house and nothing to be left behind in Jim's car.

"Why did you do this big shopping!" Bill said, "we just did big shopping at Trader Joes yesterday."

"Don't worry I will put it all away by myself, just put it on the counter for me."

I put one of the frozen chicken pot pies in the microwave for my lunch and took doggie in for tv. Bill went back to the computer to play chess.

But it was nice cutting off big slab of liverwurst as treat for my doggie before I put that in frig. Beanie only discovered liverwurst 2 days ago, and now it is the love of his life.

I'm not going to say anymore about that long endless hot sweaty afternoon. Where every bug in the world was in my house biting me the whole time, and I couldn't find anything on tv to divert me.

Bill went to the mall to see two movies and I finally

decided to go to my computer. But the bugs were all in here too biting me. There was no escape for me this afternoon. I thought "this is how someone could be driven mad."

Finally at 9 pm a tv show came on which held my interest. That is all it took. All I wanted all day long was for something to hold my interest, to entertain me, to divert me. LOL I wanted escape.

And Bill came home from the movies. "I saw 2 action thrillers, I wanted to see *Toy Story* but they wanted additional 3 dollars for the 3D glasses."

"Believe me you did exactly the right thing to go to the mall to see 2 action thrillers, if you had stayed home this long long awful afternoon you would've gone nuts......"

September 14

Publishing adventures...

Well it is a beautiful morning. September has been an interesting month so far. Nights have been very chilly which is heaven for us after long hot desert summer. The mornings are incredibly beautiful, and that is heaven for us to drink in all this beauty which was absent during long hot desert summer.

But after the most beautiful morning there ever was, clouds come in from somewhere, they bank up, day turns hot and humid. And when they don't bank up that way, the sun's heat is very intense.

Right now is cool exquisite.

Lovely September beauty out my window and sparrows playing in it. So why bother to think about the huge heat yesterday afternoon and the even huger heat they are saying will come today. Why not be like sparrows just totally enjoying what there is now, because now is perfect.

This September garden beauty is one of my favorites, and it is far more wonderful when your sight includes 4 sparrows playing in tree out my window totally enjoying it.

I have spent the past week engaged in an unusual project for me. I had been emailing with Abigail— we had met during the brief but very intense time she and Denny were in New York City. We met in Tompkins Square Park because we brought our dogs there.

Obviously 25 years before the Mass Awakening, and 4 years before the Harmonic Conversion, are going to be the most intense time our planet has ever known. They certainly were for me and for Abigail too. Because that is when the pressure is on full force to make the change in belief.

Apparently the way it works, is in order for the Mass Awakening to occur in 2012, it means that in 1987, when the Harmonic Conversion occurs, 144,000 souls on the planet have made the choice, to choose love instead of fear.

If that number is met, it is full steam ahead to the Mass Awakening. And I guess those of us who were meant to make the switch by August 1987— 4 years before (in 1983) began to be tortured to death, so it would be inevitable we would make the switch by the designated time.

Basically it boiled down to our lives collapsing. That is big motivation to seeing in new ways, being willing to switch thinking.

This is the period when Abigail and I became friends. Our time in New York City together was only during this time. I didn't meet her before this time began, and she and Denny moved to New Orleans soon after this time ended.

So altho Abigail likes to reference our time in New York together in her emails to me, and her passionate love for New York City remains intact, I don't like being reminded of this time.

I don't know what Abigail and Denny's life was like after they moved to New Orleans, her letters didn't give a picture.

I remember them being in the car in front of my building the day they were leaving NYC and Abigail telling me "we are fleeing for our lives." And I remember the day when I was leaving New York thinking the identical thing, "we are fleeing for our lives."

I don't know how long they stayed in New Orleans before they moved to New Mexico where they stayed and never left. They were both from Texas and had lived in Washington DC before they came to NYC.

My life continued to be tumultuous. I just know they settled in happily in New Mexico. I knew from Abigail's first letter that they would stay there.

They had found the place which was right for them. Denny got into free-lance Russian translation, which he had been doing all along I think. And Abigail got into free-lance book production for children's books. Which each of them is still doing.

When I was a 4 year old little girl (living in Manhattan) and my dad (a school teacher) took the subway on long ride home from Seward Park High School (on Lower East Side) to 149th Street and Riverside Drive where we then lived, he would make the ride go faster for himself by sitting with pen and paper and turning my favorite fairy tales into poems to be read to me when he got home. And I loved loved loved those poems.

They were very much written for me, the favorite things I liked to eat and the favorite things I liked to do were in the poems. There was a convergence of my life and the fairy tale.

In the first one he wrote, Cinderella, and my favorite, to make it clear that the step sisters got everything and Cinderella got nothing, the step sisters got "to eat chocolate pudding every day, got to visit grandma far away, got to play dress-up in their mother's clothes, got to dance on their toes, and had plenty of toys with which to play and didn't even have to bother putting them away."

My father described their life of all treats, as all my favorite treats. I got to hear all my favorite treats in the fairy tale. Cinderella of course got no treats at all, she was Cinderella.

I loved my daddy's poems, loved them as much as any of my favorite children's books. I thought my daddy was a great poet and they were great poems.

And the memory of how much I had loved those poems back then was always with me.

So after I put out my little Anne and Trixie book (5 tiny stories by me, the first ones I had written, a story by Trixie, and her letters to me)— I was a proofreader for a printing plant back then, and my friend Gwen, she was my best friend then, had already worked at the Women's Print Shop in Green Point, Brooklyn, so she knew about things.

The *Anne and Trixie* book was just typewritten pages. My stories were already typed up on my Smith Corona portable typewriter, so I typed up Trixie's little story, her letters. It came to 32 pages altogether.

Gwen did the press-on letters for the titles of the stories, selected the tan shade of paper for front and back cover, and did press-on letters for front cover.

We called it **Stories and Letters of Anne and Trixie**. And my print shop made 500 copies for 300 dollars. It was just 3 staples down the side.

After that Gwen and I got more ambitious and we put out **VAGUE**.

Ruthie's boyfriend Al designed the cover, it was gorgeous.

We put Ruthie's drawings inside.

Jan's story which I loved went in there.

I put a few of Trixie's stories in.

The stories by me were longer than I had put in my previous booklet.

Some little poems by Irene and a long article she wrote.

Irene had written the article for a collective and they turned it down. She came to my house in tears.

I said "don't cry, I will put it in *VAGUE*."

It was called *Marxism and Modern Art* and Cora actually read it and loved it.

Gwen found a community print shop in Brooklyn where if she did all the work herself it was very affordable. I think I paid $500. For that I got 300 copies.

Gwen had to operate all the machines. I remember being with her while she was operating the saddle stitching machine. It was a lot of work, but it did look beautiful when it was done.

And I guess some time after that I decided I would do my father's poems. I would do them the simple way we had done the *Anne and Trixie* book.

I had a selectric typewriter by now. I typed them up

and sent them to my father. I told him my plan to publish them, and he sent me a check for $300 to pay for it.

He believed I would actually accomplish it because Look! I had already accomplished these two things!

And I began to ask people I knew to do drawings for them. I gave them copies of the poems.

The first one who did drawings for them was Nellie in the park. She also took her dog to Tompkins Square Park like me and Abigail. Altho I think this was before I met Abigail.

I wonder if I still have Nellie's drawings? As soon as I saw them I knew I didn't want to use them. Because for me the poems were all about being 4 years old and having black patent leather Mary Janes, and beautiful party dresses. It was all about pretty clothes and going to the ballet and seeing how beautiful they were in their tutus and pink satin toe slippers.

It was a little girl's enchanted world. And Nellie had used herself as a model for the drawings. There was the fat lady standing on the scale naked. To me Cinderella was not a fat lady standing on the bathroom scale naked.

Cinderella was a fairy tale, the mind of fairy tales, which is all princesses who marry princes and live in a palace and eat off little gold plates and drink from gold goblets.

I didn't tell Nellie I was not going to use her drawings. Instead I asked Irene if she would do drawings for them. Irene did one for Cinderella, one for Snow White, and one for Rumpelstiltskin.

And I loved Irene's drawings.

And so that was the book I planned publish. But then as I explained that "thing" blew in. And it meant for all of us who were married, terrible wars in our marriage.

Denny and Abigail actually broke up during this time and she got her own apartment in what was then called Hell's Kitchen, the far west side of Manhattan around 54th Street. And Denny moved to Hoboken (right across the river in New Jersey).

Nellie and her husband Tex were then living in a room in a flea-bitten hotel on 14th Street and Nellie told me during her fights with Tex, she would walk out into the hall naked, which would enrage Tex beyond belief.

We were all living a nightmare.

Altho one nice thing about being friends with dog walkers in Tompkins Square Park is you got to know their husband as well as you got to know them. I had just as many long conversations with Tex while I sat on bench and our dogs played as I had with Nellie.

And I got to know Denny even better than I got to know Abigail.

Altho mainly I became close with Denny because after Abigail broke up with him and he moved to Hoboken, he and Bill played handball together in our neighborhood handball court. And Denny was hanging out in our apartment along with Bill's other friend Stuart Kaufman.

I got to know Denny so well because he was always at our apartment. I know Denny far more intimately than I know Abigail.

Then Abigail took him back and I never saw either one of them again until they stopped in front of my building to wave goodbye as they were leaving New York.

A few years after we moved to Tucson my dad went to Heaven, and I thought "I never did fulfill my promise to publish his poems and he had been happy I was going to do it."

And it was always in the back of my mind that one day I would fulfill that promise.

So even tho Abigail would reference our time in New York City together in her emails, usually I would pull away from those emails in my mind. That was a time I did not want to remember. Ever.

But when she said in an email last week, she was talking about our times together in New York, "I still have the drawings I did for the book we were going to do together back then."

I realize now it was going to be another Anne and Trixie book, a more ambitious version of our original one. Abigail was going to do the drawings for it.

But I forgot all about that planned book.

Instead I got all excited about Abigail's email thinking "I must have enlisted Abigail to do drawings for my dad's poems." And I thought "how great! she is now a children's publisher, we can do that book!"

So I emailed her back "which drawings? for which book?" and wrote her all about my dad's poems for me when I was little girl, and how I always wanted to do that book and I still want to.

And she emailed me back "Great! Let's do the book!" and I was in 7th heaven. Because I had wanted to ask Abigail all these years if she would do that book for me now that she is professional children's publisher, but I was always too shy to ask her.

So I found a folder in my file cabinet called Leon's Poems. And there were the 3 drawings Irene had done at that time. And there were my father's poems. I had copies of everything.

Nothing was on the computer, it was all on paper in my file drawer. And I sent it by first class mail to Abigail. And then began to type the poems into my computer, to a word processing program.

And I wrote an Introduction.

It turns out— I found out yesterday— Abigail is way too busy with professional commitments (she produces children's books for major commercial companies) to do the book for me.

But I am no longer dependent on publishing companies to publish any book I want published because CreateSpace and Lulu let us publish our books ourselves for free.

Altho Abigail said she would find the time to do illustrations for it. I sure appreciate her magnificent offer.

She said she will do a mock-up to send me "to see if it agrees with your vision of the book."

In real life she doesn't have to do a mock-up. Whatever illustrations she does, I would use. I am no longer fussy the way I was when I first conceived of it.

If Abigail wants to do Cinderella as a naked fat lady standing on her bathroom scale the way Nellie did, I will use it. I just want the book to be....

Post Script a year later

I hadn't realized how busy Abigail was when she made her magnificent generous offer to sneak a few minutes from her weekends to do the drawings for me. When I found out how many deadlines she is under, I decided I will do it as a simple pamphlet with the 3 drawings Irene did for it back in New York.

Anne still intends to do the book..

October 12

The booboo

I woke up before dawn. I heard the first bird chirp. Then I got out of bed to put up coffee and morning chores.

It was a little suspenseful getting out of bed because all day yesterday I had booboo in my foot. Which Bill insists is because I banged it. And which my Higher Self says is an ascension symptom (we are vibrating to faster frequency).

In any case it is not fun but not a big deal either. Altho I didn't go to the pool yesterday, I spent the day in bed.

Bill was very nice about doctoring it. He examined my foot, pronounced "No puncture! So it is not a thorn or insect bite." Rubbed it with alcohol to soothe it.

And filled up a bowl with warm water and tea tree oil for me to soak it in, which he said would make the swelling go down, also comfort my foot. And at night he brought me in a tiny ibuprofen pill, he said it would help.

All the things he said would help me did help me. And everything he did for me did help me.

It was instantly comforting to take a pill. It has been a gazillion years since I have taken a pill. It must be a form of magic, or some relationship with the mind. I put that teeny weeny thing in my mouth, washed it down with 7 Up, and thought as I was doing this, "this will help me a lot."

And instantly as if by magic it did. It took away all the discomfort.

Even tho there was suspense this morning when I decided I would get up and do my morning chores, somehow I knew before I put one foot down, that it would be ok. Somehow I knew my foot was a lot better.

I really don't know how we know what these experiences will be like ahead of time. Why yesterday I knew before I put one foot down that it would be a problem. And this morning I knew I could be secure about it, and sure enough it was fine.

I walked a little slowly and carefully at first, but did pick up the petite dog food cans in my room and put them in trash bag. And did walk into kitchen and do everything I wasn't able to do yesterday. Opened the dish washer and put all the clean dishes away (I actually had put up the dishes early yesterday morning).

And reloaded dish washer with dishes sitting in sink. Put up the coffee. Served the big cats their cat food, and the baby kitties their tuna fish. In fact I did everything. And the more I did, the more secure I got.

I even made myself toast and cream cheese because I was hungry. Having a foot booboo means you do not rush into the kitchen during the tv commercials for snacks. You just eat what is close by the bed, which in my case was big package of huge Reese's Peanut Butter Cups. I probably had six of them all thru that day and kept sipping on same warm flat soda.

But at night I asked Bill to bring me in an ice cold 7 Up, that is when he came in with the ibuprofen too and that was huge treat— ice cold delicious bubbly soda and magic pill. Plus he was so nice to me.

He hadn't been very nice in the morning when he woke up and found out about it. "O no!" he said "now we have to go thru that whole long nightmare of your foot booboo!"

It had been a long unpleasantness last winter which

isn't completely my fault. Yes last winter when it arrived it was excruciating but it probably did not really last that long.

The problem was that unbeknownst to me, when I was so unsteady on foot, I had stepped on a thorn in backyard. And I could not understand why it hurt to walk for next two weeks till Bill examined it, found the thorn and got it out. After that I was perfect.

There were one or two times after that, a few months apart, when it seemed like foot booboo was starting up again. "O no! What a drag!" I thought, "*This* I don't want!"

But it simply didn't come to pass. The slight tingling in my foot which is how it always starts didn't turn into anything. So this time when there was that slight tingling in my big toe I ignored it. I thought it will disappear as easily as it arrived. I really didn't think I would have another foot booboo.

The booboo did arrive the next morning, yesterday morning, but it wasn't that bad at all, just a little problematic. And by evening when Bill brought in the ice cold 7 Up and the ibuprofen and was happy because the Jets won, I really knew it was all over. Because my mind had moved so far away from it. It had dragged down my mind all day.

But now my mind was like a helium balloon when the child suddenly lets go in Central Park Zoo. There was nothing to hold my mind down anymore. It went up and floated where it wanted to go. Over all the buildings on 5th Avenue, up up and away and off in the distance.

I knew when my mind was free and easy and adventuring again, it was really all over.

And this morning when I made the decision to get up and do morning chores, even tho there was suspense, I knew it would be OK.

And it was. I was ok, gingerly but fine. I fed all the animals and made myself delicious hot coffee with lots of sweet cream.

October 17th

Anne puts one foot in front of other

And has no idea where she is going..

Kittens climb on their mother

The new kittens are playing in the tree. They discovered the tree two days ago. Now they are already climbing it. It is very exciting watching them climb the tree. When they first discovered it two days ago they only went one foot off the ground. But now they are adventuring quite far up.

I love the kittens so much, they are the joy of my life. O look how fast that little coal black one is shimmying up the tree. The kittens are getting good at tree climbing.

Last night before I went to sleep Bill reported a UFO was seen over New York City that afternoon hovering above Chelsea which is lower Manhattan on the West Side.

My life continues to be strangely empty. It was as if the whole long (very long) summer was an emptying out of my life.

The kittens are climbing all over their mother. She is crouched down while her babies are in the yard. They climb all over her till she turns on her side. I guess they want to nurse.

Or perhaps they are just playing with their mother. They are rolling on top of each other and on top of her. They seem too active to be nursing. Now it is all quieted down. Maybe now they are nursing.

The kittens all look like her. She is black and white and so are they. Altho one is coal black. When Mama nurses now or naps with her kitties, she uses one kitty for her pillow. She has soft pillow.

As Bill said "they are all powder puffs."

Mama cat picked her head up now and is looking around. I guess the nap they all fell into while they were nursing, she woke up now. She is licking one of the kittens giving it its bath.

Two of her kittens have gotten up and are tusseling around the tree. Mama is looking around. The other 3 kittens are still fast asleep at her breast.

O now she picked herself up, walked past the tree and changed her position in the yard.

The 3 fast asleep kittens are still fast asleep.

The two who were tusseling with each other next to the tree can't make up their mind whether to climb the tree or follow their mother.

If the summer was all about emptying out my life, I guess the autumn is having my new empty life. I guess eventually I will become accustomed to it, it will seem normal to have a totally empty life.

Last night before I went to sleep my Higher Self said "well you got thru the day."

"Is that what my life has come down to" I asked "that I got thru the day?"

"Yes" she said.

One kitten has started to climb the tree. Now another one has. They have finished wrassling on the ground and are all now going to tree climb. They play King Of The Hill and try to push the other one down.

If only I had the slightest idea what I was doing..

November 4th

Big Week!

Well it was a big week.

It began off Monday a week ago. We brought Cupcake's 5 beautiful kittens to Humane Society to be adopted. It is a serious adoption place. You pay 50 dollars plus you spend a few hours there doing the paperwork.

I could care less about the money, I just want the kittens adopted into good homes.

I think all that paperwork is ridiculous. The kittens are 8 weeks old and the most beautiful kittens there ever were. Happy, beautiful, radiantly healthy, sprites. It's like filling out a long form about a beautiful pink rose which grew in garden.

A rose is a rose, a brand new kitten is a brand new kitten. They are just there to give joy and receive joy. There is nothing to say. We are talking about love. A new kitten is love beauty joy happiness.

Even the paperwork I didn't mind, it was staying there for a few hours and doing it while people brought in their pets who didn't work out to be adopted. I prayed for each and every one that they would get a good home. But I get emotional about animals, my heart gets involved, I want so much for them to have perfect happiness.

While she was taking the kittens out of the cat carrier and looking at them, I left Bill there to do that with her. And I walked across the way to the infirmary to change the appointment for having Priscilla and Cupcake fixed. I wanted to make it for this Saturday instead of waiting an extra week.

I came back and Bill said she commented on how healthy the kittens are. Well of course they are! Then he went to the car and I did the paperwork.

And then we drove to the swim pool to be comforted by all that beauty and sweet water.

On Saturday morning we were back there with Priscilla and her daughter Cupcake to be fixed. Friday day and Friday night had been a long emotional day and night because we did not know if we would succeed in getting them both in cat carriers in time for their 8 am appointment.

Priscilla spends her time gallivanting all over the neighborhood. Only arrives back at some time in middle of the night for her food. And then takes off. And Cupcake is skitterish and runs away from me.

The 3 days after Cupcake's kittens were brought to be adopted weren't fun. I hadn't realized how much I had fallen in love with those kittens and missed them. And Cupcake spent the time looking for them all over the house and crying.

She only forgot about missing her kittens on Friday evening when she had to go thru the drama and trauma of being caught and put in her cat carrier. Which did not occur till 4 in the morning, after many previous unsuccessful attempts.

But at 8 am they were driven for their appointment. The vet assistant came out to tell me that Priscilla is a real sweetheart and Cupcake is a real scaredy cat. It was nice hearing what a sweetie Priscilla is, and I knew about Cupcake's scaredy problem.

She said "come back at 4 pm and pick them up."

We had both been up all night the night before with emotion and commotion and suspense if we would succeed in getting them both in cat carriers.

Bill watched his favorite team, the Arizona Wildcats, play a long suspenseful game. He had to stop watching when the pool would only be open for another 1/2 hour because I wanted to swim to relax myself. The pool is open till 4 pm on Saturday so we went to the one close to the Humane Society.

He sat in the car to hear the rest of the game. And I had the good fortune of arriving and there were Andrea and Ellen in the first lane saying "come in here Anne, we're just getting out." Which was good cause the pool was jam-packed.

It was heaven to arrive and find two such friendly loving faces and have a little conviviality. The cat thing was turning into an ordeal because I loved them all so much and had uneasiness until it was all accomplished and they were back home and fine and happy again.

I only got to swim for half hour but that half hour saved me. I had had too much emotion and been too rattled, I needed all that soft water.

I showered and dressed. Bill was still in the car. Thank god the Cats won the game, he has a lot of emotion when his favorite team loses. And I did not want any more emotion.

Luckily Diane, who had made the original appointment for me on the phone, was there at the desk. We got to meet in person, and she was wonderful to me. And the wonderful lady who brought out my cats was so sweet and comforting to me, a totally loving being.

"I'll get your cats now" she said.

"I hope they are ok."

"Of course they are fine" she said.

And she was right. We got them home and released them from their cat carriers. They were not groggy as Diane had said they would be. Priscilla instantly hopped the fence and went back to her gallivanting life. Cupcake also took off but she is not a gallivanter. I am sure she just hid in the yard somewhere.

Bill was worried they would be so mad at us that we did this, that neither girl would return home. He did not relax about this till both girls returned to eat their tuna fish and eat their crunchies.

Priscilla did major gallivanting for 3 days and 3 nights, to make up for her ordeal, only returning for food.

But after Cupcake calmed down she returned to her old ways. Winding herself around Beanie and kissing him.

103

She runs from me and Bill but she loves Beanie.

I think it also comforted her when her brothers arrived for food. We had kept Priscilla's first two litters. We only see Cupcake's brothers when they return for food, but I think Cupcake likes having them around now and eating with them.

It was Saturday evening when we arrived home with both cats and I truly thought "home free, now is big relax."

And Sunday we all did spend licking our wounds.

But Monday at 6 am when I woke up my computer would not connect to internet. I was on the phone for 4 hours. And finally she made an appointment for technician to arrive next morning.

My computer room which had been a kitty nursery in May, when Priscilla and both her daughters had kittens at the same time. My computer room was kitten nursery for 18 kittens. I have no idea why they chose my computer room. There is a whole big house to choose from plus fenced-in backyard.

But between the 18 kittens in May and 5 kittens this past month, the new kittens too chose it for their kitten nursery, there is no way I could let the computer technician into this room.

Bill and I planned to get to it, we just hadn't planned to do it this instant, but this instant it became.

We didn't go to swim pool Monday at all. At 10 am she said computer technician is coming next morning. We took everything out of the room and closet. It is my office, you can imagine how much stuff that means!

Bill pulled up the whole carpet and threw it in the garbage can out front. We discovered that underneath it was a linoleum from 1952, worse for wear, but still fine. Just filthy.

Bill scrubbed it for a few hours till it was perfectly clean. Then he scrubbed all the walls. The room had not been painted since we moved in 18 years ago, those walls really needed to be cleaned.

By then it was getting dark and Bill needed the last of the light to hook everything back up, the computer, the modem and the router.

After he did that, we brought everything back inside. The room was spick and span for the technician to arrive next morning.

They told us he would be arriving between ten and noon and to lock up all the pets. However at 8 am, when I just opened my eyes, the phone rang. It was Ricardo the technician. He said "I will be there in 5 minutes."

I put up the coffee, woke up Bill who grabbed Beanie on the leash and said "I will be sitting outside the house, bring me the coffee when it is ready."

It did take Ricardo two hours to locate the problem. It turned out to be the router, the router was broken. So he disconnected it from the modem and it meant I was back on internet.

I had brought Bill out a toasted roll with butter and refilled his coffee cup.

And when Ricardo left, Bill and Beanie came back in the house. Even Cupcake wandered in from backyard and made an appearance. She went over to the router and sniffed it for 5 minutes. I guess she was curious about Ricardo.

He was a beautiful young man and I was so happy he got to be in my new beautiful spick and span room.

And of course Bill and I were glad that my room was accomplished and was no longer something we had to face.

Once he started to do my room he wanted to do a major renovation. Pull up the linoleum tiles, put in some kind of new floor and paint it. He wanted to give me a beautiful room.

It was very sweet of him to want to do all that for me. But his project would have taken a month. I didn't want to be without my computer and my desk for a month.

It was an emotional fight in the midst of all the labor he was doing when he found out I did not want this plan to beautify my room, I just wanted it perfectly clean and to be able to work in it the next day.

I don't know why he got so upset with me. He misunderstood me and thought I did not appreciate what he was doing for me. Of course I appreciate it! He was a saint! I just wasn't willing to be turned out of the room and have no computer for a month.

I am sure all the fighting came from misunderstanding. There was such an abyss in our understanding. He was so hurt and enraged with me that I did not appreciate what he was doing, and I could not break thru to him that I did appreciate it. Tremendously.

We were two people who did not need more emotion stress and distress in our life after a whole week of emotions stress and distress over the cats.

And the day after, which was Tuesday, even tho every single thing in the past big week had a perfectly happy wonderful ending, we had both been thru the mill.

I think my computer room looks gorgeous now. There is no beauty to compare with perfect cleanliness. I do not care that it is not decorated. I am really happy in it. Bill did do a colossal favor for me.

Tuesday was the day we both tried to lift our spirits. I don't know why we were both so glum. I guess we had just been too rattled for too long.

But we both got miracles to help us lift our spirits. He went off to the dollar movie theater for a double feature. The first movie sounds totally creepy to me. But it was 2 and a half hours and I bet an eerie science fiction movie was the perfect thing to change his mood.

After 2 and a half hours of all the eeriness it probably wiped out clean all the emotion and commotion of the past week.

And after that he got a total treat. A very funny, very interesting, very penetrating and very real movie, which took place in New York City.

There is a whole world of New Yorker you never meet unless you yourself live there and go to college there. These are the New Yorkers in Flushing, Brooklyn and the Bronx who still live at home with their parents. And at age 35 are still living at home with their parents in Brooklyn, Flushing or the Bronx and are now either working for the civil service or who just get by.

These are boys who like girls very much but girls don't go for them and have never had a date. (They are sweet loving guys but if you want a girl to go out with you, you have to comb your hair and wear clothes which are nice to look at.)

These were Bill's friends back in NYC, he met them when he was going to community college there. I am not saying the people in the movie were identical to Bill's friends back in New York City, Marty Levine and Stuart Kaufman. But the same ilk.

I don't know how the guy who wrote the novel the movie came from met them. In the movie he met them because he answered an ad in the newspaper for a room in their apartment for rent.

The movie takes place on the Upper West Side and as a girl who went to CCNY and lived on the Upper West Side I can attest there are people like that up there. But in a way it is not so easy to find and be friends with them. These are

invisible New Yorkers, the ones under the radar. I knew

109

them at CCNY, Bill met them at community college.

For Bill they became his best friends. For me I was friends with them at college.

In any case Bill got huge treat, that the second movie he saw, all the people in it were these kind of people. It is the kind of movie Bill would understand from the inside out and would love and appreciate, which he did.

Bill's best friends in New York were all oddballs, he likes oddballs.

I would not say my best friends are oddballs, but I have always had friendships with oddballs too. I like them and I am comfortable with them. They are comfortable people to be with.

Maybe this is why Bill and I wound up in the East Village and stayed there till we were forced screaming and kicking to leave.

I don't know what the East Village is like now but when we lived there, it was where all the oddballs wound up. And if someone wasn't an oddball themselves, they were there because they like oddballs and like being friends with them, and wanted to live in their neighborhood.

All I can say is the Upper West Side oddball is a different type than East Village oddball.

And the third type, which were Bill's friends, are the ones who still live in the apartment they grew up with their parents in Brooklyn and Flushing.

In any case it was the perfect movie for Bill to watch, it is his world, the New York City oddball world. These are people he does understand, cares about and likes. Likes very much.

And for me, who is a political junkie, I got to watch 7 hours of election returns. Now that I was connected to internet again I got to finish all the emails I had started and write new emails, and after that I went in to watch the news networks on cable along with C-Span, and watched 8 straight hours of election returns until I finally fell asleep.

What a strange happy ending to the big bad week. Bill got 2 and a half hour psychological sci fi, for all the eeriness to shake it all out of him, and then a movie which was made for him.

He came home and did the chess puzzle on my computer.

Restored to being a perfectly happy man.

And I got endless hours of election returns and politicos commenting on it.

At the end of the night we had happy husband,

happy wife, and husband and wife being nice to each other again.

And Priscilla and Cupcake arriving 5 times to be fed and being together and being their happy selves again.

And then Cupcake went in and slept with Bill.

Which is a miracle.

And all is right with the world again....

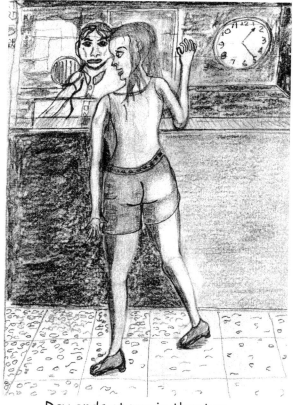

Day ends at movie theater

November 16

Bill sets up my new printer

Yesterday morning before we went to the pool Bill set up my new printer. I actually bought this printer 2 years ago. At the time my old printer was still working, but when we were in Office Depot they had a big sale on a laser printer.

And from the time I got my first computer and first printer way back in New York City, I had always dreamed of having a laser printer. I never thought it would be affordable. And now suddenly it was. I could not resist. I bought it.

It stayed in its box all this time. But in all the cat dramas over the past 6 months, 20 kittens being born, and finally two female cats being taken to vet to be fixed.

And because so much of the cat activity took place in my computer room, somehow in one of the dramas my old printer was knocked to the floor and broke.

It made no sense to hook up new printer till my room had been scrubbed from head to toe. No one sets up their new printer when the room has been a kitten nursery for 6 months.

And two weeks ago Bill tore up the old carpet, took it all to the trash, scrubbed the old linoleum underneath 3 times, and then scrubbed the walls. Room is now pristine. New printer was still in its box in fresh clean room

But on Sunday Ruthie said she would help me with the children's book I am going to publish of the poems my dad wrote for me when I was 4 years old.

Ruthie said "format the poems the way it will be in the book, print it up, and mail it to me," since her printer is broken. Her printer too got knocked off and fell on floor.

So yesterday morning Bill set up the new printer. I love my new printer and I sat at my desk while Bill took it out of the box, read all the instructions, and set it up.

Oddly enough it was a calm and productive experience. Sometimes emotions happen when things go on, but not yesterday. It was sweet and companionable and successful. Everything with Bill winds up successful, he is a good technician. But it is not always calm. Yesterday it was.

Yesterday was a day which worked. In fact the high point of yesterday was setting up the new printer. I didn't break it to him yet, that the day before I ordered a scanner on-line. And when it arrives, he will have to set that up too.

Because when he first started the enterprise of setting up my new printer, he was not happy about it. He said "this is the last printer I am setting up for you!"

I bit my tongue and did not say "the first one broke because the mice had nested in it and destroyed it." And I did not say "the second one broke because the cat knocked it down to the floor. And why is it my fault if animals destroy my printers!"

Instead I kept my mouth shut when he said 3 times "this is the last printer I am setting up for you!"

I kept my mouth shut because I thought "O no! He is not going to be happy when he finds out I have ordered a scanner and he will have to set that up too."

But when push comes to shove Bill likes doing favors for me, and he especially likes doing favors which help me with my writing or publishing my books.

He likes it when I write because he believes all artists should be doing their art, that doing art is a valuable way to spend ones time. He doesn't care about art and money, he thinks the doing of it is valuable to the artist.

Publishing my books is another story, he actually believes my books will make money.

I like it that he believes that but I no longer do. After having published 3 books over the past year, and only made $19 in toto. And even tho Create Space publishes your book for you for free, between one thing and another, each book has been a $500 investment for me.

Not that I care. It turns out all the reality, all the meaning, all the gratification in this enterprise of publishing books— for me it's all about the project itself. For me success is when I finally pull it off and the book is published and I can share the book with everyone.

And the *doing* of the project is a huge labor of love and actually a great adventure for me in many ways. Publishing a book means an idea is born, the idea of the book you will publish next. And then it is amazing how much creativity and effort is involved in bringing it off.

But I like it. I like having projects. I have been a writer a long time now, that is not new for me. Altho I still do it and I love it and it interests me. It interests me a lot because it is how I get to know myself.

But publishing a book is a monumental effort of a totally different sort and I would really say the crux of it is editing, something I never did before.

Because a book means seeing something as a whole. I love publishing even tho editing is so hard for me. It is not like writing which is like falling off a log for me at this point. Every aspect of editing is difficult for me. I have to put a lot of thought into it.

Writing does not involve any thought, it is a whole other thing. It is like going fishing. You put in your line each morning and you don't know what fish will go for your bait and what you will pull up.

Writing itself is bliss. It takes you to another world.

But editing a book is a whole different story. You have to decide what will go into the book, and where it will go. And how you will do it. And if you have to introduce certain parts of it, and write introductions. Editing a book is all decisions.

One of the books I am planning to do next is a new adventure for me in many ways. First because I am going to start off with the stories I wrote this summer. Then I want to put in stories I wrote back in the East Village. Then I want to put in Jimmy's poems, and then I want to put in Marilyn's great story about driving her car in NYC.

At first I was scared and overwhelmed about bringing off this book. I used to say to myself "Mission Impossible!" when I thought about it. And it is a bit more complicated cause Jimmy is not on email or computer.

But I have progressed so far in my thinking (altho not the actual doing of it) that now when I think of all the work involved I think "I will have a ball."

Some work I am not into doing. I actually do know a few girls who love cleaning their house. And many people love cooking and baking.

I guess I finally found a work I like doing.....

Post script a year later,

This is the book I began planning last year. It sure turned out different than I planned…. Hahaha maybe publishing books is a lot like life. You think it will go one way and it goes an opposite way…

November 19

Beautiful November

The birds are making a racket, they are chirping up a storm. Last night was the full moon, and this morning is cold wonderful beauty. We've had so much amazing beauty I have become addicted to it. I am used to it now. I take it for granted. I think "this is how life is and how it is supposed to be." I am at home in all this beauty. I cannot imagine not having it now.

Day after day of spectacular beauty seems natural to me now. It is like a state of grace. "She walks in beauty." The world is walking in beauty now. It sure is a joy, it sure is a gift.

I know it won't last forever. Even on the desert, the land of changeless weather, nothing lasts forever. December is when we get our winter rains. Altho secretly I think they are spring rains. Because right on January first our first blade of emerald green grass emerges.

And December rains are so gentle. They are gentle wet drenching. They are the counterpart to our summer rain, which arrives with such force and pounds the earth.

Summer rains or monsoons arrive with the trumpet call of tremendous thunder, stunning light show of lightning, and after that the heavens crack open and pour down rain. To bring back life to our hot as hell, dry as dust desert. They bring life back to it, they renew it.

It is a big story and the major drama of our summer. Monsoon season is a big deal on the desert, the big macher. We talk about it for a month before it arrives. It is all we talk about while it is going on. It is center stage to everything. We live for it.

It is a time when the desert (the land and trees which make up the desert), the animals, and man are all one mind. We become the desert too. We all await the great renewal of the desert. We all hold our breath till it comes. One breath sighs with relief when it finally arrives. And the release is experienced by all.

Of course the summer seems like ancient times now. Once the past is gone, it is gone, it has fallen over a cliff and been taken out to sea. The sun has set on it.

Now we are in beautiful November, a totally

beautiful month on the desert, mind blowingly beautiful. And in December comes the winter rains, the gentle female rains which bring our spring.

There are pretty Indian names for the female rains in December which bring our Spring. But I am a New Yorker, I recognize miserable weather. I know miserable weather when I see it. I come from a city which has a lot of it.

Hahaha that is what the winter rains are, cold miserable rainy days. Day after day of gray leaden skies, cold miserable wet rainy days. Without our beauty, without our bright light, without our beautiful sunshine, without our warmth.

If you go to the mall on the weekend during this time, you hear every father say to his small child in the parking lot as they are heading for the sanctuary of the warm and cozy, lit up glittering mall, "this is what the weather is like where daddy came from."

Nothing reminds us all as much of home as experiencing the weather in Tucson we all knew so well and had so much of in the town we lived in before we moved to Tucson.

All the sparrows are in the tree and so is the woodpecker. They all flew off. The woodpecker stays.

The woodpecker just inches himself up the branch pecking at the wood. I am so overjoyed my woodpecker is back.

The sparrows play all day. Flying in and out of tree. However the woodpecker remains on the thick limb. He has a job to do. Peck wood!

O there is my cat Cupcake. She stands up on her hind legs and sharpens her front claws on the wood.

The desert does not have very much wood, but what wood we have is certainly enjoyed by all. It's amazing how much pleasure this one desert tree right out my window gives to all. To the sparrows, to the woodpecker, to my cats.

And when they all had their litters of kittens and reached the age when they walked themselves out of the kitten nursery (aka my computer room) into the kitchen and out the back door and discovered the world outside, right there at edge of the patio is my tree. And there is no kitten delight like climbing trees.

Desert trees are not like trees back east, where the trunk goes high before it gets interesting. As soon as the tree springs out of the ground here it is 3 slender trunks almost immediately turning into branches.

Day after Christmas 2010
My email to a friend

I hope you had a nice Christmas.

This is the first year I celebrated Christmas.

I grew up in a Jewish neighborhood in Flushing, so no one celebrated Christmas except my friend Diane's family who lived underneath our apartment.

Diane was Polish Catholic.

They had Christmas tree and lights on their windows.

And now I realize Christmas Day they had presents and fancy dinner. And went to church.

All the rest of us just ran outside in our play clothes for a day of stick ball, jump rope, potsy, punch ball, Asses-Up, or riding our bicycles.

Christmas passed unnoticed for us.

But after almost 20 years in Tucson, I seem to have joined the regular world.

I celebrated Christmas for the first time this year and I

enjoyed it.

The day after Thanksgiving I began planning the box of gifts I would send Bill's family in San Diego. Bill was raised Catholic so Christmas was huge deal for him growing up.

I ordered yellow ruffled panties for Bill's sister and a pretty sunshine yellow nightie from internet and hoped they would arrive in time for me to wrap it for her Christmas box.

The instant they arrived I forced Bill to go to mall so he could pick out a shirt for his brother-in-law and nephew.

And I was very excited by his choices, he put so much thought and energy into them.

A week before Christmas I took all the Christmas gifts we had bought, along with wrapping paper, scissors, scotch tape, to table in sunshine in backyard.

I also took out my first two books and wrapped them up for my nephew. I love and adore my nephew.

I wrapped up all the gifts, and wrote out cards with each one. And had Bill take me to post office.

The postman said "I am not wrapping up your Christmas box" so while we were on long line, Bill got on his hands and knees and did it.

All the other ladies were on line with their Christmas box, so Bill did their box for them too.

He had been a shipping clerk in NYC and knew how to operate the tape machine the postman lent us.

And then Bill on his own wrote out 4 Christmas cards, one to his sister, one to an Italian cousin in Baltimore, and one to a new cousin, Marcy. She was researching her family and wrote to Bill asking if he was the Bill in a family photo she had come across of Bill's dad and his two year old son.

It turns out the photo was sent by Bill's dad to his father.

In Baltimore, the family they visited every week-end and celebrated everything with, was Bill's mom's family, the Italian family.

I was thrilled when the letter first arrived from Marcy with the photo of Bill's dad holding Bill in his arms and called her instantly to say "Yes! Bill is that Bill!"

But Bill was mad that I called her, he thought it was some internet fraud, and she was after his bank account.

I said "why would she do all this for the $200 you have in your bank account!"

She enthusiastically emailed Bill 10 times and sent

him a Christmas card with her family in it, her 3 young sons.

And then Bill melted, her oldest son looks just like Bill at that age.

And he got so excited at all the information that his grandmother was Blackfoot Indian.

It is so funny, that now his cousin Marcy is the new wonderful thing in his life.

On Christmas Eve he went in and spent 2 hours writing her an email, asking her which sports her son plays, which teams they follow, and about the Blackfoot Indians, and how Uncle Richard used to spend the weekends going to 3 movies a day.

Bill's sister is not a lunatic like Bill and instantly accepted that Marcy was indeed their second cousin, and called Marcy right away and they have been on email.

But then I think Mary forgot about Marcy. Mary is busy with her family, and her friends, and her church.

Whereas with Bill, altho it took him a while to warm up to Marcy (to believe she really was his second cousin) it has now become the centerpiece of our life.

He went on internet and researched the Blackfoot Indians, and tells me everything he is going to tell

Marcy in his next email.

The long email he wrote her on Christmas Eve is the first real email he ever wrote.

After we mailed off the Christmas box to Mary's family, I realized I forgot to put in the Dog Calendar I had bought for them at Thanksgiving, they have a black lab who is the love of their life, so I got them the Black Lab calendar.

I was afraid to break it to Bill we had to go back to post office next day, but Bill was eager to go, because he was so thrilled with his cousin Marcy's Christmas card with her 3 sons in it, one who looks like Bill, that he wanted to make sure his Christmas card to Marcy got there in time for Christmas.

After that I forgot about Christmas, I had accomplished everything.

But Bill decided 5 days ago to put up lights, our first lights.

He went and bought 4 strings of white l.e.d lights and wound them around the huge elephant ear cactus in front of house, it is taller than the house.

It took my breath away when I saw them at night, I never saw anything so beautiful in my whole life.

I was thrilled and overjoyed.

So I am a fan of Christmas now. I liked buying Bill's family their presents and making nice Christmas box.

And I love my Christmas lights, I want Bill to keep them on all year.

Bill cooked spaghetti on Christmas, and then went off to watch a violent revenge crime thriller at the dollar movie theater, to knock Christmas out of his system

And I watched Jean Shepherd's *A Christmas Story* two times on TV. It is my favorite movie.

Love, Anne

Bill loves drawing Skippy...

And here is our lovely Beanie

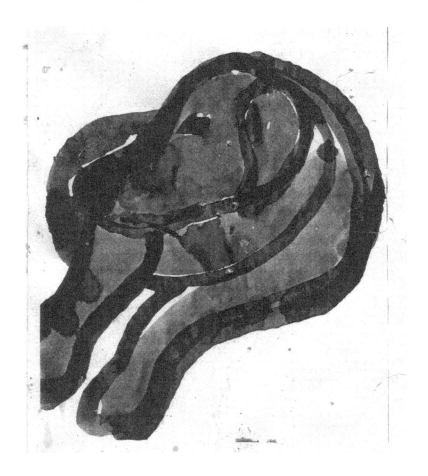

Part 2

2011

DRIVING LESSONS

Anne needs help, her friend Jim is on the spot...

Jim is not having a good time teaching Anne to drive

Luckily he finds her funny

My life in email

Look Ma no hands
Life hit me with its best shot and I came up smiling
'Twasn't easy but it is doable...

Sent: Wednesday, April 27, 2011

Dear Russ,

Bill was never sick a day in his life so it is a mystery. Bill is in Heaven. Last month he fell asleep and woke up in Heaven. Darling please do not have a booboo in your heart over me. I am perfectly happy. I have had so many ups and downs in life that I learned how to be happy no matter the circumstances.

And it sure paid off now when life hit me with its best (worst) shot. I never lost my peace and happiness. And every day my happiness deepens and expands.

My good news is my brother and I are now close.

It is very interesting, he was away on vacation for 2 months and didn't get home till early April. He was out of the country, no email, no cellphone. So April was first time I could reach him.

I was so sure that no one could understand I am perfectly happy, that it was simply impossible to understand.

My brother knows nothing about my spirituality, it has been so long since we were close.

But he knows his sister. I forgot about that. We were so very close the first 25 years of our life. We were so in synch. My parents did not understand me, but siblings who are very close do understand each other.

Russ, it was wonderful that instant I said "I am perfectly happy," he just said "great."

He believed me! He knew I was telling him the simple truth. And he was just happy it was so.

I got my brother back. We had grown apart during nearly our whole adult life, and then I stopped speaking to him last year when we had major conflict.

But 3 weeks ago on the phone we were as close as we were as children. It was so nice! It felt so good.

I said "can you help me do my income tax?"

And he said "yes." He said he will call to help me do it on the phone

I am very happy to have my brother back.

O Russ I am so happy. My brother is being wonderful to me. He just emailed me that he did my taxes, both federal and state, and paid my taxes for me.

What an angel! I love him so much. I am so happy we are close again.

And Bill's best friend Jim is teaching me to drive.

Last month the little boy (Richie) I used to play with every afternoon after nursery school found me on Facebook. So we have been emailing ever since. We have not been in contact since we were 4 years old.

Below are the emails I sent Richie about my driving lessons with Jim. Two of them made me bust out laughing as I was writing them. And I giggled all day about what happened during the driving lesson that day.

Jim is the best driver in the world, but has no experience teaching. My dad was best teacher in world, he taught me to ice skate, to play tennis, to do everything.

It is a brand new experience for me to try to learn from someone who has no idea how to teach. But I guess Jim is learning how to teach and I am learning how to drive. Meanwhile we are getting to know each other.

Jim has been swell to me, driving me to swim pool at Y every day, and to grocery store, and to pet food store for my animals.

After my catastrophic first few driving lessons with Jim, the ones I tell Richie (my boyfriend from nursery school) about, I used the excuse of "have to study the drivers manual to get my learners permit," as a way to get out of lessons.

Hugs and kisses to you and Nelma.

I love you

Annie (Below are my emails to my friend Richie about my first driving lessons.)

From: Annie
To: Richie
Sent: Friday, March 25
Subject: Re: Who is going to teach you to drive?

Hi Richie,

My wonderful friend Jim is going to teach me to drive the Mustang. He is coming by with Drivers Manual tomorrow so I can study it for my Learners Permit.

The Mustang is a manual, I hope I can learn how to do it. Encourage me!

I was so good with your Lionel trains when we were 4 years old so I figure I have inborn talent LOL.

Love, Annie

Sent: Saturday, March 26
Subject: First driving lesson was Abbott and Costello

Hi Richie

My friend Jim just came by to bring me the Drivers Manual. I lent him our truck for a few days so he could haul things. So he drove into driveway in the truck.

Since truck is a manual, he said "let me teach you the clutch on this and we'll drive around the block."

I know the Mustang is manual but Jim informed me it is a sports car. Oy gevalt!

There is a jalopy automatic in my driveway but Jim wants me to learn to drive the Mustang.

He said "let's learn on the truck and then it will be

ready for you on Mustang."

I was not prepared for a first driving lesson. I was bra-less in tank top, barefoot, in little ruffled skirt.

His idea was I back it out of driveway and drive around the block a few times. The whole thing was like a scene out of Abbott and Costello. Jim was smoking his big cigar.

He didn't bother to tell me which was the gas pedal and which was the brake. First I almost crashed it into the Mustang in front of me.

Finally I backed into road and kept backing up into neighbor's front yard. I was not able to succeed in turning the car in direction Jim wanted. I stalled and bucked 10 times before I drove one inch.

Jim kept saying "no problem, everyone goes thru this."

And he was determined I drive around the block.

But he was so focused on what I was doing since I clearly had no idea he didn't notice the cars coming or the jogger.

"O I didn't see that" he said when I pointed it out.

Finally I said "we'll do it tomorrow early morning in huge parking lot at El Con Mall."

He wanted to keep going.

"Learning how to drive is easy, I will teach you in

five minutes," he kept saying. But finally he agreed tomorrow morning.

LOL I was a mess when it was over. He said "Relax! Driving is easy you don't even have to think about it."

I hope I do better in my lesson tomorrow.

Love, Annie (PS Jim just called he is taking me swimming at the Y in 20 minutes, I have to find my bathing suit..

Sent: Monday, March 28
Subject: my second driving lesson yesterday was better

Hi Richie

My second driving lesson yesterday was better than the first. At least I did not almost crash into the Mustang in my driveway.

We went to gas station first to fill up tank of the old 2nd hand Chrysler, it is automatic. Jim showed me how to put in my credit card and insert nozzle for gas.

I did everything great and I was triumphant while I stood there filling up the car. It was the happiest, most joyous, most successful, most triumphant moment of lesson. It started off on a good note.

The mall parking lot we went to was no longer the vast empty deserted parking lot it was 10 years ago. There were no cars at 6:30 am Sunday morning, but every few feet a very small tree planted in huge cement box. Now it is an obstacle course.

Before we even began I insisted Jim show me where the brake is and I did it 5 times with my foot to get feel of foot on brake.

Then I said "show me gas pedal."

Altho I don't know if I even stepped on gas pedal once, because once car was moving slowly thru those tiny lines in and around all the obstacles I never wanted to go faster. I just wanted to learn how to steer.

But there was a limit to how much I could practice that. I just went straight and then gently turned left.

I don't think I got the hang of steering and want to get the hang of steering in my next lesson.

I will ask Jim to take me to Mervyns parking lot because that has no obstacles.

Jim is my angel and the best friend any girl could ever have.

Love, Annie

Hi Richie

Jim picked me up at 7 am this morning for my 3rd driving lesson. We went to the huge empty parking lot of Mervyns.

It was incredible beautiful morning, sun was just rising and our huge glorious Arizona sun was right in my eyes, I could not see anything at first.

But sun rose higher and I could see.

For first time I made progress. I relaxed and got happy and was actually driving the car. Jim was so happy. It made him relax and have confidence in me.

Then he noticed smoke coming out of hood. He opened it up and discovered the old car was out of oil. We both knew the old car has big problem with oil leaks.

Across the street from parking lot was gas station. Jim bought 3 quarts of oil and asked her if she sold filters. She said no. He tried to put it in without filter but it spilled all over.

Since his house is so close by he drove the car there and

got out his filter. He poured in the oil.

And next thing we knew the car was on fire. His garden hose was right there, he put out the fire. He was able to get the car to run but it was very suspenseful drive from his house to mine.

By a miracle it made it. He opened up the hood. Discovered the problem, and left hood up for car to cool down. He said the fire was caused by the oil running onto the hot exhaust.

We both agreed to never drive this car again. It is an old car 1985 and I was not even able to get my passenger door to open. I had to scooch over to get out.

It's just as well. My next driving lesson in 2 days will be on the truck with the clutch.

Jim is exhausted. He went home to take a nap. I don't think he anticipated having so much trouble teaching me how to drive LOL.

Love, Annie

Sent: Later that same day
Subject: More on today's driving lesson

Hi Richie

Thank you for your email. You are sweet to say that Jim

is brave and I will tell Jim what you said when I have my next lesson day after tomorrow. It will make him feel good.

Hahaha I think it traumatized Jim in my first lesson in truck with clutch that I almost crashed into my Mustang and then could not stop backing up and backed into neighbor's yard.

I guess he just did not comprehend that I did not know where the brake was or how to steer. He has been driving since he was 14 like everyone in Tucson.

He said my lesson with the clutch next Thursday will be "dry run," just in my driveway and no turning on motor.

This morning was the best lesson until the car caught on fire. For first time he let me relax instead of always telling me to relax, and he let me teach myself a little.

He saw how well that worked and that I made progress for the first time, so I think I will do better from now on.

He even noticed that my feet didn't quite reach the pedals and I should have the seat moved up. He didn't do it then. But I bet with truck he will notice that the pedals are too far away from me. He did not notice that in the Abbott and Costello lesson.

Today I got so relaxed that when the car stalled during my lesson (now we know why it was always stalling, no oil) but the always-stalling gave me chance to keep practicing starting up the car.

And finally I got so relaxed about doing that, that my sense of humor kicked in.

"First make my tushy comfortable in seat" I said and got in more relaxed position.

"Then tell my driving teacher how wonderful he is," and gave him big smile. "Then turn the key..."

It helped Jim relax that I said "I know how to start the car, first make my tushy comfortable in seat."

And it certainly relaxed me that I was kidding around. We made such progress in this lesson that I actually thought after we bought the oil and he put it in, we would continue the lesson. But of course when car caught on fire that ended the lesson.

He had no problem putting out the fire, but how were we to get back to my house?

His car was parked in my driveway. He was able to start up the Chrysler after the fire, he just let it cool down, but it barely ran at all. We both knew it would take a miracle to get to my house. But we did.

He immediately opened up the hood. I said "will it catch on fire again in my front yard?"

He said that is why he is sitting in chair in front yard smoking his big cigar. He wants to make sure it won't.

After 20 minutes he left. And Priscilla, my cat, hopped the fence and went in and out of the car. She loves that car.

When I went to get the mail in late afternoon I saw the hood is still up and I will leave it like that.

I called Junque for Jesus in Tucson and asked them if they will come and take the car away. They said yes. So I said I will call them back.

Love, Annie

Alas my Chrysler did not have a good day...

Hi Richie

When I am not in sunshine in backyard with doggie and kitties I am glued to TV watching the Arab Spring. I love the Arab people, I want their freedom with all my heart.

LOL Muggles (the baddest cat in whole world, he lives across the alley) is in the yard now stalking Cupcake.

She is the scaredy cat of the western world but my only cat not afraid of Big Bad Muggles. She just hip hops lightly away when he is going to pounce. She could care less.

O now he is stalking Priscilla (the mother of his children) she actually moved faster out of his way.

Which alerted Beanie since Priscilla had to go past him, so Beanie chased Muggles out of yard.

O watching animals is such a delight!

All afternoon I watched the woodpecker in yard.

It was a paradise in yard all day

Love, Annie (O Priscilla is sitting up in branch of tree now. Muggles just arrived!!! He is not allowed to come into the yard to beat up his family.

Russ emails me back

(He is my friend from swim pool)

From: Russ
To: Anne
Sent: Friday, April 29

Dear Anne:

It is great that you have gotten back with your brother and he is clearly being a great help for you. It couldn't come at a better time.

How about Jim? Is he still teaching you to drive? I was concerned that the last email on that subject was dated April 3. Are you able to drive now okay?

I must tell you that I taught Nelma to drive when our daughter Robin was less than a year old. We had a 1933 Plymouth automobile at the time.

It was an okay car except it had wooden spoke wheels that squeaked every time you turned a corner and it didn't have synchro-mesh gears.

The lack of synchro-mesh meant that you needed to take the car out of the gear it was in, put it in neutral, release the clutch while it was in neutral. Depress the clutch and move it to the next gear, and finally release the clutch in the next gear.

This process was called "double clutching" and it needed to be done on every gear change to prevent the gears from grinding.

I had learned to double clutch driving army vehicles during World War II, so it was no problem for me, but it made Nelma's task of learning to drive very difficult.

I'm sure that you can appreciate the challenge this must have been. However, we persevered and she did learn to drive.

A few years later we upgraded to a 1937 Pontiac, which did have synchro-mesh gears and it took a long time to teach Nelma to stop double clutching. It had become a reflex.

After all of this, Nelma opined that our marriage could withstand anything, and sure enough it has.

Love, Russ

To: Russ
Sent: Friday, April 29
Subject: thank you lovely Russ

Hi wonderful Russ

Thank you very much for your email. I appreciate it very much. Yes I am learning the clutch now. As you can imagine I am fascinated to read the story of Nelma's double clutching, as the clutch is now my whole life.

Jim and I had taken a break from my driving lessons because I was studying the Drivers Manual to get my Learners Permit.

Jim, my wonderful friend, who is still driving me to swim pool at the Y, to grocery store, and to pet food store, drove me to take my test for Learners Permit. I had to take it twice, but I passed the second time. Hallelujah!

That was week before last, so last Thursday Jim and I went back to me trying to learn the clutch in Mervyns parking lot.

That was a total disaster. Jim had to go home and take a tranquilizer and I did not want to continue driving lessons.

But Helen researched internet for learning the clutch. She had just bought her son his first car, a second-hand car with clutch. She was finding it impossible to teach him the clutch so she researched the internet.

She found one thing very helpful and emailed it to me.

It begins off with the no-gas method, and Helen said Jim can do it with me in my driveway.

That was 2 days ago, and by a miracle, it worked. We had our first successful driving lesson. It was all about finding the pressure point.

I am immensely encouraged by your email, if Nelma can learn to double clutch, then surely I can learn to single clutch.

I love you

Annie

From: Russ
To: Anne
Sent: Friday, April 29, 3:34 PM

I am so delighted to get this email. It makes me think you are really doing very well, and I was not sure before. Thank goodness for Helen and Jim! They are the heroes of the day. Love, Russ

To: Russ
Sent: Friday, April 29, 6:30 PM
Subject: I love you

O Russ I am smiling ear-to-ear at this email from you. You have made me so happy. You are exactly right when you say "Thank goodness for Helen and Jim! They are the heroes of the day."

Jim is the greatest friend any girl could possibly have, plus he is my angel. He has his heart set on teaching me how to drive, he believes it is the biggest favor he could do for me.

He himself is a great driver and has been driving forever, but he is not used to teaching. Which seems to be all about how you relate to the person who is trying to learn from you.

After last Thursday's disastrous lesson I came home and thought "it is impossible for me to learn to drive from Jim."

Which is why Helen saved me when she sent that email and said "practice it in your driveway with Jim."

It is the first thing which worked. As a result both Jim and I were both so happy.

Jim corrects me if I suggest something like "Let me relax instead of only telling me to relax."

He says "I told you to relax, you can't drive until you relax." He and I both realize it is necessary for me to relax, but he thinks telling me to relax will do it.

However this friendship is very valuable to both of us in this point in our lives. There are so many things he offers me, there are so many things I offer him, we can bring great happiness to each other, and enrich our lives.

So altho I could hire a professional driving teacher, I have come to realize that process is everything in my learning how to drive from Jim.

Altho it has introduced conflict and stress into our friendship, it is also making us much closer. And helping us really get to know each other.

And of course meanwhile it is a tremendous favor that Jim is willing to drive me anywhere for anything. He drove me out to the Indian Reservation to buy my 10 cartons of cigarettes cheaper there than in town. Cigarettes cost a fortune in town now.

When I decided to buy a designer dress to take my Learners Permit test in, and the only store which sold that designer was in downtown Tucson, Jim drove me there.

And there was no parking, he had to drive around the block the whole time I was in the store.

Naturally I will never ask for that favor again. The woman had told me there was parking on Sunday behind her store, but she was wrong.

Jim was not mad at me, and all the way home we giggled and cracked jokes about my designer dress.

And it did bring me luck, I have my Learners Permit.

And I like the dress too!

Also because of the drama which goes on during the driving lessons, we have things to kid around about when he drives me to swim at the Y or to grocery store or pet food store.

And he was so proud when I got my Learners Permit.

It is truly a beautiful friendship.

Helen is helpful too because she is the best teacher in the world, she understands it from Jim's point of view and my point of view, and says encouraging and helpful things to me on the phone.

As she pointed out, "Jim is learning how to teach and you are learning how to drive."

My Higher Self says "Jim is the most experienced driver in the world, but he is new at teaching.

"But driving lessons with Jim are the best thing to be happening in your life now.

"As the only purpose in your life now is to be completely happy.

"So even tho Jim has to take a tranquilizer each time he returns home after a driving lesson with you, and you have to plotz in front of the TV for 5 hours to calm down after a driving lesson with Jim," my Higher Self pointed out "the next day both of your happiness has increased exponentially."

Love, Annie

Here I am at MVD
Anne wears designer dress to take learners permit test

From: Russ
To: Anne
Sent: Wednesday, May 11
Subject: Ft. Lowell Pool, etc.

Dear Anne:

First, I want to say that I really enjoyed your picture on your learner's permit. You looked very happy.

How are the driving lessons progressing?

About a week ago, I started getting emails from Aevya asking me to come to the pool and telling me about Lifeguard Mike having finally gone to the Coast Guard.

I was pleased to find out that his sister Kristin has taken her brother's place as the chief life guard and that the pool was immaculate and the water delightful. In the future, I think I'll try to go once a week, probably on Wednesday.

You may know all of this, but I thought I'd let you know, just in case.

Love, Russ

From: Anne
To: Russ

O Russ thank you very much for this report of our

beloved Fort Lowell Pool. I am so interested in hearing about it.

Wow what an adventure Lifeguard Mike is off in the Coast Guard! That is a huge adventure, leaving home, leaving his parents and sister, leaving Tucson, leaving the pool. And having a totally new life. I think it is great.

I think it is wonderful his sister is now Head Lifeguard. I am sure she is excellent.

We had a big break from driving lessons because Jim was away. This break turned out to be wonderful for me.

It gave me the time and peace to go back to working on editing and publishing my 4th book, and I do totally enjoy the enterprise of editing and publishing.

I love work if it is a work I like to do. And this is work I love. My friend Marsha loves cooking and baking and Bill liked to clean, but none of that interests me. So I don't do any of it. I snack instead of cook. And a bare minimum of housework.

With publishing it is the reverse. As you remember from doing your book, the temptation is always to overwork. You get caught up in it!

So Monday of last week we had our first lesson after the disaster I wrote you about last, when Jim had to take a tranquilizer afterwards, and it took me hours in front of TV to calm down.

We went back to Mervyns parking lot and it was total success. Jim was glowing, he was proud of me and so happy.

I still don't think I got the hang of the clutch because the 3 times I started it up, the truck bucked like crazy.

But Jim was thrilled when I switched to 2nd gear and 3rd gear as I was driving around Mervyns parking lot, when I followed his instructions and did it.

So now for first time I have confidence. I did steer beautifully around Mervyns parking lot last Monday.

So my whole attitude has changed. For first time I no longer dread the lessons, and no longer think they will be traumatic. Now I have confidence in both Jim and me. I have turned a corner!

Jim has quite ambitious ideas for our driving lesson tomorrow. I don't know what they are and I am not yet at the point where I want to know.

But I do trust now he knows what he is doing in teaching me to drive. So I will leave it all in his hands.

I love you

Annie

From: Russ
To: Anne
Sent: Wednesday, May 11, 4:24 PM

Dear Anne:

I knew you could do it! Keep up the good work. You are almost there.

Love,

Russ

Anne catches the ball

Anne refuses to drive on Aviation Highway

To: Russ
Sent: Monday, May 16
Subject: Driving lesson yesterday

Hi Russ

Our next driving lesson got postponed to Sunday (yesterday). It was not one bit what I expected when Jim told me last week he would take me to dirt roads where there are no cars. I pictured way out in the countryside in the beautiful desert.

Instead we drove a long time on a highway thru the industrial part of Tucson, outside the city, thru barren desert. And then he stopped the car and said "Switch seats, you will have your lesson here!"

"Are you crazy!" I said. "You want me to drive on Aviation Highway! I won't do it!"

"There are hardly any cars," he said.

But there was traffic in both directions, just not a whole lot of it.

I refused and neither of us would back down.

"If I say it is safe, it is safe! I am right here next to you," he said.

"I won't do it!" I said. "Can't you take me to a country road."

A few feet up the highway was turn-off to a two lane road. So he turned up that. That turned out to be OK.

There must have been some hotel at the end of it because the cars who passed us headed to the highway all said Airport Taxi.

Maybe we were near the airport, and the people who stayed at a hotel in that barren ugly area were businessmen involved with the companies in the industrial area we had just gone thru.

The lesson went well. The truck still bucked like crazy each time I tried to start it up with the clutch. And when it didn't buck, the engine just went off, and I had to start it again. And again and again and again.

But still I was driving very very very slowly on an actual road and keeping to my side of it.

And Jim had me switch to 2nd and 3rd and 4th gears as I was driving, telling me how to do that.

The lesson was 45 minutes, it took us 45 minutes to get there. And I would have wanted to continue. But I knew I had to go to PetSmart to get a ton of canned dog food and canned cat food, and that takes so much energy.

I stopped the lesson so Jim could take me.

It's too bad I couldn't continue the lesson, I was learning, but I am glad I saved energy for the pet food store experience.

It was an awful long drive into and thru town to get there, the store was crowded, the dogs were having their lessons in the store. I just so much wanted to be home. I didn't even unload it all from the truck when we reached the house.

I am glad I did it tho. Some time late in that afternoon I started having a train of thought which unsettled me. I went in and opened up the new canned food for the kitties and the new canned food for the doggie. They were all so happy. And I discovered that made me totally happy and at peace too.

So I went into the backyard with my books, my iced coca cola, lounged on the comforter I had put on the ground. And watched the beautiful Sun set. And then the beautiful Full Moon rise. My animals were all around me enjoying the lovely air too.

We were all very happy. So all is well.

Have a lovely evening. Love, Anne

Stand off in the desert

To: Russ
Sent: Tuesday, May 24
Subject: I have aced the parking brake...

Hi Russ

Jim and I finally had another driving lesson yesterday. The previous one was last Sunday, the week before.

Jim took me back to that 2 lane road which led off Aviation Highway. Again I was stunned that last week he had planned for me to drive on Aviation Highway.

And the lesson yesterday was best ever.

I am brilliant at releasing the parking brake.

Jim thinks I am silly to be proud of myself for having aced the parking brake. He says "the parking brake is only used if you are parked on a hill and Tucson has no hills."

So what! I am glad to be great at something having to do with driving the truck.

Finally I got him to concede I might be one of the best at parking brake in Tucson.

Everything else I was not so hot at, I am still learning.

Altho I was quite good at turning the key and starting the engine. Maybe not as magnificent as I am at parking brake, but close to excellent.

Everything else was D minus. Altho better than I was before, which was an F.

LOL I was a failure, now I am not! I did a lot better.

I still don't get the car to start running each time I put in the clutch and try to let it out slowly, as I slowly step on the gas.

At the beginning of yesterday's lesson all I did was stall and have to do it again and again. And again and again.

But midway into the lesson, I started to try what Layla had told me to do on email when I told her about the truck always bucking on me.

She said "the engine wants more gas."

Jim had said "you are not giving it enough gas," but it didn't sink in till Layla wrote me that on email in the middle of last week.

So when it simply bucked and stalled after my first 10 tries yesterday morning, I started pressing on the gas pedal a lot harder.

And that turned out to be the secret. After that almost every time I got it on the second try and once or twice on the first try.

Miracle! Jim was so proud of me he could burst.

Of course with my foot pressed down so hard on gas pedal so the truck would move, when it did I was speeding. I was going 40 miles an hour on road which the limit is 35. I did not want to go that fast but I have not yet learned how to slow down.

Jim had no idea I was going a lot faster than I wanted to go, he just thought it was great I was going that fast.

But of course when there was a stop sign way up ahead, I had to stop for that, so Jim said "put in the clutch, foot off the gas, and slowly brake."

I did that 3 times, the 3 times we arrived at stop sign. I was OK at it, not good but OK. I was very proud of myself for being OK at stopping at stop sign.

I have still not learned how to slow down when I am going 40 miles an hour. I do not want to go that fast. I know how to slow down for a stop sign, foot off the gas.

Maybe that is the same way to slow down when truck is going a lot faster than I want it to. I tried that at first, but Jim said "you're slowing down, why did you take your foot off the gas." So I stepped on the gas again. And again I was going too fast.

I really have not had any chance to practice steering. Because as soon as I am driving along Jim has me shift to second and then to 3rd, and then to 4th.

And then because of my speeding problem we have reached the stop sign and there is a highway. So Jim and I change places and he turns the truck around for me.

One stop sign leads back to Aviation Highway, the one at the other end is not such a major highway. And Jim wanted me to try to drive across it to wherever the two lane road continued.

On the 3rd time I was willing to try, but when I stalled in the middle of the intersection, I instantly got out and made Jim drive the truck across that small highway.

Then I got back in and drove it till it reached another huge highway. I got out, Jim turned it around. So whole lesson was going back and forth like this.

We both got really good at getting out of the truck and changing seats. We had to do it so many times.

165

Jim said "There is a coyote!"

"Where?" I said, "Where? I have always wanted to see a coyote."

So I tried to scour the desert close to me to see the coyote. "There!" Jim said "there!"

I forgot I was driving and should pay attention to what I was doing. I didn't see the coyote and truck nearly went off the road. I won't do that again until I know what I am doing driving, not even to see a coyote which is a lifelong dream of mine.

Love, Annie

After driving lesson we stop at 7-11 so I can buy ice cold can of soda for me and Jim

To: **Russ**
Sent: Sunday, June 12
Subject: today's driving lesson, finally progress!

You took me back to Aviation Highway!!

Hi Russ

Finally some progress with driving.

I didn't have any lesson for two weeks, so Saturday

(yesterday) I was terrible. But during second half of

lesson the progress which I had made kicked in. So I was back to where I left off 2 weeks ago. Not the disaster I was at start of yesterday's lesson.

So today I was able to pick up where we left off yesterday.

Jim said "I am taking you to a beautiful country road with no traffic at all, and you will like the blue sky and beautiful countryside and you can see wild animals coyotes, rabbits, and even deer."

"Great!" I said "everything I love."

I got the impression it was a dirt road.

It was pretty far out of town. It turned out not to be a country road at all, what Jim meant is it goes thru pretty country. It had 3 lanes and tons of traffic whizzing by. I refused to get out of truck and go to driver's seat.

Lots of traffic in both directions, altho speed limit is 50 they were all going 60 at least.

We had our usual fight.

"I can't do this!"

"I am your teacher, I say you can!"

I refused.

So he drove a little further down the road and there was turn-off for the fair grounds. Since the fair grounds are closed, it was practically zero cars, and just 2 lanes. Perfect for me!

I forgot my sunglasses, the glare was so intense I could not see the signs on the road ahead. Luckily there were only 3 or 4, and after 2 or 3 trips around the fairgrounds I had an idea of when they were coming up.

I made a mistake when we got to the end, at the stop sign because it leads back to that same whizzing road which we had started on.

I mixed up the clutch with the brake and could not understand why the car was not slowing and not stopping.

I just have not had enuf practice with stopping. Jan's husband Harry had taken me 2 weeks ago to Mervyns parking lot and he gave me my first practice in stopping.

I don't know why Jim has not had me practice at all on using the brake and stopping. I think it is because he simply finds it incomprehensible a person would not know how to do this.

His entire focus from first to last has been on shifting gears. As a result today I did get the hang of it. And I am now able to start the car up in first gear pretty smoothly most of the time.

Since nearly all my experience in steering has been in

Mervyns huge parking lot, where I am quite good at it, I was surprised to notice that in the long stretch of road around the fairgrounds half the time I did not stay in my own lane, I was driving down the middle of the road.

After the big booboo the first time at stop sign leading back to that hugely trafficked road, where I kept mistaking the clutch for the brake the whole time and didn't know why I wasn't slowing down and did not stop when I pressed it all the way.

The next time we arrived there I said it all aloud to myself as I was doing it.

"Foot off the gas, lightly on brake, B-r-r-r-a-a-a-ake."

I succeeded in doing it perfectly. But Jim went nuts.

"This is going to be a long Sunday," he mumbled.

So after that I kept quiet and just said it silently to myself.

In my final tour around the fairgrounds Jim said "I'm not going to tell you when to change gears and how to do it. You do it by yourself."

So I did. And Jim was pleased as punch.

But he still had to go home and take a tranquilizer because I was getting on his nerves.

And I came home and plotzed in front of TV because

it was stressful and by end I had lost my mind.

The good news is I now have confidence in Jim as my driving teacher, and he now has confidence in me as a driving student.

Altho we argue more now, our cooperation is better because of this new confidence we have in each other.

Love, Annie

Anne loves stopping at Circle K on way home for ice cold sodas for her and Jim

May 16

I start writing my little women's lib book

Helen and Anne had so much fun in women's liberation

To: Helen
Sent: Monday evening, May 16
Subject: I just wrote my last chapter for our women's liberation book

Anne loves her book

Hi Helen

Yesterday morning while I was waiting for Jim to call me and say when he will come by for driving lesson, since I was up so very early, I decided to come in from the backyard and write the one chapter about women's liberation in its first year that I never got around to writing when I was writing about it few years ago.

It is about how we all went out to a restaurant together after the meeting. It was such a happy experience that writing about it was fun for me.

It is not long at all. I think it took me 2 hours to write it.

And practically as soon as I finished writing it and was wondering what to do next, Jim called and said sorry he overslept and do I want my driving lesson.

And I said "I am glad you overslept because there was something I wanted to write about women's liberation, and I finally did it. It all worked out perfectly."

And he arrived 10 minutes later for our driving lesson.

My first early chapters are about our meetings, our actions, and the fights which broke out at meetings. They are so much fun.

It was fascinating watching our leaders duke it out at meetings..

But Helen this last chapter is simple and sweet.

I loved writing it.

It was a breeze and it made me so happy.

I love you.

Annie

Girl in book store

June 16th

Publishing the book

It took a month to edit and format the little book for publication. But I had a ball doing it. It was such an interesting project.

The fun part for me was putting in Bill's cartoons. I opened up his art box and found cartoons he did that I never saw before.

I scanned several and the one Helen chose for back cover is the one where the girl's tushy shows. Which made me whoop with joy when Helen put that on back cover.

But the absolute most fun of all was 5 minutes before I ordered a proof copy. I found a cartoon Bill had done of bad girls smoking pot in the car.

How could I resist!

During the first year of women's liberation in a hot steamy September 1968, Helen was driving her parents' car.

She came into the city and drove us all to Jones Beach.

Of course we were smoking pot in the car.

So I stopped the presses to add the cartoon

Women's liberationists on way to Jones Beach

And the next day I went back to my writing....

Girl friends

June 17   6 am

The Birds and the Bees
(not about sex about waking up at dawn)

It was lovely being in the yard at dawn, lying on my sweet fluffy comforter on the sweet ground. Reading my *Letter from God* for today, smoking cigarettes, drinking my coffee.

Watching the birds alight around me to eat the icing from the cupcakes which encrusted on the plastic box they came in.

My dog Beanie lying near me. And my cat Cupcake under the sun couch right next to my head. Crouched there, watching the birds and occasionally springing into motion as she sped after one.

She is fast but they are faster, they just flew off.

The sun must be peeping over mountains to the East now because the leaves on tree right outside my window have lit up with iridescent green. They have turned into green light. The first ray of sunlight has touched them, has lit them up.

I really do get a bird's eye view of the birds when I lie on the ground so close to them while they are pecking at the hard crusty cupcake icing. It turns out they like frosting.

The birds are the sparrows and the baby cactus wrens, which are the same size as sparrows when they are babies.

Also the morning dove who is not a baby, she may be a mother bird. Naturally she is much bigger than they are and arrives like a queen. She likes the icing too. I see her from my open window now pecking at it.

I actually woke up at a normal time this morning, I can't believe it. I had been waking up in middle of night and then staying up. Today I woke up the instant dawn began. I opened my eyes, looked out the window, and there was the lightening of the sky starting in the East.

Just as dawn is starting is perfect time to wake up. I like beginning my day at same time the day begins its day.

And now that the huge summer heat has arrived, the cool early morning (before the sun is high enough to be furnace) is a nice time. All in all it really is the nicest time of the day.

A new day is starting and that is always full of promise, it's made up of promise. It's like a present before you have unwrapped your gift.

The pretty wrapping paper, the colorful bow, and the anticipation of the wonderful treat inside. That is what dawn is. The package is delivered and it is still in its pretty wrapping paper and its wonderful bow. You have not opened it yet. It is still in a gift box.

O Cupcake just took off! And the birds flew off the icing! I guess she likes that hidden spot under my sun couch where no one can see her. But she can watch the birds intently with her eyes as wide as saucers. Then she springs into action!

She made beeline to where they were all at the icing. But they were too fast for her, they just flew off! And now she went back to her hidey spot.

O look her mother, Priscilla, has arrived. I wonder what Priscilla is heading for. O she is switching her tail. Back and forth her tail is going as she stands there deciding where to go. O she is heading off towards the back of the yard.

What a funny world I live in now. Priscilla, Cupcake, my dog Beanie and the birds. And it all takes place in the amphitheater of my yard.

The house is another story. Of course the birds are not in the house, they live in the backyard. And Beanie has strict rules about letting the cats come near me, he is possessive.

O I see Priscilla. She is in back of yard. O she stopped and is switching her tail again. I see her huge black fluffy tail switching. Just her tail and paws are black. She has the coloring of a bobcat with a lot of red in there too.

Cupcake looks more like her father. I don't even want to talk about Cupcake's father, big bad Muggles who lives across the alley. She has her mom's multicolor but I don't think the red in it. Blacks and greys and whites and that huge white bib her dad has. Big bad Muggles.

O there is Priscilla! She is at the woodpile, almost camouflaged. O now she hopped across one of the tree trunks and is nesting.

It is still in shadow, the sun is not that high yet, so she blends with the shadows and tree trunks in wood pile. She is in a direct line of sight from me at my desk. I look at her thru my open window. I think she chose that spot, nesting and looking at me, because she likes to be in my vibe.

All the animals are sensitive to my vibe but Priscilla most of all. And she most of all likes to bask in my vibe.

Occasionally she turns her head and looks around

but mostly she is facing in my direction. She likes a spot where my vibe reaches her. And where I can see her and focus on her, so she is in the middle of my attention and my vibe.

It is almost our whole relationship, me and Priscilla together in my vibe. She chooses a spot where my attention reaches her. She is looking at me and I am looking at her. We love each other. We are very happy together.

I have to lean way over as I type to keep my eyes on her. Because of course there is perfect clarity where the window is wide open. But on the other side where the two windows are pushed together, I have not washed those windows in years. I would not be able to see her thru those double windows.

When I lean over I can see her perfectly thru the open window. It is just that it is not comfortable to type, leaning way over to my side. But worth it to keep my eyes on her.

There she is! Right in my line of sight. She has her paws stretched out over a slender log right in front of her. She likes nesting in the woodpile, I wonder why.

Well it is day light now. Regular full daylight. Priscilla is still in shadow, there is still big shadow in middle of yard and she is in the shadow.

But the sky is a regular blue now and all the trees are lit up. It is no longer dawn turning into morning, it is now full morning. No trace of the dawn is left, full morning is here.

The birds are no longer on the ground. All are flying into my tree right out my window. They are all roosting there. They seem to be doing their morning ablutions. There are four of them, each on their own branch. They peck at their feathers and fluff their feathers.

O now birds are flying into the tree. But these new ones are hopping from branch to branch. O well they like that. Flying into tree and swinging on the branches which are lighter than they are. It's probably the sparrows. The sparrows are fond of that tree. O a huge pigeon flew in overhead and landed on the telephone wire.

Priscilla is still there. She has not moved. She found her spot.

In a few hours Jim will arrive to take me swimming at the Y. I would like to get a blouse at Target afterwards but I don't like to impose on him. I will decide after my swim whether to say "let's stop at Walgreens on way home so I can get sunglasses."

Sunglasses turns out to be a necessity on desert when you drive. I didn't have sunglasses for my driving lesson last weekend and the glare was too intense for me to be able to see at all.

I guess I would like to go to Target, get sunglasses there, and buy a blouse there. But it is very hot at noon now. Jim won't want to come into the store and he won't want to wait in car in all that heat either. But it is a favor I would like.

Maybe I will talk it over with my Higher Self. I can always order the blouses on-line and then not have to ask Jim to drive me. Maybe that is a good solution.

If they are not cute or don't fit or I don't like the material, I am sure he would take me over to return them.

Target is close to where Jim and I live. He lives in my own neighborhood and Target is practically right behind his house. We can go on an early morning before it gets hot. And they may have a way to return which is fast so he does not have to wait long. It is not such a bad idea.

It means waiting a week for the blouses to arrive instead of getting them today. But it simplifies the day and does not mean I am imposing on Jim.

Post script an hour later, *I watered baby trees in yard. I fed my animals. I ordered the blouses on-line per my Higher Self's suggestion.*

Sunday afternoon, June 19

Driving lesson today

Anne acts up during her driving lesson

Well I had a driving lesson this morning. Jim called when I had been up for about 15 minutes. I was still drinking my first cup of coffee in backyard and had just finished reading the two page *Letter from God* for today.

"What time is it?" I asked

"6:35" he said, "I'll pick you up at 7."

"Perfect!" I said.

We had planned to have back-to-back lessons yesterday and today (Saturday and Sunday) but yesterday Jim overslept till 9 am so we canceled that lesson. He just took me swimming when the pool opened at 10:30 and then we went to the Chinese restaurant for take out.

I didn't fall asleep till 2 am last night, I was trying to untangle the necklaces around my neck. Finally I got out my nail scissors and cut the red string on the little green jade Buddha pendant I had bought at the Chinese restaurant that afternoon.

That turned out to be a mistake. I thought I could slip the little Buddha pendant onto one of my other necklaces and not have so many necklace chains around my neck.

But the little jade pendant doesn't have a hook, it has a hole in it, which the red thread is knotted into. And I cut too close to it to be able to reknot the red string.

I was up for 2 hours trying to fix my necklaces. To take off the ones which were knotted around other ones. To fix what I had done to my new jade pendant. Finally when it was 1:30 am I gave up because I knew Jim would arrive early for driving lesson.

I used to dread my lessons and always hoped Jim would have reason to cancel. And when he did I would be so happy. But yesterday when he canceled I had been up for the lesson, nervous, but still up for it.

And this morning same thing, nervous but still up for it. I was able to get ready for it quickly because yesterday I had gotten everything ready for the lesson which turned out be cancelled.

I had 2 pairs of sunglasses in a little padded pocketbook. I will never go to a driving lesson without sunglasses after last week's lesson when I forgot sunglasses and could not see a thing from the glare. Now I have the pair I bought few years ago and never used and much darker ones I bought at Walgreen's two days ago. I am prepared.

So I didn't jump right up when Jim said he will be here at 7 and it is 6:35. I read 2 pages in *A Course In Miracles* and then watered the baby trees which sprang up around the mesquite trees. They sprang up from the seeds from the wild mesquite trees.

We have not had a drop of rain on the desert in months and it is over 100 degrees every day now with huge bright hot sun. I like to water the new baby trees each morning now when it is cool early morning.

I am sure there are gazillions of them all over my huge yard but I only water the ones I discovered in my line of sight when I am hanging out in yard with my animals or when I look out my open window while I am at my desk.

There are about 13 altogether that I discovered this past week and have now been watering each morning.

And they look much greener and happier as a result.

I put on swamp coolers for the dog and kitties so house will be cool when big heat arrives at noon.

And did a few odds and ends before I put on a skirt and blouse for driving lesson. I like driving barefoot.

Because I am still nervous and scared before my lesson I was quiet in truck and tried to keep my focus. I was curious which road he was going to take me to. Recently we have been going to a two lane road which branches off Aviation Highway.

There are no houses on it, just desert on both sides, but at one end is parking lot for airport, 4 dollars a day for parking and shuttle bus for airport which leaves from there. I guess all the traffic on that road is involved with that, unless they come down the big road at the end of it.

It was a beautiful morning, lovely blue sky, and not a single car on the big highway we drove on to get there this early Sunday morning. And not a single car on the two lane road when we first arrived.

The truck started up beautifully when Jim and I switched seats. Nearly all my driving lessons till this point have been all about that. Press down on clutch, shift to first, and give it gas while slowly releasing the clutch.

And for the longest time I seemed to make zero progress. Truck was bucking bronco and I was stalling and starting again. This period seemed to go on forever. Altho to be fair about it Jim and I only had one lesson a week on Sunday mornings.

I'm not sure when I discovered that things had reversed themselves. Instead of it being miracle when it did start and was not bucking bronco which stalled, most of the time it did start up nicely, and only rarely did stalling and bucking bronco occur.

Maybe it was last week's lesson I had noticed the difference. I'm not sure what I am doing right now that I did wrong before. Perhaps my feet know how to do it. I work my feet and this time it works, where before when I worked my feet it didn't.

Jim and I went thru so much to get to this point that we are both pleased as punch. Our confidence soars when I actually do start the car. It is a good way to start the lesson. We feel that I am on my way.

And the effort Jim put in last Sunday when he took me to the road around the fair grounds (way far out of Tucson) to go from first to second to third and 4th as soon as I start driving did pay off. I was able to do it on my own this time without instruction from him.

Altho I am not so good at remembering where 4th is. And there is an awful grinding sound when I miss it. I got nervous when I screwed up 4th when a stop sign was coming up. I panicked and forgot how to stop at the stop sign. Because of the clutch a lot is involved in stopping at stop sign and I am not good at it yet.

When I finally stopped it was suspenseful because I was screwing up. We were both yelling at each other by this point.

"Why do I always have to switch to 4th! Why can't I drive in 3rd!"

"Because you need to learn how to switch to 4th!"

"Why isn't the fucking car stopping!" I'm now yelling. We were now at major intersection.

"Step on the fucking brake!" he yelled back at me.

I was pressing on the clutch instead of the brake.

(It is the first time I heard Jim say fuck, it is the first time he heard me say fuck. Tucson is not like NYC where it is every other word in conversation. Men may say it to each other, but they are a gentleman when they talk to a lady. And girls are ladylike in their speech in Tucson.

When Bill was taking his driving lessons our first month in Tucson from a teacher at Sears driving school, he told Bill one of his students had been a girl who had just arrived from New York City and he was stunned when she said fuck.

She said it all the time. He thought it was a remarkable thing to happen during a driving lesson, no other girl student of his had ever done that. He got a crush on her as a result, she was a knockout New Yorker with language he had never heard a girl use before.)

When I finally did succeed in stopping the car I flounced out of it and said "That's it! Take me home!"

Jim responded imperturbably. It didn't occur to him I was mad at him, he thought I just had enuf.

"OK" he said, "if you think you've had enuf, but I think we should continue."

I was taken aback that he didn't realize I was pissed, and just thought my mind had shut down and I had enough. So I got sweetly back in the car and we continued the lesson. And I didn't make a fuss about shifting to 4th gear after that. When it grinded because I did it wrong, I just let him tell me what to do to get it into 4th.

Many times I think I am in one gear but it turns out I am in another, but Jim always knows which gear I am in, or when I miss the gear, and tells me what to do.

It has been a long haul for us to arrive at this point where I have total confidence in him as my driving teacher and he has total confidence in me as driving student. At the beginning we each thought the other was a disaster and I was convinced the problem was him and he was convinced the problem was me.

We finally turned the corner on this in last week's driving lesson just as in last week's driving lesson I turned the corner in starting up the truck and in switching gears.

I always knew Jim was a great driver, I just thought he didn't know how to teach. But I have now come full circle on this. I think he is an excellent driving teacher, maybe because I am finally learning how to drive. And hahaha he probably thinks I am an excellent driving student because I am finally learning how to drive.

And also because finally we are both relaxed about it or a lot more relaxed than we used to be. And have confidence, or at least a lot more confidence than we used to have. So we don't aggravate each other as much. And I am understanding how he teaches and he is understanding how I learn.

It is like before we were dancing partners who kept stepping on each others shoes and could never move together to the music.

We bumped into each other instead. And knocked each other down. Hahaha both of us spent most of the time on the floor.

But now we are actually partners in the enterprise, we have learned how to be partners to each other.

And all his patience with me has paid off. There were so many things I was scared to do, like to start up the truck when I stopped at the intersection.

I was scared of stalling in the middle of the intersection. So we both had to get out of truck and change places. We spent tons of time changing places and actually became very good at changing places.

I don't think he always wanted to change places, sometimes he thought I should try to do it. But when I did and stalled in the middle of the intersection and panicked, after that we changed places without murmur of protest by him.

And I think he really appreciated it today that when we got to that intersection I said "I am going to try it," and I did it. And after that I did it each time, he did not have to change places. And when I stalled in middle I did not panic, I just started it up again.

So this is what progress looks like.

As a result neither of us was wrecked after the lesson for very first time. And I don't think I will ever have dread before another lesson and I think the nervousness before a lesson will be less too. We were both calm and harmonious on trip home which was a nice change too.

Anne storms off in middle of lesson

Tuesday June 21

Phone call with Marty

Anne is a mess after her phone call

Yesterday I got phone call out of the blue from Marty, a friend of Bill's in NYC.

Marty had recently gotten on internet. Queensborough Community College which he had graduated from offers its alumni free use of their computers. So he goes there to look up stuff on internet.

He found out Bill is in Heaven and he was able to find our phone number on free people search so he called.

He and Bill had a falling out quite a long time ago, years before we left NYC. Bill never has falling out with his friends, but I guess Marty, who is an impossible friend, just went too far.

I don't think it was impulsive or emotional, my guess is Bill just wanted the friendship over, and so he said or did what would make Marty never call again.

Bill really did like Marty and they went fishing together and had met at the chess club at Queensborough Community College when they were both going to school there.

I don't know if Marty had any other friends. He said on the phone yesterday Bill was the best friend he ever had.

Bill would have welcomed a phone call from Marty last year when he started to play chess on the computer, they shared passion for chess, they could have played on email or both joined the chess site Bill found.

Bill was thrilled with finding that chess site and sent the link to every person he knows who plays chess, but none of them were interested. But he is right Marty would have loved it. They would have been on it together.

"I was afraid to call Bill because of the falling out we had," Marty said.

"How come Bill never called me?" he asked.

"He didn't know your phone number," I said.

"But I am sure he took his address book with him," he said. But Bill never had an address book.

I love Marty the way Bill does, but I can see why Marty has no friends except Bill and why Bill finally couldn't take it anymore.

Altho since Bill was friends with Marty for years and was used to the way he was and didn't mind it, I can't imagine what Marty did to go too far. Bill usually puts up with anything and everything. He is an exceptionally easy going friend.

Not such an easy going husband.

I guess we were the reverse in this, I bent over backwards to put up with any nonsense from Bill but if I had a friend who gave me as much nonsense as Marty did, that would end the friendship before it started.

I understand why Bill loved Marty because I did too. He is a warm affectionate friend and is very friendly and so easy to talk to because he never bothered to become an image when he became a teenager.

He dresses, talks, thinks, exactly like a boy in 5th grade. He digs women of course, but won't make the effort to dress nicely, get a nice haircut, and talk like a gentleman.

I was 27 and Bill was 24 when he first brought Marty home. I instantly loved Marty because in a world of image it's relaxing to be with someone who has no image at all.

And because he is so revealing and holds nothing back. It made me so sweet on Bill that this was the first friend he had made in NYC.

But a person would have to be a saint to put up with the phone call I put up with him yesterday afternoon.

It is perfectly understandable he would begin off telling me how shocked he was to find it out. And it was nice to hear that Bill was the best friend he ever had.

Marty's emotions and shock at finding out were a thread thru the phone call. Every 15 minutes he would return to it. Say again how shocked he was and go into detail about it.

I didn't mind any of that.

I did not enjoy the half hour he spent speculating on the diseases Bill might have had and what caused it. Bill had no diseases and nothing caused it, but of course Marty did not believe me. He spent 45 minutes discussing diseases in detail. Which is my least favorite topic in the world.

The first 45 minutes as it relates to Bill. Oy what a drag!

But it got worse! Then he talked about all the movie

stars and what they died of and I had to hear disease in detail about all the movie stars. He reads a scandal sheet and learns all this.

I made it all thru learning about Peter Falk's dementia. And about midway into John Ritter I couldn't take it and moved the phone away from my ear for the half hour Marty talked about his blood disease or whatever it was.

I happen to like Peter Falk and John Ritter a lot and cannot stand talk of disease, it was impossible to keep listening.

I really don't know how I listened as long as I did. The phone conversation had now gone on for an hour almost two hours. And all of it had been awful.

Then I had to hear about Marty's mom's disease, she went to Heaven a few years ago. And his dad's dementia, he went to a Home a few months ago.

There was one moment when the conversation got normal. Marty finally asked "did Bill do good art?"

I had said we moved to Tucson and Bill followed his dream and went to art school.

"Yes," I said, "his art is wonderful."

And I tried to think of how to send Marty one of his paintings. Then I mentioned that recently Bill had been doing cartooning.

And Marty got excited and happy. He was actually like a normal person.

"Cartoons!" he said. He was so happy and interested Bill had done cartoons, Marty loves cartoons.

"Yes, he posted some of them on the internet. Wait! Let me go to my computer! And I will give you the web address and you can look at them when you go back to Queensborough Community College."

So I came to my desk, I had been in back bedroom watching tv when he called.

But we only spent one minute on that because he said "they brought back the show where Ted Knight is a cartoonist."

I said "I never saw that show, I liked *Three's Company*."

That is what started him on John Ritter's blood disease or whatever it was.

I refused to listen to all the gory details. That is when I moved the phone away from my ear.

Even tho Marty worked for the civil service, for the courts, somehow they found a way to get rid of him, which is impossible, but I guess they couldn't stand Marty.

Now that his dad is in the Home, it seems they want

the co-op apartment back. It is the co-op where Marty was born and lived his whole life. They are willing to give him $150 thousand and he has to be out in 2 months.

But Marty doesn't want that, he doesn't know where to go. He is trying to fight it but he can't win.

I said "New York is too expensive to live but there are other places. Tucson is very nice."

But Marty has so many fears, he is afraid of twisters, he is afraid of hurricanes, he is afraid of flood and earthquakes.

"Tucson doesn't have any of that" I said.

He is afraid of black widows and scorpions.

"Tucson does not have any of that," I said.

"What about bats?"

Tucson does have bats altho they are not in the area where I live. I just lied and said "I have never seen a bat."

"I wouldn't want a big house" Marty said. I thought it is because he knows how much work there is involved in having a house. But Marty said it is because every time he got home he would have to check all the rooms for burglars.

"Maybe you should just move to Albany" I said.

"It is way too cold and I don't know how to drive."

"Food is too expensive in Tucson," he said, "it is cheap here."

But when he asked me the price of steak, it is less than what he pays. That made him excited about Tucson. "You and Bill moved to a good place," he said.

Our best time on phone was when we talked about fishing. He loved those fishing trips with Bill and I had heard all about them when Bill came home.

They sounded so good to me that one time I made Bill take me. It was a nightmare. You have to be up all night. You take the Long Island Railroad at 11 at night to Babylon.

And then sit there in the dark till the boat rental place opens at dawn.

Then Bill rents a motor boat or row boat and you fish. Then you do the whole thing again to come home. And it is not pretty around the water. It is all industrial around there. I hated it.

But Bill and Marty loved it. He'd get to our house at 5 pm and hang out in our apartment till it was time to get the train to Babylon. And then Bill would come home with a lot of fish and clean them.

Bill said "Marty is like a little boy, he just dumps the fish in the sink, admires them, and his mother has to clean

203

them. "

Marty loved the fishing trips and always said "Bill and I had a banner trip."

I remembered all the places they had been and fish they got but Marty remembered better. They got porgies at Babylon, and fluke somewhere else, and he told me Bill actually got striped bass.

I understand now why Bill and Marty were such good friends. They both love fishing and they loved going on their fishing trips together. Bill never went fishing after he ended the friendship with Marty, he had no one to go with.

Altho his fishing rods were one of the few things he took to Tucson, he took his fishing rods and his climbing gear and that's it.

Bill had told me when they fish, the fish they don't want to hook is a hacklehead. When I was 30 I was briefly friends with a girl who every time she called I was totally confused when I got off the phone.

When I mentioned it to Bill, he said picking up the phone and finding out it is her on the line is like hooking a hacklehead.

So when Marty was talking about the bottom fish I said about hackleheads. Marty got excited.

So I said "when Bill finally did go on email and had to choose a screenname, guess which name he chose for himself?"

"Hacklehead!" Marty sang out with huge merriment and glee.

"Yup!"

Only Marty, the only one in the whole wide world, would guess that Bill chose hacklehead for his email name.

It was our one instant of pure joy on the telephone. He and I were both so happy and loved it so much. He loves Bill so much and was laughing at his email name.

And then he told me some of the things Bill told him which used to make him laugh so much. I didn't find it funny, it was way too earthy to talk to a girl.

Bill would never say those things to me. But Marty found it hysterical and is not sensitive to what you say to a girl. He just enjoyed it so much and assumed I would too.

I tried to say "Bill is not dead, we are all immortal eternal beings and he is in Heaven and I chit-chat with him all the time."

But Marty thinks it is better to be 95 and have dementia and living in a Home than to be in Heaven (which doesn't exist in his belief). So he thinks his dad is better off than Bill.

Since he just got on email that day (he said Queensborough Community College offers free mail) I didn't ask for his email address. But he said he will call me again.

And I knew now that I got that phone call from Marty and understand the lay of the land with him, I am going to make an all-out effort to lighten and sweeten his mind.

After the phone call I spent a lot of time sending him love directly to his mind. And I will do that every day.

When I chatted with Bill right after the phone call, he said "Heaven really wants you to help Marty." And I will.

And when the next phone call from Marty arrives I will be more prepared. I won't be so swamped by the density of it. I will keep a space, and use that space to send love directly into his mind as he is talking.

I tried to do it in this phone call but the density was way too dense. But now that I know what I am up against, I will find a way not to let the density get so close to me.

And I will focus on sending love to him as he talks. That should have the effect of lightening his mind during the conversation. That is how it works. Which will enable me to focus more love into his mind.

And meanwhile I will spend some of each day sending love to his mind and connecting to his Higher Self.

Once I am in full communication with his Higher Self, which I already am, that will bring a lot more light and love into his mind too, and some of his fears will have to lighten up.

I don't think I ever understood before how a person's fears turn their life into a prison house.

I realized there is no way Marty would actually move anywhere in the state of mind he is in. Altho he did find a trailer on Long Island in a trailer camp and he is considering buying that with the money they would give him when they force him to move.

It is a perfect idea because it is the only one he is willing to consider.

When they switched the TV from analog to digital, his kid brother, the wealthy dentist, bought Marty and his dad two new television sets.

But Marty is not able to get the channels on it. He can get 3 channels on one, 3 channels on another, but still misses a lot of channels.

"Why don't you get cable TV?" I asked.

"90 dollars a month!" he said, "I can't afford it."

But he can. When they forced him out of the courts a few months ago they gave him his pension. It's just a bad habit not to spend a penny on making your life more comfortable. I am glad my Higher Self finally broke me of that habit.

And I thought Marty should get his own computer and pay for internet access. But I can't see him doing that as long as he is allowed to use the computer at Queensboro Community College.

And I don't think he will get cable tv either. He goes back and forth between the two televisions.

But I do think that Heaven is determined to help Marty, and I will do everything I can from my end to lighten and sweeten his mind. His only problem is he needs his mind to be freed.

It really is like meeting my past. I too lived behind bars in a prison of my own making until I moved to Tucson, read *A Course In Miracles,* and let my Higher Self remove the bars one by one.

In fact I never could have moved to Tucson if I had not found my Higher Self and been in constant communication with Her the summer before I moved to Tucson. I followed Her suggestions and that set me on the path to freedom, or the way out of prison.

It is the job of Marty's Higher Self to do for Marty what my Higher Self did for me. All I can do is send a lot of love his way. But they say there is nothing as powerful as love....

June 22 Middle of the night

Swan Lake

Well I am up at 1:30 again for second morning in a row. It seems like such an odd time to wake up, the middle of the night. It takes a while to dawn on me that I am not going to fall back asleep, go in and make coffee and print up the *Letter From God* for that day.

Then back on bed with my coffee and my *Letter from God* and read it by the lamp next to the open window. And drink coffee and smoke cigs and then start to think about things.

The cats are up at whatever time I wake up and like to be fed. But my dog Beanie is usually still sound asleep in the yard.

We have hit the time of the dramatic heat. It's hard to fathom right now at 2 am when it is so cool (and with the swamp coolers still on, even a tad chilly) but the forecast for today is 110.

And yesterday must have been sizzling too because when I tried to walk on the ground in bare feet it burned the soles of my feet. When the ground is too warm to walk on you know the era of big heat has arrived.

But I have a new relaxed attitude about it because I remembered our monsoons cannot arrive until we have stratospheric heat.

So when I woke up this morning and thought "today is the day they said it will be 110," I remembered that, and thought "OK if this is what it takes to make the monsoons."

This is the first year I am not looking forward to monsoons. The thunder scares Beanie and I won't be able to lounge in yard if everything is soaking wet.

And altho I myself love terrific storms with huge thunder, great great lightning, pounding rain, it all scares Beanie. And right now I am still enjoying the peaceful stable weather.

But now our desert is drying up and needs to be watered. And massive wildfires are going on now. And those fighting the fires are praying for rain.

So I have to put the land and its vegetation first. Their happiness has to come first now. It is time for them to have their water.

Beanie and I will just have to love each other and get thru it. We have had it so good for so long, it is the turn of the land and the vegetation. It is time for the plant world to have its day.

And the shake-up caused by the storm may be good for me too. The summer monsoons are always revivifying, bring new life to the world I live in, my desert world. It is really the break-up of the old and start of the new and fresh.

A new beginning. And I am in the middle of such a huge transformation this may be good for me.

And there are nice benefits to the storms and rains too. Watching the desert turn green, all that beauty and happiness. The plant world on the desert transformed into love and beauty and green and joy, and delight.

They bathe in the rain, they drink the rain, it is their spa, their refreshment. They all grow a foot taller and become big and bushy and full. They luxuriate in the water world.

My cats won't like it. Me and Beanie and the cats love being dry. But earth and plants love water, they will be very very happy.

Me and Beanie and the cats will all have to pull

together while wild storms rage around us, while earth and sky have their huge lightning show.

It is odd that I should feel so close to both Andrea and my friend Cora now. Even tho I have only had one phone conversation with Cora in past year, we had a long wonderful phone conversation last month.

And I have only received 2 emails from Andrea in my whole life. We are pool friends. Which means for past 10 years each time I saw her in the pool I would look around and sure enough there was my friend Ellen.

Andrea and Ellen have been the couple I have been closest to in my years in Tucson. We go back a long way, Andrea and Ellen, me and Bill.

And although Bill and Ellen talked movies together in the pool, when you are a swimmer at the public pools, it is under the shower and in the dressing room that friendships blossom. That is when conversation takes place.

I became friends with Ellen first because her work schedule meant she was at the pool same time Bill brought me. But when Andrea's schedule changed the two girls arrived together, and I got to know Andrea too, and the two girls as a couple. That was nice too.

Ellen is the only friend I made in Tucson who is

exactly my age and whose experiences in life parallel my own. We were both hippies in the '60s. We had so much in common because of so many similar experiences.

We had so much to talk about and we loved making each other laugh. My friend Jan (from NYC) moved to Tucson 12 years ago but she has this everywhere. For some reason wherever she goes she finds people she has so much in common with, so much to talk about with, and so much fun making each other laugh.

She has this with the people at work, she has this with her neighbors. She is always going out to lunch with the people from her job and having so much fun as they all make each other laugh at the table.

I only had this with Ellen. We would make each other laugh while we were under the shower together or putting on our clothes.

And a big thing we had in common too was that both of us was in a couple. It was never topic A in our conversation because when you are in a long time couple, and so close, you relish the time when you are not being in a couple, when you are kicking up your heels, and getting wild.

And of course you need someone to kick up your heels with. Ellen was my person to kick up my heels with.

That's really what we did in the shower room while under the shower or putting on our clothes. The whole time was spent kicking up our heels.

But I always knew every instant that Ellen's whole heart was Andrea and she knew my whole heart was Bill. I knew the background to giggles in shower room was her home and life with Andrea, she knew Bill was my home and life.

Our relationship was bumping into each other in the pool. I was never on email with them, or telephone, or seeing them anywhere else. But I had both of their email addresses, and some time in April I emailed both of them about the big change in my life.

And I braced myself for getting back a return email how shocked they are.

But what made Ellen such an ideal friend for me was that she always blew my mind. It is so much fun to have your mind blown. And I guess Andrea really was Ellen's mate.

I never heard back from Ellen but I got email from Andrea that day. And instead of the email I had braced myself for, how shocked she was, how sad she was, and how am I doing? Andrea emailed me she is in the same boat as me because she and Ellen have separated. Each has gone their own way.

It totally blew my mind. I had braced myself for all her sympathy. I had postponed emailing them because of the wave of sympathy I was sure would come. Instead her email was bracing to me. Andrea and I were going thru the identical thing at the identical time. She was making a new life for herself without Ellen, I was making a new life for myself without Bill.

An unfathomable thing had happened to both of us. And most unfathomable of all, was as Andrea pointed out in her email, both of us were doing so well.

I actually thought I would be best friends with Andrea on email now. To have the same experience at the same time, to have such a big experience at the same time, to understand so perfectly where the other is coming from, it's a lot to know about each other.

We perfectly knew what the others life had been, we perfectly knew what each others life was now. It's no wonder I felt so close to Andrea.

But it wasn't meant to be. I never got another email from her.

It is an interesting thing about life, that when you have an amazing unexpected blossom of closeness, which you totally cherish, which is lovely gift from Heaven, which really hits the spot, which is just what the doctor ordered, you don't know if it is the start of a beautiful relationship, or that is it. An amazing unexpected gift just at the moment when you most needed it.

I had the odd feeling reading Andrea's email yesterday, her second one and as it turned out her last one, that she and I have been climbing a mountain, and we have both arrived at the place for the final ascent.

That this is what it is all about. This is what we got ourselves into. We had decided to stop at the point we reached, but Ellen was whisked away from her, Bill was whisked away from me, which means we have no choice but to continue climbing up.

Because the top of the mountain is in Heaven, and who does not want to turn their mind into Heaven. Hahaha but it takes a lot of motivation to go for that final ascent. Andrea and I were pushed into it.

Cora is the dearest friend of my youth, our friendship blossomed at the exact same time Bill moved in with me. Because it turns out Cora's favorite thing in the whole world is to sit at kitchen table with a girlfriend, drink coffee, and unburden herself. Tell her all about her day.

I had never met anyone like Cora who loved everyone, judged no one. And who gave me total unconditional love. And the misadventures of her day were something else!

It was the oddest combination, in one way compared to me Cora was a total mess, what went on in her day-to-day life. But Cora was a fully enlightened being, at the center of her mind and heart was crystal clear light blazing out.

Blazing from all the love in her heart. And the clarity in her mind. Whereas my mind was dark as pitch.

She was the most enlightened being on the planet, I was the least enlightened. But because Cora was round peg in square hole in terms of the world, or because she marched to her own drummer, things were never working out for her. She was always in my kitchen for help. She never went under, she never climbed out, she was always caught.

She was the perfect first teacher for me, introducer to the spiritual path, introducer to spirituality. What a great way to learn! To think you are helping someone, not knowing you are the one being helped.

But of course it was her love. I never in my whole life received that much love, no judging at all, and sweet warm unconditional love. I had no sisters, I was not close to my mother, it was my first experience of female love.

I shake my head now, nod in disbelief, at the wonderfulness of it, that first experience of female love. I had had my brother, my cousin Richie, even my daddy, I knew boy love, I had boy love, but never girl love.

There's just nothing like it. Even now that I live in divine love, and yes divine love is the ultimate love, I couldn't live without it now, there is still something very wonderful about human female love.

If divine love is the blue sky and bright sunshine, then human female love is the sweet blessed rain.

Cora left the neighborhood when she got evicted and in a way you could say I never saw her again. Because when she returned to the neighborhood she had a different best girlfriend who she spent every evening in her kitchen. And I was spending my evenings differently too.

And now that she is in Tucson she has her Tucson best friend next door and her sister lives here too.

We have almost zero contact. But my Higher Self insisted I call her and tell her about Bill.

There are trillion gazillion suggestions my Higher Self has made for me and I do carry out each one of them, and each one has turned out to be wonderful.

But there was nothing like calling Cora that night last month and telling her about Bill.

Of all my girlfriends from NYC she is the only one who really knew him. He and his friend from San Diego had been her roommates when she couldn't come up with the rent (this was before he moved in with me).

And he was home in our apt. every evening studying while she was in the kitchen having coffee with me. There was a spillover of closeness all around.

I worshipped Cora but Bill never did. He always said she is like the girl in 6th grade who cries because she can't get long division.

She was my first savior and my first teacher and to Bill she was a girl who cries in sixth grade because she can't get long division.

I guess that is marriage in a nutshell and what makes marriage so wonderful.

It is so interesting to live with another mind, and another mind who sees it all differently from you. It makes life so rich, so interesting, so soft and fluid and ever flowing.

It is Cora's tenderness. That is the word I was looking for. My experience of her tenderness. I always felt completely safe with Cora because all I ever experienced from her is tenderness. Really it is all she is capable of. It is her expression and being in the world. She is a completely tender being.

She was the ideal person for me to confide it all to in our phone conversation last month. Her tenderness, her mind power and clear intelligence, and all the love in her heart for me. And the years of our total intimacy which still remain in both of our hearts.

She was so relieved and so gratified when I told her at end of the conversation how much she had helped me. That's how I discovered how much she had wanted to, and been in suspense if she would be able to.

It was simply the degree of intimacy between us. That was it. That was the whole thing. Maybe it was difficult for her and she was in suspense about trying to help her dear friend Anne, but she didn't have to be.

Because it was the intimacy between us from our early friendship. It all resurfaced now that it was needed, and I bathed in it. I bathed in that intimacy and it took away the aloneness of the experience.

I opened up the whole experience to her and bathed in the intimacy.

Some girls have this with their mother, some girls have this with their sister, and now that we are grown up some have it with their daughter. I never had intimacy with my mother, I had it with Cora.

I did long for my mother right after it happened but my mother is in Heaven. Just as my mother longed for her mother when she went thru what I did with her husband. And my mother had horrible relationship with her mother. But her mother was in Heaven too.

We all long for our mothers at a moment like that. And I truly have no idea what it would be like if I did have my mom. A relationship of almost zero intimacy and almost total judgment, does it turn on the dime and become Cora and me?

I don't know and there is no way for me to know. I just know the Universe has everything designed perfectly for us. When that was the intimacy I most needed, Cora was there, the one who embodied it best for me.

I experienced total comfort from that conversation. I had not realized how much I needed it till I had it. All her tenderness in the place where the booboo was. I guess I needed Cora to kiss the booboo and make it better. Which happens to be the girl's gift in life.

It's the tale of the ugly duckling who is really a swan. Cora was always a swan but she has now fully transformed into it. Now my only experience of her is her swan-ness. The traces of the ugly duckling are gone.

That phone call I had with her a month ago was the most amazing phone call of my life. What her beautiful swan-ness did for me, how deeply I am blessed to have this beautiful swan in my life..

The first morning dove has called. I guess dawn must be starting.

June 30th   6:36 am

First monsoon arrived last night

Beanie and Annie spend the monsoon together

It rained last night. Or to be exact at 3 am. I happened to be up when it happened. I was up at 2:30 am. My strange new weird routine seems to be I wake up at 2 am, put up coffee, do a few things, and then go in and watch tv.

Finally my eyes get heavy after an hour or two, and my new waking up time is 6:30. It's like my second morning. I've already had my coffee. I already did my morning routine at my first waking up at 2:30 am.

I did more little things than I generally do when I first wake up at 2:30 am. I mean I always put up the coffee and always print out the *Letter from God* for that morning and take it in to read with my coffee. And I do check my email to see if anything interesting arrived.

But this time I took out the trash. It was so odd and interesting walking out in that deep of night very hot air. It is something which never happens, it is something which is impossible to happen, that 3 am be hot air.

It's just not the way the desert works. The afternoon could have been 118 degrees and yet 3 am is always cool and delightful.

It was just such a totally strange, totally unusual, experience— to walk into my front yard with bag of empty soda cans, to walk into all that night— and to walk into all that hot air. It was so unusual it blew my mind.

It fascinated me. I could have been on another planet. It was so interesting being out in it that I walked over to my mailbox too.

I could tell from the porch night light it was junk mail, I put it in recycle bin. My dog Beanie was waiting for me at the door. I guess he finally woke up. He must have been sound asleep in backyard when I first got up.

I didn't want to go back to bed and watch tv yet, I liked being up. I put new cans of soda in the frig so they would be cold.

Finally I couldn't think of anything else to do, so I poured myself a glass of juice, poured myself a cup of coffee, prepared wonderful ice water for Beanie, and took it all in to my back bedroom where tv is.

I musta assumed I would be tv watching because I brought it all in, one by one, and put it by the side of the bed where I watch tv.

But when I finally did go in, the sky out the open window was so very very interesting. A night sky, but it looked like white cloud shapes all over it.

So I moved the cup o'coffee to the little chair next to bed by open window, propped myself up on my elbows. And prepared to watch the night sky, drink coffee and smoke cigs, instead of watching tv drink coffee and smoke cigs.

And instant I was in position, had my first sip of coffee and first puff of cigarette, it all began. Thunder and lightning and rain.

Actually now I remember when I was bringing my coffee and juice, and ice water for Beanie, and *Letter from God*, when I went out my kitchen back door and into my bedroom back door, I remember the first tiny drops of the sweetest rain. I loved it but I didn't count it for anything.

A few little drops of the sweetest of rains had fallen the evening before. It hadn't meant anything, it hadn't amounted into anything, it had just been the sweetest of treats and the sweetest of promises.

But now right before my eyes, still propped up on my pillows and elbows right by open window, the real deal was happening, what you wait all year for, the very first arrival of the monsoons, the very first monsoon. It arrived in Tucson at 3 am on June 30th.

The roar of thunder scared Beanie. He tried to make his way to cubby hole near the bed. He didn't want to be on the bed, he didn't try to, but he wanted to be as close to where I was on the bed as possible.

He changed his cubby hole 3 times, each time the sound of thunder rousted him, to find a spot closer to where I was lying on bed.

And then finally he settled down and I settled down, and my thoughts got less inspired and began to drag in mud, and I closed my eyes and we both fell asleep.....

July 1

The day the roofers came

Friday morning of July 4th weekend

Hi Richie

Roofers are on my roof now. Our big rains on the desert (they are called monsoons) start right about now. I am so grateful the roofers are fixing the roof right now.

Since desert summer heat is tremendous but early mornings are still very cool, they arrived at 7 am to start working.

My friend Jim will take me to swim pool when roofers leave.

Also he will take me to post office again to mail my books to you. Yesterday they were back in my mail box again! I can't believe it.

This is second time they were returned to me, because they said I had to hand it to the person behind counter at post office.

Jim drove me few days ago to do that, and I did.

But I guess the postman at counter I handed the package to didn't understand.

So now Jim is driving me to post office again today for me to do it again.

This time I will not hand it to just anyone behind the counter, I will look for Michelle.

She is my friend who works there and she understands how this all works.

I guess my big mistake was trying to do 2 day mail. If I had just sent it book rate, they would not have put me thru all this nonsense.

Hahaha I thought it would get to you faster by 2 day rate, now it will be a miracle if it gets to you at all.

Happy July 4th weekend

Love, Annie

Friday evening

Hi Richie,

Today was no picnic, a team of roofers up on roof for 8 straight hours putting in a new roof.

I had to shut off the swamp coolers so they could move them.

It was tremendously hot day on desert today.

And Beanie was spooked by all the commotion on roof.

It had to be done, roof was leaking like a sieve.

Bob's crew were angels (Bob's custom roofing, Tucson).

O Richie they were all such sweet Mexicans.

They had the radio tuned to a Mexican station while they worked.

They were heroic, what they accomplished in this great heat!

And working so hard!

I sent them up ice cold coca colas a few times.

One of the roofers must have long arm, I put 6 cans of ice cold coca colas in a plastic bag.

I reached the bag up with my arm and was just about to bring over a chair to stand on.

But he said I don't have to, he reached his arm down and got it from my hand.

I brought out more cold sodas when they broke for lunch.

By the time they finished the job I had lost my mind.

It had been too hot for too long trapped in house with a spooked dog.

I just wanted Jim to come and drop me off at swim pool while he went on to his swim club.

I just wanted to be in the water and cool down and refresh.

Luckily Jim had the brilliant idea of taking me to post

office earlier when the roofers broke for lunch to mail the books to you.

Because as I told Jim on way to pool, "my mind is so shot now, I would have waited till post office reopened on Tuesday to mail the books."

There is no way I could have gone before or after swim pool.

Actually taking your books to post office when the workers broke for lunch at 11 am was the high point of my day.

The post office was so cool and air conditioned.

Michelle was right there at her station.

She was so happy to see me and gave me so much love.

And she was so expert at arranging the package of books would actually be mailed to you and not returned to me for the 3rd time.

I love Michelle.

Of course Jim teased me all the way back home that tomorrow the books will be back in my own mailbox.

The roofers worked heroically for another 3 hours and when they said I can turn the coolers back on and began preparing to leave I called Jim and said "they are leaving now, can you take me to swim pool."

I was a complete mess in car on way to swim pool, it had been so hard for so long.

I knew Jim couldn't stand it that I was expressing myself on this.

He likes it when I am happy and kid around with him in car.

It was a long hot day for him too, I think he found it oppressive that I was saying my feelings, he would have been much happier with just the radio on tuned to the sports station.

But it would have been beyond human ability for me to have sat there with my mouth shut, and not have said in 20 different ways "O god that was so intense!"

Finally he said "I see you let little things rattle you."

So I promised myself I would be upbeat on the way home from the pool.

I guess husbands are used to tuning out their wife when she is a drag in the car.

So they don't have to be subjected to it.

But Jim doesn't have enuf experience to know how to do this.

LOL the funny thing is I have had a husband for a million years, I have tons of experience of tuning out a husband when he is being a drag in the car.

So when Jim talks about the body and disease, a topic I cannot stand, but which fascinates Jim.

I just look out the window and tune him out, the way I would do when Bill would complain too much while we were driving.

Actually what I do is the exact same thing I did with Bill, I connect with my Higher Self.

Which lightens and brightens Jim's mind too and next thing I know he is making jokes about me which I find very funny.

All the way home from the pool he kept cracking jokes about how the package I had mailed to you will be back in my mailbox.

I said "O I see the mailman is at my mailbox now, is he bringing back the books?"

Jim said "No, first it has to go to the central Tucson post office, it will be returned to you on Tuesday."

For some reason I found that a riot.

Love, Annie

July 2 Saturday morning 6:24 am

Morning after the roofers leave

The roofing experience yesterday was so intense that to wake up this morning to my front yard, my backyard, my home, be restored to quiet and peace.

To birds flighting and alighting in back yard. To sound of bird whistles again.

To see my plants in backyard (the new baby trees arising).

To catch glimpses of my cats again.

It is like having heaven back.

Yesterday was like living in Times Square.

I am not surprised I did not see hide nor hair of my two cats till this morning, and why little Beanie was shell shocked all evening.

The happy miracle is that this morning it was all disappeared without a trace.

Front yard is not filled with major machinery. All the huge big trucks are gone. The hard working workmen are gone.

It is just me, Beanie, Priscilla, and Cupcake again. And the birds of course. All my wonderful birds in backyard.

O here is a big pigeon too.

I can't believe my luck that all is quiet and peace again. I will never again take it for granted. It is fortuitous thing.

To be in the middle of major construction is way too intense. Major construction machinery is a huge big deal.

I feel heroic for having gone thru it. I will never do it again.

O there is big morning dove. I have fallen in love with morning doves. I got to know the look of them intimately when I spent all that time lying in the yard. And now I recognize them instantly.

A pigeon is a giant compared to them. Morning doves actually are dove grey, which is a very nice grey with a blush of blue in it. But what makes them recognizable is their white racing stripe, which must actually be a ribbon of white feathers underneath the gray ones.

But just the edge of white shows, not exactly a ruffle, not like the bottom of a petticoat, because it appears to have a straight line edge all around.

How this can be I do not know? How can the edge of all the white feathers line up so perfectly that it appears like a straight white line edge on both sides of the bird.

But in any case I love the morning doves and love the look of them. Gray with that white line racing stripe on both sides. It is such a trippy bird in its own way, and ubiquitous on the desert and ubiquitous in my yard.

And its call which I have fallen in love with too. A very deep call which goes out everywhere.

It is such a quiet looking bird, what can be quieter looking than a bird which is all dove gray. Even the sparrows have interesting patterns all over them.

The morning doves have very quiet personalities too. They aren't vivacious like sparrows. They are not flighty. They are just being. It is like looking at being, or being with being.

They are an experience of being. They rule my yard, if rule meant being a mother or a backdrop or a foundation. It's as if my whole yard and every living being on it rests on the sweet quiet beingness of the morning doves.

It is the morning dove world in my yard. It is their world, and we are all the guests and visitors in it. The morning doves graciously share it with us, welcome us to the morning dove world. And I am so happy living in my dreamy morning dove world.

Their call is very throaty. It is the most distinctive of all the bird calls. It lasts long, and very deep and throaty, and a call which goes out to all.

July 9

My life is starting to change

Drawing Bill did of me when he started art school

Well my life is starting to change. By that I mean my inner life, what I think and how I think about things. The huge thing in my life of course is losing Bill. We were together for 40 years which is a long time. Almost our whole adult life we spent together.

But it's not about the shared past. All that amounted

to in our present relationship is we knew all the same people, the same restaurants, the same stores. We shared the same reference points.

The huge thing is how entwined our current present daily life had been. I could almost say Bill was my whole life. It certainly all revolved around him, the way planets go around the sun or the way the moon is satellite to the earth.

For one thing the boy liked a lot of attention. And for another thing he was so dramatic. He dramatized all his emotions, always. It was always like living with Ralph Kramden in the *Honey Mooners*. He was almost always carrying on.

The other thing is my tremendous devotion. At the heart of my being is devotion. It was natural for me to be so devoted to him. It is my natural way. I couldn't be any other way. To not be devoted would mean I would not be me. It's like asking a cat not to purr or a dog not to bark. It is my expression and being. It fulfills me.

The other thing is how deeply I loved him and how greatly I loved him.

The other thing is how happy he made me. The boy had extraordinary talent for making me happy. It was his forte. He was my cup of tea. I dug him.

And at first all I thought about was the happiness he brought me and how much I missed it.

For me he was both things, all my happiness plus the bane of my existence. So to be without him now is to be without the bane of my existence. I can't believe how calm and peaceful and quiet my life is now. It's like being able to hear myself think. It's like getting to know myself. Before all my attention was on him. This is the first time since I have been grown up that my attention is on me.

In some ways it was like having a volcano in the house. It was always erupting. Half of my energy went to holding on to my peace while sharing a home with a volcano which erupted on a regular basis.

That was the first thing which struck me when I first had my home to myself— not only the quiet, not only that I had so much more time, but the relationship had consumed so much energy, that energy was now at my disposal.

Not that I knew what to do with it! I had built my life around him. It is just that I noticed so much more. I got time to notice.

In a way I could say I never noticed anything while I was with him. I don't see how I could. The combination of all my attention on him, and the energy always being consumed. Noticing is a very specific thing. It means being quiet and looking around.

I never noticed how dilapidated my house had become. It was something Bill always talked about, always noticed, and always planned to do something about. He really wanted to fix up the house. It was his plan and intention.

He was always mad at me that I did not notice how much work had to be done and didn't appreciate that he wanted and intended to do it.

Now I do notice how dilapidated the house is and now I do appreciate that he wanted to fix it up for me. Now I would be so grateful for the beautiful new house he wanted to give me.

Also now I do notice everything he did for me. He was always mad at me that I didn't notice it and didn't appreciate it.

I do notice it now and I do appreciate it now. I notice everything he did for me and I appreciate it so much.

So now I think while we are in the world, it is a mixed bag. Some things we get to appreciate about them while it is going on. And some things you need deep peace and quiet to notice…

July 13

Beautiful morning

It is a beautiful morning in Tucson. I can't believe it. We have not had a beautiful morning since monsoon season started over two weeks ago. And before that it was boiling hot, you couldn't even think of walking outside.

Now it is both pretty (incredibly pretty, completely lovely) and very pleasant to be outside at 6 am.

It is such a treat, this lovely day. And such a promise of things to come. I don't think monsoon season is over, I think this is just an intermission. I don't think the big heat is over, it is a respite.

But O what a treat to have it now! To be able to lounge in my backyard with coffee and cigs and *Letter from God* and be outside and be so happy to be outside.

I had forgotten what a total joy it is. No wonder I was so happy all Spring. To have had that. I had it all day long.

Day after day, every day, it was my life. My life was paradise.

To have this beautiful day now makes me feel like a new chapter is starting. Because there is something fresh and something new is this new beauty. And because it is promise filled.

There is no way I can understand my life now, it is so different from how it was. But it is surprisingly easy to live it.

All I know right at this instant is that to spend 20 minutes this morning back in my yard lounging on the thick felt comforter on ground and looking at all the birds around me brings me huge happiness.

It is how I spent my winter and how I spent my spring and I loved every instant of it. And I loved having it back for the miracle 20 minutes this morning.

July 16

Sharon at the door last evening

Last evening while I was sitting here formatting my new book on the computer, Beanie was barking like crazy at the front door. I didn't hear anyone call out my name. Just the screen door was on the latch.

But finally I went to take a look and when I did Sharon with her dog Shiva were just leaving my front door. I called her back.

She said she was at my door because no one had seen me for the past few days, and she had been to my door many times in the evening knocking and there had never been any answer.

And I had heard from Frank, another neighbor, the morning before, while I was getting in the car with Jim to go swimming, that "everyone has been worried about you because they had knocked and knocked and you hadn't appeared, and nobody has seen you for the past few days."

Jim had gone on a fishing trip to the White Mountains with his friend Bob for Friday Saturday and Sunday so those 3 days I had not appeared in front yard except to get my mail. And I guess when he picked me up and returned me from swimming Monday, Tuesday, Wednesday, Thursday, Friday, Sharon had not seen me.

Altho Frank had seen me getting into the car on Thursday because that is when he said "everyone was worried about you, nobody had seen you and they were knocking at your door."

When Frank first said it to me on Thursday I didn't think too much of it. I had gone to brunch with Jan on Wednesday and Jim said he had arrived 3 times to take me swimming, banged on my door but only Beanie was there. So he thought I was taking a nap. I thought Frank was referring to that.

But when Sharon used almost the same words, "nobody has seen you for the past few days, when I banged on the door there was no answer," LOL then I knew there had been a confab about me among my neighbors.

And I knew what was going on. They all jumped to the conclusion that if they hadn't seen me, and there was no answer when they banged on the door, that I must have committed suicide out of my grief over losing my husband.

Which makes zero sense at all. As they had all seen me day after day for the past 4 months perfectly happy. And they had all seen the huge machinery in my yard two weeks ago for putting in the new roof.

It was major machinery, a major enterprise and it lasted all day. And last week the roofers came back to put on the plastic coating which keeps the heat from penetrating.

It just shows how irrational fear is. Every bit of logic would have shown them that I was perfectly fine. And if they hadn't seen me and if I hadn't come to the door when they knocked there had to be some other reason.

Sharon claims she was knocking at my door in the evening. There is no way I could hear her in back room watching TV. And if Beanie is carrying on at the door, he does that when someone is walking their dog across the street.

I had a wonderful time seeing Sharon at my door tho. I love her, she loves me, we are so happy to see each other.

We had delightful conversation even tho it was short.

She said her cousin is visiting, "he drove all the way down from Minnesota on his motorcycle."

And I said "cousins are so much fun."

And she said "he is exactly my age, so we were always very close."

And I said "That is how it was for me with my cousin Richie. He was born two weeks before me so we were very close and best friends and had so much fun together. But when we were 30 we drifted apart. I didn't want to. But he got married and had children."

So I knew exactly what Sharon was talking about when she said her cousin is here and it is so much fun. She had stayed close with her cousin her whole life.

My cousin Richie had a motorcycle too. Maybe Sharon's cousin is like Richie. That is why she is so happy, she is enjoying her cousin staying.

I guess she knocked on my door because she was taking Shiva for a walk. I'm sure that is always the time she tried knocking at my door, taking Shiva for her evening walk, but if I am in back room watching TV I wouldn't hear her.

And she asked how am I doing. They are all so concerned. The whole world is concerned about how I am doing without Bill. I don't like being concerned about, and there is no cause for concern, I am doing fine.

And she asked about my driving and I said I am still having my lessons with Jim. I said "Let's hope the Russian proverb, *the slower you go the further you get,* is right." And we both giggled.

I had given Sharon all 3 of my books last time she was here which was over a month ago. I hadn't seen her since then. I don't know if she read the books, I don't know if she liked the books.

In Tucson I give my books to everyone. But most of the time I have no idea if the person read the books, if the person liked the books.

It's like an odd limbo. Altho what I do have— is when I write another book and I am carrying around copies in my purse and I see them and say "I wrote another book, do you want it?" and take it out of my purse to hand it to them, their eyes light up, they want it.

So I guess this means they like my books.

I said to Sharon "I just wrote another book. Wait!" I got out my little womens lib book. I said "it's a lot of fun and it's short you can read it in an hour." I couldn't tell if Sharon was happy to get another book from me.

But she was willing to take it. The logistics at the

door to hand it to her were tremendous. Beanie was barking like crazy at the door because of Shiva, Sharon's dog, right next to her. Altho Shiva didn't like Beanie.

Shiva is not on a leash and Shiva was trying to walk away, really keep her distance from the lunatic dog behind the screen door.

My screen door which Bill had put in when we first bought the house, the latch stopped working years and years and years ago, so Bill uses a climbing carabineer to keep it shut.

I would not open the door with a lunatic dog barking ferociously at Shiva, but I was able to push the door onto the carabineer so the crack it was open was bigger and slipped Sharon the tiny book thru the crack.

"Give it to your cousin to read," I said. "Boys like this book" I said.

And then the conversation turned to Jim. She asked about my friend. She even remembered his name. I thought it's about me, "yes he takes me swimming every day, yes he is still teaching me to drive."

Then I said how much he likes Sharon which he really does. Jim likes Sharon a lot. She's a tremendously nice girl and fun and laughs easily and is outgoing and friendly.

Jim likes people like that and he likes girls like that. He really does like Sharon, his eyes light up when he sees her.

So when I told Sharon how much Jim likes her she got very happy and said "tell him to ask me out on a date."

Which is how I found out Sharon digs Jim.

Sharon is slender and blond which is Jim's type. But because of the way Jim's marriage ended, she left, she came back, she left, she came back, she left, came back, and when she left again Jim couldn't take it.

"Never come back again!" he said. He really loves his wife. The way she left was too much torture.

Altho he is tremendously interested in women and adores them and is always flirting with them and dreams Meg Ryan will be his girlfriend, Jim always tells me and tells every woman when we meet a woman when we are together "I have my cat, that's all I want."

Jim and I have been very close friends for 4 months but I was with Bill for 40 years. There is no possible way for me to understand Jim, to know what he really wants, to know where he is coming from.

It's possible he really does not want a girlfriend, that when he closed the door on his wife that last time, that was it for a woman in his life. I have no idea. I can go by what he says, but what people say is often not the truth in their heart.

Now that Jim is the guy I spend time with instead of my husband, and because Jim is single, I am becoming aware there is a world out there of men and women aware of each other, and their friendly interaction on the surface could be only half of the story.

LOL I am hanging out with a single guy, when we bump into a woman, best thing is for me to get out of the way, and let the two of them have their thing whatever it is.

I think what I will do tho is tell Jim all the nice things Sharon said about him. I mean how attractive she finds him...

Jim is a great guy. In some ways he is the counterpart to Sharon. He too is so easy to talk to, so friendly, so warm, so fun, so easy going, so outgoing, such a nice person.

And obviously if she wanted him to ask her out on a date she must find him good looking.

In any case Jim is picking me up in half an hour to take me swimming. Maybe best thing is to play it cool. Just say "Sharon was here. I gave her the book. I like her so much. She is such a nice girl and she told me she likes you."

And leave it at that. I'll see how Jim picks it up.

Thursday evening July 22

My crazy morning

Last night I had just finished fixing the typos in story I wrote Wednesday morning about Tuesday night's rain, I was just about to send it to Jan on email.

Just at that instant wind picked up like crazy. I rushed to press send, but internet went down before I could send anything. So I went in to watch tv. But my cable tv was down.

This morning everything was still down. Internet, tv, and telephone. It didn't come back on till 10 am.

At 7 am I walked out front door to see if anyone was on the street. I wanted to find out if it was just me, or storm had done something to whole neighborhood.

I didn't see a soul.

At 8 am I heard Beanie barking at dog being walked across the street.

I rushed out, it was Sharon.

So I told her.

She had no idea what was knocked out for her, she does not have cable tv, she does not have internet, and she has cell phone.

She offered to let me call Jim on her cell phone.

So I told him everything is knocked out and he can't call me on the phone about going to supermarket early this morning or swimming later.

Sharon got on the phone and said "if you need to call her, I live across the street, you have my phone number."

Since Sharon had told me the other night I should tell Jim to ask her out on a date, I was in awe at her finesse in slipping in he has her phone number.

Sharon is a girl in a million, whichever boy does wind up getting her will get a diamond.

I still assumed it was out for whole neighborhood. So I just did word processing on my computer, formatting my new book.

There was knock at door, it was Frank our neighbor, he used to be good friends with Bill.

He said Sharon told him I have no power, no phone, no cable tv, no internet.

He came to help me.

"Where is your switch box? Is it out back?"

I said "I have power, but my phone is dead and no cable tv or internet."

We went into backyard, I showed him the switchbox on back wall of my house right next to my open window.

He switched it on and off, and said "I heard something, power is back."

I said "the power wasn't off, my frig is running and my coffeemaker."

So he said he will go home to see if his cable tv is working, since he has cell phone and no internet.

When he first opened the huge switch box, he said "OOO Black Widow!" and there was the hugest black spider I ever saw in my life.

Frank was not fazed by it, he gingerly shut everything off and back on and closed the door to it.

I thought "O my God a huge black widow right outside my window!"

Then he went back to his house to check his cable tv, he said it is on.

So after he did my switch box, he said "let me go home and get my cell phone, we can call Cox and tell them to come and fix everything."

I was sitting in front yard barefoot in my nightie, stunned at all the events in my morning.

Frank came back and called Cox. They said wait time is 10 minutes. He said "I will come back in half an hour for my phone."

I never used a cell phone before but he showed me how.

He left it on speaker. For 15 minutes there were advertisements while telling me to wait.

I took it inside to my desk.

Finally a man came on, I said "I thought it was knocked out by the storm, but I am the only one."

"Which storm? Where? Where are you?"

"Tucson" I said

"Just a minute" he said

While I was waiting for him to come back, I heard my own phone make a popping noise, like it was popping into life again.

Meanwhile I got disconnected from customer service on Frank's cell, it went back to calling out the advertisements.

I couldn't figure out how to shut off Frank's phone, I didn't want to use up his minutes.

I called Jim on my phone and told him my own

phone is working again and how do I shut off Frank's cell, he told me how.

I walked down the block to Frank's house to return it to him. I am still in a nightie and barefoot, and thanked him very much. I said "it is all back on."

When I came home to check, tv is on, internet back on.

I had to reprogram phone and microwave from when Frank shut off the power.

I refused to think about the huge black widow.

I made another cup of coffee and decided to have it in front of tv in my bedroom.

I had no choice then but to think about the huge Black Widow.

I talked it over with my Higher Self.

"Aren't I supposed to kill it, it could hurt my Beanie?"

"No" my Higher Self said, "just make sure door to switch box is shut securely on it, leave it alone, it won't bother you."

"I will do what you say, I hope you are right."

I liked Her answer, because I wanted to just ignore it, and that is what She said to do.

Also Frank set a good example for me. He is American Indian. Yes he stepped back when he saw it, but he just closed the door on it.

At 11:30 Jim called. I said "Too late for me to go to pool, it closes in 5 minutes, you get a day off from having to take me anywhere or do anything for me. Tomorrow we'll have driving lesson and then pool."

Jim said "You need practice, we have to have driving lessons a lot. I'll pick you up early, we'll have lesson. Then I'll take you to the pool."

"Thank you" I said

He said "I tried to call you on the phone a little while ago, your phone wasn't working."

"But I put in a new message."

"I didn't get it."

"And I came to your door but both doors were shut like when you leave the house to go somewhere."

"How could that be! I never went anywhere! Let me put in a new phone message. Call me back and see if it works now."

I put in a new message.

He called me back and said he got it.

And that was the end of my crazy morning.

July 25th evening

God says, "call Jim on phone, I want to talk to him about your driving lessons"

This morning's driving lesson, good that it was brief!

It's not that I did not drive well or do well, I just felt off.

My big progress is when I went over the curb in the middle of the lesson, I simply took it in stride and kept driving, instead of my usual flounce-out-of-car and make Jim get in drivers seat and drive me home.

However Jim did not understand why that was progress, he said we didn't make progress because he did not get to teach me anything.

He wanted me to continue till he teached me a new thing.

But God told me "time to end the lesson."

Jim was adamant, "I am your driving instructor! You have to listen to me!"

"I won't" I said

I got out of truck to change seats. When we were both back in truck, he was still insisting I have to listen to him, and I should continue another 10 to 20 minutes.

I said "I'm not talking to you."

He said "Then I'm not talking to you."

I said "It's Monday, the Jewish bakery is back from vacation, let me buy you a cheesecake."

I said "Come inside this time, in case they don't have cheesecake their first day back from vacation, you can choose whatever you like."

We both told the bakery lady about the driving lesson.

I said, "He is my driving teacher, he is a wonderful teacher."

He said "She is a pissy student and I have to take a tranquilizer before a lesson with her."

She was laughing at everything he said, he cracked so many jokes about me as a driving student.

Then he drove me to the pool.

In the late afternoon I was chitchatting with God, God said, "Call Jim on the phone and let me talk to him.

"I want to tell him my suggestion for your driving lessons.

"Something is not working.

"You have to be allowed to stop the lesson when I tell you to stop."

I really didn't want to.

I have only mentioned God two times in the car in all the time we have been together, and both times Jim instantly got me on another topic.

How was I supposed to call Jim on the phone and say "God wants to talk to you about my driving lessons!"

But by some miracle it all did work

God said "*You* know Anne is doing very well because you see it, but Anne goes by her feelings. Because she is anxious she thinks she doesn't know anything and can't do anything.

"This is why she always hopes you will oversleep and cancel the lesson.

"You always tell Anne to relax and I try to reassure her all day and all night but neither of us have succeeded.

"So we have to come up with a solution."

Jim said "I know a solution, we will take breaks, we will stop every 15 minutes, and Anne can have a snack."

God said "No that is not a good idea, because the lesson will last too long that way. She doesn't like to be away from Beanie and her kitties for a long time. If you do that she will give up her swim. And her swim makes her so happy."

God said "Let's do half hour every other day. Anne can have her swim bag and swim suit in the truck. You put your swim bag in there too. And then just head down Craycroft to the pool after the lesson.

"That way you both will be home in time to watch *Loony Tunes*."

(Jim and I both like to watch *Loony Tunes* at noon.)

Jim said "But I like Anne to progress in every lesson, to learn something new, half hour is too short."

God said "I am God, you are not, I live inside Anne's mind, you do not. I know when her concentration starts to flag. When she continues past that point she makes mistakes, and that frustrates her, so then she gets stressed and you both lock horns.

"It's OK that you have been locking horns a lot, it gives you something to crack jokes about and have fun in the car on way to pool.

"You both laugh about it.

"But you've had enough of locking horns.

"From now on let's do 'leave the party while the party is good.'"

Jim was tickled pink to find out my secret, that I

always hope he will oversleep and cancel the lesson.

He agreed to everything but said to God, "Tell Anne she has to practice in her driveway, she won't practice.

"She has to practice going thru all the gears and then back again.

"She has to practice starting and stopping, get used to the pedals.

"And she has to practice glancing at all the mirrors."

God said "she lies to you and tells you she glances at the mirrors but she doesn't."

Jim said "I know."

Jim said "She has to practice for ten minutes."

God said "This is a good idea, I will have Anne practice every other day, the day she does not have her lesson. And when I tell Anne to do something she always does it. She can practice for 15 minutes."

Jim said "10 minutes is enough."

God said "fine."

Then Jim said to me "I had your cheesecake, it is delicious."

And I went out of my mind with joy.

And then Jim said about something which happened in one of my driving lessons which made me laugh for 5 minutes, I couldn't stop giggling.

I love laughing at myself.

I actually think Jim liked the conversation, he has been dying to have a serious conversation with me about my driving lessons, but whenever he starts one, which is all the time, I tune into love and look out the window because the topic made me anxious.

We'll see what happens.

Hahaha we will find out if God had any luck solving my problem..

Epilogue, The phone call made a huge difference. Yesterday I practiced in my driveway both morning and evening, per God's instruction.

Today was lesson. It went swimmingly. We were both happy after the lesson. We were both so proud of ourselves, so pleased with ourselves. And so pleased with each other.

Big joy all around.

A New Chapter

Jim always helps me

August 1

The adventure of the new doorknob

Friday
My Peculiar Morning

Such a peculiar morning. I finally fell asleep at 1 am. Then opened my eyes just as first light of dawn was starting. I went to open the closed front door so Beanie could plant himself at the screen door, let cool morning air blow on him, and look out.

His favorite thing is bark like a maniac when he espies a dog being taken for its early morning walk. He likes to give the dog the dickens.

But I could not open the wood front door, the lock was jammed.

I tried every which way to open it with no success.

Finally I called Jim. It was 5 am.

"Come over" I said, "the front door lock is broken."

"Are you locked out of the house?"

"More like locked in the house." I wasn't really locked in, there is a back entrance to get out of house.

"Be right over!" he said.

"Bring WD 40 with you!" I said.

He came right over and fixed it. Beanie was ecstatic that his darling friend arrived at dawn to play with him. Big love affair between Jim and Beanie.

So I thanked him and said "Go back to sleep."

We had driving lesson scheduled at 9:30 am.

Driving lesson at Mervyns parking lot went fine.

Altho right before driving lesson I went to get something in my yard in bare feet (of course) and the pail of tar which roofers left on roof, which had blown over. I had thrown out the half-filled pail of tar, but there was still a pool of tar in yard.

I stepped in it.

So I put my foot in the sand in back yard and got a little off. It still covered my toes and bottom of my foot.

I assumed it would erode off, like my nail polish, from swims and showers, but Jim said in car "you have to get nail polish remover to remove the tar." But I don't plan to actually do that.

Of course I had not locked the front door because I did not want the same problem to reoccur. But after Jim brought me home from pool and started to drive off the door was locked anyway and my key would not open it.

I yelled out "Jim come back!"

He no longer had his WD 40 with him but he found screw driver in Bill's tool chest. He was able to take out the lock and open the door after half hour.

So now I will not close the door at all until I get new lock. Beanie can have his dream come true. Only the screen door shut all night. He can spend all night in front of it.

Jim was tremendously good sport about everything. And an angel to help me .

The swim in the midst of my peculiar morning was a godsend. The water was so lovely, it is very hot again, and it sure was a treat to be in lovely water.

There was only one little boy in pool with me. LOL we each did handstands in the water.

And the lifeguard said mine was good! Hahaha I have been doing handstands in the water since I was 7 years old and this is the first time I was complimented on it. I was thrilled.

He said to the little boy, "let me see you swim."

The little boy said "I wont! Make me!"

Lifeguard said "if you don't show me how you swim, you'll have to get out of the water."

So the little boy did.

I giggled for 10 minutes.

Who says "Make me!" to lifeguard. A lifeguard can make you do anything.

I didn't know if the little boy would like to be teased about saying Make me! to a lifeguard.

But I could not resist kidding around with the lifeguard about it. "If I say *Make me!* are you going to make me get out of water?"

Anne is in a dream after her peculiar morning...

Saturday

We drive to Ace for new door knob..

Next day my plan was we drive to Ace, buy new knob with lock, Jim put it in, then we swim. But when next day arrived Jim had different ideas.

"I'll pick you up at 1 pm for your swim" he said.

"Fine" I said.

He called at a quarter to one and said "are you ready now, I can come over right now."

I said "I have been killing time all morning waiting till 1 pm. I can't just jump into my bathing suit and be out the door waiting for you, I need 6 minutes to organize."

I said "what about putting in the new door knob and lock in my door, are we going to Ace to get it?"

He said "We will go to Ace after the swim."

"When will you put it in?"

"Maybe later on in the day," he said.

"OK" I said.

I instantly got off the phone. But when I pictured dragging all my stuff for swim pool out the back door, thru side door gate, and arriving that way in front of house for Jim, with just rickety screen door closed in front the whole time we were gone, I knew I wouldn't do it.

I called him right back. "Forget swimming today! Forget driving on Corona Road tomorrow! Forget everything! I am not going swimming. I am not having any more driving lessons. I am not going to do a thing until I have a front door I can open and close.

"I am not leaving the house. Just take me to Ace right now for new door knob and then I will sit in the house with it until the time comes when you are willing to put it in for me.

"Come over right now!" I said, "let's go to Ace."

He came right over.

It was too much for me. It had been two full days of doorknob drama starting at first light the morning before.

We arrived at Ace parking lot. It was the first time I had been back there since last fall with Bill. He and I went there all the time, it was on the way home from the pool. He would go to Ace, I would go to bakery and we would meet up at the books in the charity store. We both like to read.

It is more familiar to me than any place in Tucson. He and I were there together more than at any place in

271

Tucson. We passed it on way to pool every day, on way home from pool every day, and 3 times a week we were in there.

And I had not been back since.

I got out of car with Jim confused and overdressed. Bra, panties, skirt and blouse, heels.

I couldn't face walking back into Ace, the scene of all my memories. All the time we had been in Ace together.

I started to tear up and was walking very slowly.

"I don't know how can I do this" I said to Jim, "I haven't been back here since I was with Bill, we used to come all the time."

Jim was hot and bothered himself. He had not put in a door knob with lock since he had built the house in the foothills for him and his wife 25 years ago. He didn't know if he was able to do it.

The last thing he wanted to be doing right now was walking into Ace to buy new lock and then coming back to my house to put it in.

His plan for the day was to take me swimming, go to his club for his swim and then come right home and get stoned on pot.

No wonder when I said "When will you put in the

new door knob?" he said "maybe later, much later."

All he was willing to do at that point was stop at Ace on way home from swim and buy it.

But best laid plans of mice and men...

I had a different idea. I wasn't going to step one foot out of the house and go on with my life until that new door knob with lock which works was in there.

Hence at 1 pm we were walking into Ace, me with tears in my eyes.

"I'll meet you at locks" I said, "I am going to buy new trash bags."

Jim chose the doorknob which looked the same as the one he had taken out which had been in there since house was built 50 years ago, with a simple little push button to lock it from inside. It was the kind I wanted.

When the man came over to help us, Doug, Jim consulted with him if it was the right one. Doug said it was. I had my new women's lib book in my pocketbook and offered one to Doug.

"I just wrote a new book, would you like it?"

He looked at the title *How the women's liberation movement started* and said "No thank you" and handed it back to me.

LOL I guess Bill was wrong when he said "everyone wants to know about that." Doug in Ace Hardware did not.

I told Doug the story how I had called Jim the morning before at 5 am because the lock had jammed. And what an angel he was to come and open my front door for me so doggie could have the joy of being at his screen door and watching the street.

I said to Doug "Jim was an angel to do that for me. Who comes over at 5 am to open your front door for you!"

Doug agreed Jim was a wonderful friend.

I paid for my purchases. We went home. Instantly I slipped into an airy sundress.

And Jim opened up the package to start the work on it. He got out the screw driver from Bill's tool chest. I had bought WD 40 while I was there so Jim would not have to bring over his whenever he was doing me a favor. Bill's WD 40 had disappeared.

When Jim had everything opened out and it was on the table in front of sofa and was trying to read the small print of the directions, he said "There are no keys."

I looked at it myself and saw there was no keyhole in knob.

"We bought the wrong one, this is for a bathroom

door. We have to go right back," I said.

It was the last thing he wanted to do. Bill always jumped up with alacrity when it meant returning to Ace because something was wrong or something else was needed.

But this is a mistake Bill would not have made. He and Jim are almost the opposite in this kind of thing. Bill was almost obsessive with his care and concentration.

Jim is like me, casual.

The schmacta sundress must have looked like hell but I was far more comfortable driving over in the convertible to Ace in it.

I even made Jim take down the top. The claustrophobia of the top up on the way over and back had bummed me out, and I was already bummed out to start with.

I wanted to get back some oomph. I wanted to get my mind back.

"Open the top," I said to Jim, "I want the light."

He hates that. He likes to drive with the top down, windows up, and AC on. He hates driving out in the sunshine and heat.

He always indulges me in it. I don't know why. I guess because he is my angel. Or because he was Bill's friend and loved Bill, and he knew how much Bill loved me. He is taking care of his friend's wife. It is the favor he is doing for his friend Bill.

As soon as the top was down and we were driving in light and air, and cool schmacta sundress and naked underneath, I was more comfortable and happier. More with it, more confident.

"You checked with Doug, he said it was the right one. I wonder how he screwed up? He heard the whole story, he knew it was for my front door."

I wasn't feeling that warmly to Doug, it smarted when he looked at my book, looked at the title and handed it right back to me and he had screwed up about the lock.

Jim really did not like having to make the return trip. He is not like my husband in that department, who when he decided to undertake a project was gung ho to do it right.

I never remember Bill dragging his feet and having resistance in the middle of undertaking a project. Maybe ahead of time if it was something he didn't want to do, but not once it had been undertaken.

Luckily the lady at cash register had suggested I hold on to the receipt. And I put everything Jim had taken out of package and was on table back in the Ace bag along with package it had all come in.

I walked right over to her and said "it's the wrong lock, it is for bathroom, I need for front door."

And placed it all on the counter. She said "I have to check it's all in here." And she got on phone, Doug came over.

He was much nicer to me this time. He really apologized for the error. He was very nice to me. He was on my side. He was loving to me. He was a friend. It really helped. He brought over the right one.

She did the exchange and gave me back $1.50. I have no idea why the right one was $1.50 cheaper, but altogether it made it a nicer visit— It was right one, Doug checked it carefully, Jim looked at it, we all knew it was the right one this time. Doug was so nice to me. And she gave me 1.50.

Jim looked at the car clock on the way home, it was only 1:30. "It won't take long," I said, "we can have our swim."

"If I remember how to do it," Jim said.

"You'll remember" I said.

He wasn't sure, he didn't have confidence.

I made him a huge coca cola with a ton of ice instant we walked in the door.

He sat on sofa opened up the package and began the process all over again.

It took him half an hour but he got it.

It was beautiful and worked like a charm. I was overjoyed with it. "My hero!" I said to him.

He said "Put the WD 40 on top of tool chest so we know where to find it."

And I grabbed my bathing suit and jumped into it in the bathroom.

I didn't lock the front door but I closed it good and it gleamed. I was very happy with it.

I was happy on way to pool. And divinely happy to be in the pool. I was happiest girl in the world to be in a swimming pool with everything all sorted out beautifully at home.

My new doorknob and lock put in, all back in place. Everything upgraded. Instead of old door knob from 50 years ago, brand new one bought at Ace less than an hour ago. The same one but the new version, the beautiful new gleaming one.

I never was so happy to be in the water as I was that Saturday afternoon two days ago. I was so grateful to be in the water. I relished every instant of it. There was no instant I did not totally enjoy and was not totally grateful to be in it.

I would have stayed longer but Jim had said he'd be back in an hour.

So I showered and washed my hair and put on pretty clothes and walked out the door and Jim drove up at that instant.

"Wasn't that the most wonderful swim you ever had in your whole life!" I said to him glowing.

"No" he said

"Why not?" I said

"There was no one there."

I was overjoyed to be alone in my pool with just one little boy doing everything same as me, just playing in the water.

I was so surprised Jim was not happy to have his pool to himself.

But Jim has now been a bachelor for a long time. And he has been at the Club since his wife left. He knows everyone there, he is friends with everyone. It is his social life and companionship. He likes to flirt with the "hot blonds" and see his friends.

For him that there was no one there meant the treat of going to his pool didn't exist. I was completely gratified but he felt completely cheated.

Then I asked him to stop at Paco's, a fast food Mexican place, for us to get burritos to go. And I ordered a tamarind drink too.

Jim couldn't wait to get home and smoke a joint. He hated his Saturday and was looking forward to his evening making it up to him. I heard all his plans for getting stoned.

My spirits had soared back up, I had fun teasing him on way home about his Saturday night at Casa Jim's.

That tickled him. "Every night is Saturday night at Casa Jim," he informed me.

"Every night is Saturday night at Casa Jim" I sang out.

"Every night is Saturday night at Casa Jaime," he said. "That's my name in Spanish." Jim speaks fluent Spanish.

We were making each other laugh again, which raised both our spirits.

And on that happy note he dropped me off at my house.

And my door opened like butter. He had done a good job and it gleamed like gold.

I was very happy.

And I went in to have my burrito and my tamarind drink in front of the TV.

All was right with the world again...

August 3

Fixing the typos saved me..

It's a beautiful morning and it was a night full of beautiful stars. I don't remember when last we had a beautiful morning. I don't remember when last we had a night filled with stars. It is a huge treat to have it this morning, it was huge treat to have had all those stars in the sky last night.

Yesterday afternoon was the kind of hot sweaty afternoon which went on forever. It's almost as if the same weather was in my head as it was outside, nothing going on, just trying to get thru time.

I kept thinking if evening would only arrive, if I can just make it to the evening, I will have relief. It will get interesting, there will be something my mind will enjoy, it will cool down and become more comfortable.

But evening brought no change at all. Finally I fell into another nap. And this time when I woke from nap and went to computer, instead of only frustrating myself that there was nothing to hold my mind on computer, I found I was able to start fixing the typos on the story I had written yesterday morning.

All day long I had hoped that would be my escape, that I would edit and format my new book, or edit and fix typos on story I wrote yesterday. But no go! For some reason I was unwilling to do it.

Work on the computer turns out to be great escape for me from endless hot sweaty boring afternoons and evenings.

I thought it was something I could count on, but whatever blah place my mind was in yesterday it didn't want to do it. LOL I wonder if I had a bad case of the blahs.

But evening tv didn't work for me either, and this time I don't know if it was tv's fault. I had gone in to watch with high hopes, it was the time the shows I usually enjoy are on. But I couldn't stand any of my regular shows.

I got up hoping to find something fun on computer. It didn't happen. I went back to give tv a try again. This is when I fell into another nap.

And this time when I went back to computer, after trying and trying to find something fun or interesting, I clicked on my story from yesterday morning. And this time a miracle took place, it caught hold! I began to fix the typos and that solved everything.

Because I got caught up in my own story, and caught up in the labor of making it readable. Finally I had the joy of concentration again, the escape that concentration gives you, work I liked doing.

The story is pretty bizarre but for some reason it fitted my mood. It was what I had written yesterday morning when I woke up and finally by mid evening, just before 8 pm, my mind finally caught. I started the labor of fixing the typos. I was focused on the story.

It was like I had spent the whole day starved out of my mind for communication, starved for some self expression, starved for some attention.

I couldn't find it anywhere on computer no matter how hard I looked. And TV was not supplying me with any diversion, entertainment or interest either. It is completely peculiar that my story finally supplied it for me.

Nothing in my own mind had either. I had bad case of the blahs. Not one single thought entered my mind all day. It was dullsville in there. The only thing which did work was the story, the story held my interest and fixing the typos held my concentration, it saved me, my own story saved me.

There is a very interesting bird in my tree now. I wonder which one it is? It has that long beak so it is not morning dove, altho it has the same grey coloring. Perhaps it is a yearling cactus wren, before it gets its beautiful speckles and is the size of the morning dove.

My own story saved me and when I went back to tv two hours later I had different head. I was capable of being interested in things again. It was such a relief.

It's odd that the relief I had waited for all that long day turned out not to be in the weather at all, turned out to be the weather in my mind.

O well I am just glad that finally the idea of working on something did not totally turn me off, that I was willing to try and I did and it worked. I was saved by the work.

I don't know why yesterday was the way it was. Maybe I was tired. Maybe things have to be that boring so you will nap more in the day. Or maybe I just needed all that pressure. It was like an endurance test, all day was about enduring the day.

But perhaps that is one of the ways cleansing of the mind takes place. You endure that weight on you all day. Weighed down by boredom, by dullness, by heat, by complete emptiness.

But maybe it is a cleansing process. As weird as it sounds perhaps when it is over the mind is refreshed.

Saturday August 6th

Car Missing in Frys Parking Lot

It was a huge morning.

Incredibly intense.

Began off so well.

Jim called and said "let's go to Frys I'll be there in ten minutes."

It was perfect time to get off computer, get dressed, brush teeth, spray on a little perfume, and organize for big grocery shopping.

I was just about to walk out the door when I saw him drive up. "It's almost 9, credit union is open on Saturday, can you take me there first so I can pay car payment, credit card bill?

"Wait let me get something!"

I went back in house and re-emerged one minute later. "My friend Jimmy from New York City just published his book of poems.

"Here is proof copy he sent me which arrived yesterday. Each poem is one page long and reads right off the page.

"And because of Jimmy's job you will get to know a side of New York that even the New Yorkers at your club don't know.

"They aren't all about that. There are poems about animals, his own life, the countryside."

I knew he would want to read it because he had loved Jimmy's poem in my little womens lib book.

I said "it is perfect for you to read while you are sitting in the car waiting for me to come out."

And when I went out in the middle of my transaction at credit union to give him the money order for his cigars, there he was engrossed in the book. Obviously he loved it.

And when I came out at the very end because I was finished he was engrossed in the book again.

He talked about the poem half way to Frys. "He's driving across country," Jim told me, "on his way to San Francisco and going thru all this snow."

Of course Jim would love the driving poem. Jim is always driving to California himself. LOL he didn't sound happy I had interrupted, he had wanted to finish the poem.

I had a lovely time at the credit union. I was first one there. The woman, Jana, was so wonderful to me.

I twirled around to show her the skirt I had just ordered from a designer in Hawaii.

"It just arrived yesterday so let me pay last month's credit card bill plus for the skirt."

It is first time I was wearing it. I had taken it out of its packing bag when Jim called and said "I will take you to Frys now."

And I gave her copy of my little womens lib book. She was happy to get it. "It sounds interesting," she said.

"It is, but the man in Ace hardware didn't want it, it didn't sound interesting to him."

She said something very sweet to me, in case I had taken the rejection with bitter taste. She said something so sweet to make the taste sweet.

So I was walking on air when I returned to car to find Jim engrossed in Jimmy's book. Which multiplied my happiness exponentially. Jim never reads, but he loves Jimmy's book.

We were so happy on the way to Frys. I told him I had been practicing shifting gears in my driveway. And he was proud and pleased.

And I said "I am sure we will meet our goal, drivers test by your birthday December 4th.

"I am going to buy a new designer skirt for my drivers test, she described the new one coming in and said it is beautiful and she will put one aside for me and call me when it comes in.

"I can't decide whether to wear it for my test, or as reward when I pass the test."

"When you pass the test I will buy you something."

"Perfect!" I said, "you can go buy me a blouse at Target to go with my beautiful new skirt."

We were still planning out with delight when we pulled in Frys parking lot.

"Drive me over to the beauty parlor. I want to see if it is open. If it is open I want to give them copies of my new book, they love all my other books. And I want to get more shampoo and conditioner and other stuff for swimming."

He pulled over, it said *open*. Since it is the other end of the parking lot I said "let me off here and then we'll meet in the car after our shopping."

"We'll meet in Frys" he said.

"Great!" I said.

I bought out the store because I hadn't been back since February and I didn't want to make Jim take me again soon.

I don't like to impose on him.

I didn't know the girl who was working there, I was used to the other girls. But she stopped in the middle of doing a lady's hair when it was time to let something set in.

And came over. I took out 6 books and said "the girls like my books, here is one for each of them and one for you."

She said "thank you."

My purchases were all on the counter and she rang them up and put them in a plastic bag. I got out the little shopping bag I had bought at Petsmart for her to put them in there and she loved the bag (it had kitties and puppies on it).

She said "I collect bags like this, I never thought of going to Petsmart."

I said "you can have this one, I have two just like it at home. But this one is so used, I have been putting my shampoo and conditioner for the pool in it. Do you want me to come back with a new one?"

"No, this one is fine, I will just put it in the washing

machine."

She was totally delighted. She loved it and wanted it.

So I was even more walking on air.

I started to try to find the car in the middle of the parking lot but it was too long a walk. I decided just to lug everything to Frys.

I was so happy I had not exhausted myself and was still able to do my shopping. I really wanted to do my shopping. That is why we were doing all this.

I did small shopping. I have finally broken the habit of totally overdoing it. I bought exactly what I wanted. I was very happy.

And Jim found me at check out, he was finished.

"I'll meet you at the car" he said, "it is in the middle of the parking lot."

I was just about to go out when I saw Frys shopping bag for 99 cents. I wanted to put my heavy bag of beauty goods in there.

I asked the Help Lady "can I just give you a dollar ten, I finished my shopping."

It turned out to be bit complicated. I had to have my Frys card, and my change purse did not have a dollar bill, just some change.

I handed her a ten from my wallet. A nickel and two pennies fell on the floor. "Leave it" I said to her, "the little children will find it and be so excited."

When this was finally over I could not find my change purse. "It doesn't matter" I said to myself, "there was only 35 cents in there." But I loved my red change purse.

I wheeled the shopping cart to Jim's groceries in his shopping cart. I couldn't figure out why he hadn't put them in the car. He was standing there in middle of parking lot. He called out something to me. I did not hear him.

I said "I spent $157 in beauty store."

He said "Did you hear what I told you. The car is gone. It's been stolen. The car is not here."

I came down from the cloud nine I had been on all morning. It was very long, very fast, descent. I landed with a thud.

"Don't worry" Jim said, "I have had 3 cars stolen, the police always find it."

Which would have comforted me but the lifeguard at the Y had just had her car stolen from Y's parking lot and when the police found it two weeks later there was nothing left of it.

He told them at Frys. And then called the police on

his cell phone. The manager came over. He was very nice. He said "I'm so surprised, this almost never happens."

I said "That reassures me. We didn't put the top up and lock it, I thought maybe we did something wrong."

But Jim's conversation with the police seemed to go on forever. I began to desperately want something cold to drink and a cigarette.

I had finally taken the cigarettes out of my purse the day before. I thought, 'We never have stress in our driving lessons anymore. I never flounce out and sit on curb and smoke a cigarette. Why do I need cigarettes in my purse! We never go anywhere where I might want one.'

Then Jim wanted to call credit union to stop payment on the money order for his cigars. "It is in the car."

I didn't think we really had to do that. The money order was for $117 how did that stack up with losing the Mustang.

He told the woman at credit union but she wanted to talk to me.

Then he talked to the police again for a long time and she wanted to talk to me.

For some reason she could not spell Bill's name.

Finally in frustration I handed phone back to Jim.

"This is ridiculous. It's been 20 minutes on phone with her. You tell her how to spell Bill's name."

She wanted a lot of information I didn't know.

"Which year is the Mustang?"

"We got it used, I don't remember, maybe 2004?" I told Jim to tell her.

"What's the license plate?"

I didn't know. I remembered once Bill remarking "Look it says (I don't remember now). That is good luck."

"Maybe it begins AYR" I said to Jim to tell her.

She kept wanting me to be definite. I could not be.

"What's the VIN number?"

"I don't know. It's back in the house. Can't she find it on the computer?"

"She can't find Bill on the computer, she has his name spelled wrong."

When he finally got off the phone with her I said "I am so thirsty and I want a cigarette."

I went to try to buy cigarettes but the line at customer service was too long.

I sat down again.

"I'm so thirsty" I said again.

"The manager said there is water fountain around the

corner."

But I wanted to sit there with cold drink in my hand. I couldn't believe the manager would not bring over an ice cold coke for me and Jim. And help me buy cigarettes.

I was starting to get unhappy.

I just wanted to go home.

We had been waiting half an hour.

I just wanted to go home to cigarettes, my ice cold coke, and be with my doggie.

I hadn't locked my door either.

I really wanted to go home.

"We are waiting for the police to come" Jim said.

"Then will they take us home?"

"No" he said, "I will call a friend."

Finally a police car drove up and Jim and I went to greet it.

To my surprise it was a girl.

Sweet girl medium size with beautiful eyes. She was just my height and I was looking into hazel eyes.

My eyes are hazel, I have never seen another girl with hazel eyes.

"Aren't her eyes beautiful Jim. Look!"

"Let me stand next to her, tell me if they are the same

color."

Jim said "she needs to take your information Anne."

But when she looked down to begin writing I saw her violet iridescent eye shadow.

And light touch of mascara on her lashes.

"O Jim look at her beautiful eye shadow it is violet."

Jim was getting very impatient.

"She just wants your information" he said.

It occurs to me now that she did not mind at all being told how beautiful her eyes were and her eye shadow.

It was Jim who assumed she was impatient about writing down my information.

It was so easy for me to give her my address and phone number because of internet, I had been writing it 100 times a day it seems.

When it came to registration, I said "it is registered to my husband, he went to Heaven a few months ago."

"O I'm sorry," she said

"It's OK" I shrugged, "I believe we live forever, it is just a change of address."

She said "I like that."

Then I said to Jim "here's a 20, there's a smoke shop over there at end of parking lot, buy me a pack of Marlboros"

(I have not had Marlboros in 15 years ever since price sky rocketed but if ever there was a time for Marlboros this is it.)

"And buy yourself a package of cigars you must be dying for a cigar.

"And buy us a lighter."

"I have a lighter."

"You do?" I said

"O that's right it's in the car."

I didn't care about the money, I was so grateful Jim was willing to walk all across the parking lot to buy it.

I had given the manager in Frys while we were waiting for the police to come a ten dollar bill to buy me and Jim both ice cold cokes.

"You want a 20 ounce?"

"Perfect!" I said.

When I saw that drinking my ice cold coke completely lifted my spirits and I was happy again, I realized the whole problem had been I wanted something cold to drink and I wanted a cigarette.

My impatience to be home was all about that.

The coke made me so happy and Jim was so happy with his too when he came back with that Crime Stopper from Frys to look for the car.

She was a plump brunette with long hair and looked very confident and efficient in a very good way.

"We have the footage of the parking lot inside. You can look at that."

I guess it is what the surveillance camera took.

Jim told her "we probably arrived around 9:30 and were back out at 10."

"They were fast," she said.

"Yes" Jim said, "here are the keys," he brought them out of his pocket.

When he got back from looking at surveillance tape with her, he was so glad I handed him the ice cold coke.

I was 100 per cent happier sitting there drinking my ice cold coke. All I wanted now was a cigarette, but it wasn't as intense because I was so happy with my coke.

I was no longer a hot unhappy girl who just wanted to be home. I was content sitting on the bench drinking my coke waiting for the police to arrive.

So Jim and I both walked out with our half finished cokes when we saw the police car drive up.

I have no idea why I was so happy. I guess I thought, 'the police are here, I will ask them to drive me home.'

I said to Jim "will they drive us home?"

He said "I will call my friend."

But when he went to get the cigs and cigars I said "will you drive us home?"

"Yes" she said, "let me just call my sergeant."

Jim must have still been there then because when she asked "do you live in the same place?"

He said "take me to her house and then I will drive her truck home."

While he was at smoke shop brouhaha about the police report broke out between her and me.

It was friendly of course but I dug in my heels.

I had already signed some things.

Now she brought out something else for me to sign.

"This says you are willing to prosecute."

"I don't want anyone punished. I just want my car back," I said.

"And it also says if we see someone driving your car we can make them get out at gunpoint."

"I don't want you to punish anyone.

"I don't want you to point a gun at anyone.

"I am not signing it.

"I just want my car back."

"I can't put in a report of stolen car without it," she said.

I gathered that meant they wouldn't look for my car. And I would have nothing to show insurance.

I couldn't accept that.

But I couldn't accept punishment and gunpoint either.

I was stymied.

Just then Jim arrived back with my Marlboros, lighter, and change.

"We'll ask Jim, altho he is not New Age like me. I'm sure he will be on your side."

"I have no side," she said, "it is completely up to you."

"OK, Jim you're here, maybe you can mediate."

I told him everything. But before he finished talking I knew I had no choice but to sign it.

"OK OK" I said, "let me sign."

"Do you want me to read it to you?" she asked.

"No, I just want to sign."

Then there was dig-in-my-heels about being victim. "I am not a victim, I am a person a citizen. You have to say citizen, you can't say victim."

I didn't say to her "it is a new age thing, you are not allowed to see yourself or anyone else as a victim."

So she changed it to *citizen* and I signed.

Then she came to employment. I said I am a writer. "O wait!" My womens lib book was still in my purse.

"Here I just wrote this one! Do you like to read?"

"I love to read."

"O you will love this. It is a lot of fun and it is real. It is history. But very personal and *very* revealing. And my husband's cartoons make it so much fun."

She really wanted it but refused to take it.

"I am not allowed."

I tried every which way. But no way would she take it!

"I am not allowed."

"What if I just leave it behind when you drive us home?"

"Then I will have to put in a lost property report."

"OK" I said, I threw the book on the ground.

"O there is some trash! Pick it up, you can take it to garbage can."

When I threw it to the ground she said "that's littering."

There was just no way I could get the girl to take the book.

She really wanted it. "I love to read." She said "I will buy it," and she wrote down its title and Anne Wilensky.

Jim had gone to get his groceries and she loaded

mine in trunk of cop car along with all my beauty supplies.

When Jim started to unload his in, the zaftig Crime Fighter from Frys arrived.

"Come with me," she said to Jim, "I am looking at the surveillance tapes I think I see your Mustang."

I didn't pay much attention to Jim going off with her. I didn't understand.

I was having so much fun chatting it up with the police woman.

But the two of them arrived back together. And they both said it sure looks like my Mustang at the very edge of parking lot, hidden behind the gas pumps, by the big street.

So Jim and I got in the backseat, the police woman drove us over there. And the zaftig Frys crime fighter showed up soon after.

As soon as police woman drove us over there we recognized our Mustang. It was our car. Jim checked and everything was in there, including the money order.

It is a miracle. I had trusted all along that God would not let me down.

But I had still assumed a whole bunch of inconvenience before I got my car back. Or a whole insurance deal and the getting of replacement car. I didn't think of it as an ordeal, but just as something I would have to go thru before I got my happy ending.

But miracle of miracles the happy ending was right now. My car was right here and it was all perfect.

The first thing I said was to the police woman. "Tear up that thing I signed! No prosecution! No punishment!"

"Do you want me to keep any police report?" she said.

"Why! I have my car back, I am so happy."

I had kissed the zaftig Frys Crime Stopper when she first came back with Jim and they both said it looks like our Mustang on the tape. I wanted to kiss her again but she pulled away shyly.

So I thanked both her and the police lady very much with all my heart.

And Jim got in the car and drove us home.

"Well it wasn't the morning we expected," I said to Jim when we were driving home.

We were both so happy to have the car back.

I had him help me bring all my stuff to doorstep, he couldn't wait to take off to put his ice pops in the freezer.

Practically my last words to police lady were "I can't wait to be home, smoke my head off, drink ice cold coca cola and be with my dog."

For some reason Jim burst out laughing at "smoke my head off."

When I would not let her use the word victim in the paper I had to sign earlier and had her change it to citizen, "I don't like the word victim" — Jim said "you see what I have to put up with when I give her a driving lesson." And they both laughed.

On the way home Jim said "well that cop will never give you a ticket."

"You mean she loves me?" I said

He said "She has never seen someone so happy right after their car was stolen."

When I got home...

Jim and I got home from Frys and I was waiting 2 hours for him to take me swimming.

The first hour I could not budge from lying on bed, drinking ice cold orange soda, and smoking one cigarette after another. I didn't even turn on the tv.

All I did was say "O my god" each time I thought about my morning. It had been such a big experience! It didn't matter which aspect of it came into my mind I would still say "O my god" about the whole experience.

I guess this is what being blitzed means. I was totally blitzed. I couldn't get past "O my god! I can't believe it happened! What a thing to happen! Such a big thing to happen!"

It was the refrain no matter which part I remembered. And for first hour I couldn't do anything else but this. My mind would go back to it and I would say "O my god."

My ice cold orange soda was empty. I was still thirsty. I didn't want to move. Finally I forced myself up off bed to get ice water and to call Jim to give him the address of the

Indian Reservation in upstate New York to send the money order for his cigars.

There was no answer on his cell phone. I guess he was plotzed too. I just left message "call me for address for money order."

I made huge ice water with plenty of ice and went back to lie on bed.

But my mind was more organized.

I asked my Higher Self about the car.

My Higher Self said:

"It happened at 9:30 right after Jim parked it and walked into Frys."

She said "9 am on a Saturday morning is when kids go into Frys to shoplift. Almost all kids shoplift. You shoplifted at Woolworths when you were that age.

"That manager is very sweet. But you saw how preoccupied he became each time an old lady walked in and asked him with help with her coupons. She wanted him to show her where everything was.

"There you were in the middle of your car being stolen, just 3 feet away from him, he never once came over to ask how it was going, what he could do to help. Can he bring you something cold to drink. When you said 'I am dying of thirst,' all he said is 'there is water fountain around the corner.'

"But when the old lady came in with her coupons and asked for his help he gave her 20 minutes of devoted attention. That is what he likes to do. This is why it is easy for the kids to get past him with the stuff they have shoplifted.

"And Jim had parked the open convertible Mustang right in the middle. Just the way they would walk out of Frys to leave and go home.

"It was too tempting. They really hadn't gotten that big a bang out of shoplifting. They knew how to start the car without the key and all 4 got in and drove off. They never intended to keep the car, they just wanted the excitement of going for a ride in it.

"They timed their joy ride perfectly. The policeman didn't finally arrive till 11. They drove it for an hour and then parked it all the way in that dark corner of the gas station by Grant Boulevard. Then they all dashed across the street.

"They had a banner morning but you and Jim did not.

"Jim likes shopping at Frys at 9 am on Saturday

morning, but this is the same time the kids are in Frys shoplifting. It is too tempting to leave an open convertible Mustang in full view like that.

"I suggest from now on you take the red truck. It is so dilapidated looking now, it will not catch anyone's eye. An old faded pick-up. A dime a dozen in Tucson.

"Also it will make everything easier just piling in the groceries in back of truck.

"Then Jim can move his stuff to the Mustang while you are bringing your stuff into the house. He won't have to sit there worrying about his ice cream and ice pops melting.

"He can just take off in the Mustang as soon he puts his own stuff in it.

"He can park truck close to house so it is shorter walk for you back and forth with your groceries.

"Plus when he drives the truck you pay attention to what he is doing with gears and pedals. It helps your driving awareness.

"The manager is a tremendously nice man, he was tremendously nice to you and Jim. But it was a huge thing which happened and he said it almost never happens.

"He should have instantly brought you over ice cold cokes without you having to pay for it. And bought you a pack of cigarettes and Jim a pack of cigars. He has all the stuff right there.

"He should have tried to make you both a little more comfortable while you sat there half an hour waiting for police to arrive.

"Although Jim was totally appreciative when he offered to put his groceries in freezer while waiting for the cops.

"The girl policeman was a total sweetheart, but it is never good to be too compulsive about rules. She should have been willing to take your little book. It only costs the same as an Archie comic book. That is hardly police corruption!"

Email from Layla later that afternoon

From: Layla
Subject: Re: very big drama in Frys parking lot this morning

Yes Jim told me in the pool. He was in very altered mood about all this and you not wanting to sign the paper left him bewildered.

I had such a laff at all the weirdness.

The swim was refreshing and Jim's puzzled face was great.

Love you Layla

Jim wonders how Bill ever put up with me

Emails with Jimmy

Jimmy grew up in Flatbush Brooklyn, we walked our dogs together on Lower East Side of Manhattan, now he lives in Margaretville NY

Sunday August 14

My banner morning

Hi Jimmy

My friend Jim drove me out to Corona Road by airport for my driving lesson today.

The driving lesson went spectacularly well.

And I saw a one year old coyote running and jumping in the desert next to me.

I was in bliss.

What a perfect morning, coyote pup and great driving lesson

I am the happiest girl in USA

Love, Annie

From: Jimmy
To: Anne

How thrilling must have been the puppy coyote...all i get up here is deer doe...

the coyotes are very shy...usually you'll hear them feeding their young at night...

love
jimmy

From: Anne
To: Jimmy
Re: coyote pup looked one year old..

Yes Jimmy seeing him was the most thrilling experience in my whole life.

It was about 10 am and was not boiling hot yet.

The road went thru desert on both sides.

He was crossing the road. When he went back to the first side of road there was barbed wire. He easily and gracefully jumped it like a gazelle.

It was a thing of beauty watching him jump.

His youth was outstanding.

I knew right away how young he was, not only from his size (I was in Tompkins Square Park so many times when someone arrived with their new german shepherd mix they had just adopted from pound).

But you felt his youth because there was a sense of play about him.

You knew he was out playing, you knew he was out in the morning to play.

That was what he was doing

just playing

like children hanging out on Saturday morning

that sense of freedom

Yes he did seem shy. I talked to him in love talk, I called him endearments. I didn't call him over, just called out words of love to him.

I won't say he ignored me but I guess he did.

He just gamboled a bit in the desert after he jumped the barbed wire the whole time I was calling out love words to him. Of course he stayed close to where I could see him.

And only finally at end he slipped thru barbed wire and came onto the street where I was.

Perhaps if I had not been in truck he would have found me more interesting. But in any case it sure made my day.

Love, Annie

To: Jimmy
Subject: I tell Jim Yiddish joke on Corona Road

Hi Jimmy

When we arrived at Corona Road Sunday morning so I could drive on a road and not around and around Mervyns empty parking lot, when Jim and I changed seats so I would be in drivers seat,

He said "this will give you a chance to have the *vind* in your face."

Where this boy who has never been out of Arizona in his life learned *vind* is Yiddish pronunciation of wind I have no idea.

When he said "you will like a chance to have the *vind* in your face," I busted out giggling.

I said "When I was 7 years old my parents moved from Riverside Drive to a housing project in Flushing which had just been built.

"Everyone else moved there from the Lower East Side which is a Jewish neighborhood.

"On rainy days my friends and I sat in the hall together and told knock knock jokes.

"They learned the knock knock jokes on the Lower East Side, I had never heard one. This is the very first knock knock joke I ever heard in my life.

"Knock knock" I said to Jim.

"Who's there?" Jim said

"The **VIPER!**" I said

"The viper who?" Jim said

"The **VINDOW VIPER!**" I said.

And I cracked up for 5 minutes.

Jim groaned and said "it is going to be a long Sunday and he will have to take a whole bottle of tranquilizers after my lesson."

But Jimmy I heard that joke at 7 years old and completely forgot about it till I was in the middle of the desert on the outskirts of Tucson in coyote land on Sunday morning.

It tickled my funny bone to shriek out *the vindow viper*.

I was still laughing when I tried to remember my concentration to push clutch in all the way, step on gas lightly, lightly let clutch out and start the truck.

Love, Annie

I drive a lot and love every instant

But big fight before lesson starts

Well today's driving lesson was sensational.

I drove a lot and loved every instant of it.

Of course I am still very amateurish at all the changing of gears at stop sign, at light, etc.

Hahaha there is so much to remember to do for stopping at stop sign that one time the one thing I forgot to do was to stop.

Jim said "that's ok you didn't hit nothing."

I said "good."

Which for some reason cracked him up. That my response was such an off hand "good" at being told "you didn't hit nothing."

But I was so happy to be actually driving, and driving long distance for me, that I didn't care that I still fumble around and am not so good at all the mechanics yet of stopping and starting with clutch.

I'll get better in time.

The lesson began off with a huge drama.

I had printed up my story about car missing in Frys parking lot for my neighbor Teresa and her husband Floyd.

Teresa was born here in South Tucson, she is Mexican. Floyd was born in Minnesota, his parents are immigrants from Norway.

They married when Teresa was 16 (if she was 16 yet or she fibbed and told them she was already 16).

When they built their house Tucson did not go up this far. It was all pristine desert. Teresa told me "all there was were coyotes, bob cats, javelinas." They had to drive long distance to market.

Teresa spent her whole life as check-out girl in Safeway, they are unionized so Teresa always had good job.

And one of their sons is now a manager at a Frys supermarket.

Now that they are both retired Floyd does the shopping and he goes to same Frys I do for his shopping.

I thought they would both enjoy reading a story where they know every inch of it and the people involved, etc.

So I said to Jim "I'll drive truck out of driveway and up Arcadia Street to Teresa and Floyd's house. It is just one block up."

Doing the U turn (they are on other side of road) turned out to be endless process since I didn't give myself enuf space originally.

And so I had to reverse, turn, and go.

It took 40 steps. Motor would go off. Clutch in to turn motor on. Clutch in. Reverse. Clutch in to go to First.

Jim could have driven us all the way to Corona Road by airport in the time it took me to turn around truck in front of Teresa's house.

Finally I succeeded and slipped story thru their fence.

So then God suggested I drive truck to Swan Road (at end of my street) and let Jim drive us to Corona Road.

But Jim refused to get out of passenger seat.

He said "Drive us to Corona Road you can do it."

It was very early Sunday morning, not a car on the road.

But lots of freeways and huge streets to get there.

God told me "No way!"

I said to Jim "God said you drive us to Corona Road and then I'll drive, but I should drive you on Arcadia Street all the way to Swan."

Jim said "Fuck God! I am your instructor! I'm telling you to drive us to Corona Road. You can do it! There's not a car on the road. You have to listen to your instructor!"

"I won't!" I said, "I listen to God."

"Fuck God" Jim said again "I don't care what God says."

"Well I listen to God" I said. "Get out! you can walk back to my house."

I tried to pick him up as I was driving back to my house, but he stubbornly refused to get back in truck.

In my driveway we switched places.

And he drove us to Corona Road.

It was not such a fun ride because he spent the whole ride proving to me he was right.

"You see there's not a car on the road, you could have done it!"

I tried to sweet talk him and distract him to another topic.

"I dreamt last night that Bill and I were offered an apartment in NYC, and I was considering taking it.

"Having both a house in Tucson and apt. in NYC.

"In my dream Bill and I were talking it over.

"I wonder what NYC symbolizes? Since in real life I have zero desire to move to NYC.

"But in dream I was very interested in the idea."

That took us to Corona Road.

We had wonderful drive. I took us on Los Rialles Road (off Corona Road) for a long drive. And then another road which branched off Los Rialles for another long drive.

Since Jim had never been on these country roads which go nowhere, he found it interesting.

And he loved it that I was so happy and enjoying it so much.

At the end we were back on Corona and I had to do another U turn.

"O no! Another U turn! Another 40 steps! And this time there is traffic, they are going to hate me," I said to Jim.

But I did it in 6 steps, I am getting addicted to U turns, it is suspenseful.

Drive back was fine, he was very proud of me.

Altho the fight took it all out of him, he said "refill his prescription for tranquilizers." And again I am called "a pissy pupil!"

God talked all kinds of love talk to Jim before we switched seats for ride home.

I have no idea what to think about the big drama.

I could care less that Jim says "fuck God," but at some point I hope he realizes I will do what God says, not what he says.

But the driving itself was totally swell and that made up for everything.

Anne loves her drive

The next day

God talks to Jim on phone again

Hi Robin,

God is serious about no more locking horns in the car. He doesn't want any more of it.

Jim is stubborn tho. This morning God had me call Jim and said He will talk to him on phone.

It was very interesting for me to listen to the conversation between the two of them. Jim started off impenetratably stubborn.

I wondered where it would go since I knew God would not back down.

It was clear all during the early part of conversation Jim had no intention of backing down at all. He was not one bit fazed that he was talking to God, he did not intend to back down. But I knew God would not.

So I was very interested hearing the conversation.

Basically the first part of the conversation was God

reiterating He does not want any more locking of horns in the car.

Jim's response was basically to brush it off and dig in his heels deeper. It was clear Jim just intended to ignore God and was ready to end the conversation.

There wasn't any movement at all in the conversation (hahaha they locked horns) until God said

"I don't care that you said 'Fuck God.' You can say Fuck God from here to tomorrow. You can say Fuck God day and night, I am not a baby you can say Fuck God as much as you want, I could care less. And Anne is not a baby either, you can say Fuck God from today till tomorrow and Anne could care less either.

"I just do not want you and Anne locking horns in the car."

That changed the entire dynamic. Because at that point Jim fully engaged in the conversation.

Jim said "I want her to learn something new in each lesson. That will give her confidence."

God said "Do you know where confidence comes from?"

He did not press Jim to come up with answer. Instead He answered it.

He said "Confidence comes when Anne finally relaxes and does it and sees that she does it, then she has confidence. And then she makes progress.

"Confidence is what makes her progress possible. You have reached a plateau where for first time Anne has confidence and first time she is making progress.

"This did not happen for first 4 months because she dreaded her lesson and always hoped you would oversleep and cancel the lesson."

Jim giggled at that.

God said "No matter what we can't return to Anne dreading her lesson and hoping you oversleep and cancel the lesson."

God said "Yes you accurately judge what her abilities are but you do not understand her feelings. Only I can know her feelings because I live inside her mind. I live inside everyone's mind. I don't want Anne to do what she is not comfortable doing, I don't want her to be anxious.

"Last lesson for first time she enjoyed it. She was relaxed, she had confidence, she enjoyed driving, she had a ball."

So then Jim said all he wants is for Anne to have fun.

And God said "Yes, good thinking, we want Anne to

have fun."

And Jim said he does not want Anne to be uncomfortable.

And God said "Yes, let her be relaxed."

And then they had long detailed conversation about me learning how to stop at lights.

Jim told God "She has to learn to stop at the red light and to stop at the line."

Since I had no idea what the line was, I tuned out during the long detailed conversation about what I had to learn.

I had been up all night worrying about how this would be resolved.

Since I knew God would not give in, and knew Jim would not give in

But it was resolved (at least in the phone call) by the end of it.

Love and kisses, Annie

From: Robin
To: Anne

A good conversation! I hope it translates into real life!

From: Anne
To: Robin

O lovely Robin, thank you for this email.

And guess what! That phone conversation helped.

Jim and I had driving lesson at Mervyns parking lot this morning. For first time it was total joy for both Jim and me.

We were both so happy.

I drove so well.

We kibitzed and joked and teased each other the whole lesson, we were both so happy, so relaxed, and in such good spirits.

And Robin my driving really was top notch. I took those tight curves in parking lot exquisitely.

I was completely relaxed driving around parking lot, and confident too.

We were there so I could learn how to pull into and back out of one of their 3 trillion empty parking spots.

Of course I have not aced this, I am still learning.

But my new confidence paid off, I was so much more relaxed while trying to learn how to do it.

Which meant I learned faster.

Love, Annie

Anne is happy it all worked out

August 30th

Dirt roads

To: Jimmy in Margaretville
Sent: Tuesday, August 30, 5:06 PM
Subject: I am getting the hang of driving

Hi Jimmy

We went to Corona Road again this morning.

I drove the whole area including dirt roads.

I don't see why driving all that distance on dirt roads helped my driving but I had no idea they went on forever.

However Jim is enthusiastic about my driving on dirt roads. He thinks it is good I learn how to drive on a dirt road.

It is a very good thing I drove all over that area and had a ball doing it.

Of course there was no traffic, no lights, only 1 or 2 STOP signs.

But my confidence has reached a new plateau and I

think that is big.

Jim of course is out of his mind with joy.

It was exciting when I looked in the mirror and saw a car had started to pass me. I felt like a real driver.

I had fun driving. And the desert countryside is pretty.

The blue sky had a tint of purple in it. And the mountains in the distance looked charcoal with purple in it. It was very pretty. .

Love, Annie

From: Jimmy
To: Anne
Sent: Friday, September 02
Subject: dirt roads

the thing about dirt roads is that they can be somewhat unpredictable because of the roughness of the surface...

and it's good to become so accustomed to the unpredictability that it can feel ...

almost normal...

not really normal but you can handle the unpredictable as a matter of fact...

you sound like you're doing good at the wheel and liking it...

i'm taking care of joan's brother's dog while she and her brother are visiting their father...

i think she's a red bone hound...

her name is pogue...

it means something in czech...

his daughter spent her junior year there...

very nice red haired coat and an unusual face...

and overweight at three years...

she steals food...

margaretville is trying to put its self back together after hurricane Irene swept thru...

she destroyed almost the whole town...

we're lucky we're on a hill...

it's hard to find food...

and kingston which is about 50 miles away has no power…

i hope i don't starve to death...

if i do...

i'll send my love to you
now..jimmy

From: Anne
To: Jan
Subject: I had a wonderful Saturday

Saturday evening, Labor Day Weekend

Hi Jan

Jim and I had driving lesson in Mervyns parking lot this morning. To practice pulling into parking spots, because the store closed years ago there are gazillion spots.

I had a wonderful time, Jim and I teased each other and kidded around all thru lesson and I did so well in my lesson which of course delights Jim. I am making real progress now.

I even told him about the **Moment of Quantum Awakening**.

Naturally he had never heard of it.

I said "During it we'll all be given 2 choices, return to our bodies on earth or just be in Heaven.

"Of course I will want to be with Bill in Heaven."

"Not before you take your driving test!!!" he roared.

Last night Layla had prophetic dream it could happen any night now.

"It could even be tonight," she was told.

But I asked my Higher self and She said "the earliest would be 6 months from now."

It is only fair to Jim I take my Drivers Test before it happens.

Love and kisses, Anne

I tell Jim about the Mass Awakening

September 15th

the mystery of it all

How does a girl from New York City who can do nothing at all.

Who had a husband who could do everything.

And did everything for her.

Manage having a house in Tucson?

LOL!! Yesterday morning the phone went off, the technician from Cox arrived when Jim got me back from pool.

Before we left for pool Jim was on phone with Cox technician for whole hour on his cell phone.

Trying to fix it without sending techie to house.

Troy (the Cox techie) had Jim find all 3 of my phones, disconnect them, pull out plug, pull out phone connection etc.

Jim assumed the one on my desk went to my computer

so I pulled out computer and Jim tried to see where the telephone plugged into it.

Turns out Jim didn't realize I have cable internet, phone is not connected to computer.

But Cox techie was so happy dealing with Jim on phone, who was technician for gas company here in Arizona for 20 years, rather than dealing with me.

He started out dealing with me and was so enthusiastic when I suggested "Jim is right here, he is the techie for the gas company."

Jim is the one who arrives in middle of night when there is gas leak or whatever.

He left that job before we became friends to take care of his mom.

Or he was fired for refusing to take the drug test.

Or was fired because he started a union.

Or some combination of all 3.

It was the job his dad had whole life before him, so Jim as a little boy went out on all the calls with his dad.

And the job Jim got when he graduated college.

Jim is really good at it but he said to Cox telephone guy, "I am a gas man, I know nothing about phones."

I still think he did fine.

He did whatever the guy said to do.

But none of it accomplished the job, with all 3 phones disconnected, it seems I had no service, because it appeared someone was talking on the phone.

So Cox guy, Troy, said he will send technician at 1 pm.

Jim instantly took me swimming, there was 40 minutes till pool closed.

And also took me for breakfast burrito and flan at take-out Mexican joint, Paco's.

Jim is a sweetie pie.

Robin, the phone technician arrived soon after I got home and ate my lunch.

He worked like a dog for 4 hours.

First on the outside box.

Then inside house.

Then on roof.

By 5 pm he got two phones to work, but the line to the one in my bedroom he could not get to work.

"That's OK, I don't need it" I said, "you were heroic."

Inadvertently it turned out while trying to open my front door, not the wood front door where Jim had replaced the doorknob. But the one with the metal lattices which lets in all the air.

That lock had busted years ago, Bill nailed in a carabineer so we could lock the door.

Well Robin inadvertently, while trying to open it, locked it.

Dog is barking hysterically, Robin has worked over 4 hours, I am ready for him to leave, at least I have a phone to call.

I go right in and call Jim "metal front door is locked, I can't get in or out, come right over!"

He arrives as Robin is leaving.

I've now had it! The dog locked in bedroom whole time because of his barking at Robin.

But of course while Robin was trying to fix the phone in my bedroom, I had to sit with Beanie in living room while he barked his head off.

Quelle drag!

I was holding Beanie by the collar, he won't settle down

When Robin leaves, at least I can let go of Beanie, he and Jim is huge love affair.

Jim tries using WD40.

And inserts a key that I think might be right one, it doesn't turn.

So we plan to buy new screen door to replace that

one this morning.

Meanwhile I cannot get into or out of my front door.

It is locked solid.

This morning I walk out back door, thru side gate.

I see Sharon, my angel, who lives across the way.

She said "Frank is not here, but Danny is."

She will call Danny.

Danny says he can come at 3:30 when he gets off work to put in my new screen door.

Caren's brother Jack is there with Sharon.

Jack comes over at 1 pm and says he knows a good locksmith, he calls Mitch on his cell. Mitch says he is on another job, will arrive between 1:30 and two.

Mitch picks the lock so it opens. WOW! I thought it would never open.

It was thrilling I could walk out my front door.

I put Beanie in bedroom.

Then he examined the lock, pronounced it totally broken, said "door was bought at Home Depot."

Who knew! I had called "The Door Man" in yellow pages when we first bought house 20 years ago.

Mitch said "they don't make replacement parts for this door, you need new handle and new lock."

He said "they put in the handle backwards, that is why it didn't fit, so they just jammed it in there."

I guess that is why it always dangled in that weird way.

"Look how loose it is!" he said, "you need a new door, this handle won't last much longer."

He takes out the lock for me because what if someone else arrives who doesn't know and inadvertently locks it! I will be up the creek again.

2 hours later Danny arrives, Sharon brings him over.

I say "Will you go to Home Depot for me and try to get a door like this one.

"And put it in.

"Here is $100 for the door, and $100 to put it in.

"If the door costs more than $100 I will give you more."

He comes back with a screen door.

It is a lot flimsier than the one which now has to be retired, which had iron lattices and iron frame etc.

This is plastic.

But Danny said "the only 2 choices now are this one or security door, the one you have is in the middle, they don't make it anymore."

I didn't want security door.

He made the right choice.

It came to $93.

"Keep the change" I said.

"I am so grateful you went to Home Depot for me and I didn't have to go with you."

He said "You better put dog in bedroom, it will be wide open the whole time."

"Good thinking!" I said, "I will stay in there with him, then he won't be so upset this time."

I honestly thought it would only take Danny an hour.

But of course there was *some problem*.

And the problem is what took up all the time.

(It took him hours.)

He was a saint to persevere and accomplish it.

The new screen door is so pretty, so much prettier than the other one (which was black and heavy).

Danny chose white for me which goes with the color Bill painted the house.

(When Bill bought the paint he said "it is the color of khakis." I guess he means those pants our dads wore when we were little. It is a nice color.)

I am just praying the door will be sturdy enuf for all the activity Beanie does when he has a fit at the door.

He likes to give Sharon's dog, Shiva, the dickens

when she is having her walkie.

Danny is an angel of course.

They all are, Sharon, Frank, Danny, Jack, and my Jim.

So I guess that is the answer to my question

"How can a girl who can do nothing

"Manage without her husband who did everything for her?"

The answer is the angels help her.

I love you

Annie

My wonderful friend Linda in NYC emails back

Amazing story. I am laughing now, as a NY girl myself who becomes unhinged with house disasters.

Great angels saved you.

Love, Linda

Sharon is my angel

Whenever I need help of any kind

Anne hits a flat

I turn around and there is Sharon with her dog
Shiva

Sharon

Last chapter of book

Back to driving

My baffling experience

Trying to drive in town

Sunday afternoon September 18th

ça marche (hahaha French for progress in my driving lesson this weekend)

Well what a trip!

We had not had lesson since before tv broke, before phone went out, before front screen door fell apart.

Yesterday at noon we did. At Mervyns.

I just drove around the empty parking lot, it is perfect way for me to break the ice after long break. I know that parking lot by heart now, so it was just nice for me to drive and drive and chat with Jim whole time.

I told him all about Selma as we were driving. Of all my friends back in NYC she was definitely the wildest.

I told Jim everything.

How much she loved her husband Gilbert.

How she always had lesbian girlfriend on the side during her marriage.

How she forged the doctor's signature on the prescriptions for her dexedrine.

We were both private secretary to a psychiatrist, we both had to write out Rx for patients for her to sign.

But Selma who loved her dexedrine, whenever her pills ran out, simply wrote out a new Rx for herself and because she is a genius artist, also did the doc's signature.

Selma is in Heaven now, so I can reveal her secrets.

So yesterday morning was very pleasant, just driving Jim around Mervyns parking lot for an hour.

Just the right amount of time for him to learn all about Selma.

Her wildness started at 16 years old because of her rebelliousness. Her father was from the old country and very strict. He said "you can't take the subway at night because you are a young woman, men will try to have sex with you."

So Selma rushed out, took the subway, met a young man on the train, and went home to his apartment and had sex with him.

I met Selma in women's lib of course. I wonder if I met all my wildest friends in women's lib.

She was a great artist and a wonderful friend, but we had major blow up when she visited me in Tucson a few years after we moved here. And she never talked to me after that... I haven't even mentioned her since then until I was in truck driving around Mervyns yesterday morning.

I don't know if Jim is interested hearing all about Selma. He lives and breathes for football, fast cars, and of course his favorite, flirting with hot blonds.

Altho when I got to the part in the story of Selma and the forged prescriptions where she had just handed the forged prescription to the druggist. And it turned out the man behind the counter with him was a Fed investigating his prescriptions.

The druggist turned to the Fed and said, "Look! this one just came in, what do you want me to do with it?"

Lucky for Selma, who must have been plotzing, the Fed didn't even look at it.

The druggist said to Selma "I'm busy now can you come back later."

Selma who is always cool as a cucumber just said "give it back to me, I'll come back tomorrow." And got out of there fast!

Jim who had zero interest in hearing about sex, lesbianism, drugs, forgery. Actually responded to hearing about Selma's forged prescription shown to the Fed who was investigating.

He grunted.

He only got interested when I told him Selma's experience taking her driving test.

He is completely 100 per cent involved in me learning to drive. All the way to the pool after Mervyns, driving is all he talked about. He pointed out how he popped clutch in neutral and coasted to red light. Etc.

I was Bill's wife a long time. I had to act in a way becoming to a wife. I have zero desire to return to being the wild girl I was when Bill met me.

But it is fun for me now to kick up my heels with Jim and laugh about it all.

My friend Selma is wild

And this morning I learned red lights..

Jim decided that it is time for me to learn how to stop at red lights. Alas the last thing which happened in my last driving lesson 2 weeks ago, we came to a major intersection at Valencia and I ran the red light.

It was my first red light after the tiny one, way out on Corona Road, which is just country road and no traffic.

Jim has not told a soul I ran that red light, and advises me "don't tell anyone, then no one will know."

I don't know why he thinks it is so tragic that I did this.

There is just too much involved with the clutch and changing gears with red lights. *So what* if the one thing I forgot to do is wait for it to turn green, before slowly and carefully made my way across the big intersection!

It was only on the other side that Jim informed me I had run a red light.

So he decided this morning we would both get up at 4 am and we would drive around Tucson so I could practice stopping at red lights.

He chose 4 am because there is no car nor person on road on Sunday morning at 4 am.

So we both got up at 4 am, but when he called I said "this is silly, why do I have to drive in pitch dark, can't I have a little light."

So he called again at dawn

Everything went fine for first half hour. But then we were heading back East and sun rose above the mountains. I was on Broadway, such a major street, lotsa cars and bicyclists and was totally blinded.

I kept changing to darker sunglasses. Nothing helped. The light was right in my eyes and blinded me. He wanted me to move to middle lane to be away from bicyclists.

But I just wanted to turn the wheel over to him. I can't believe I actually did drive half a mile totally blinded by the light. But finally he said "OK pull over" when I kept saying "I can't stand this."

So he drove to Columbus. How he drove in blinding light I don't know!

Since my Y is at the other end of Columbus and is driving north, not into the light, the idea was I would drive to my Y.

But I had sort of had it. Altho I had done fine (more or less) in the first hour, I did make mistakes. Plus I never once looked in any of my mirrors. I just let Jim do all the looking for me.

So instead of driving the 6 miles on Columbus to where my Y is, I said "why don't I just drive us home."

Bill's route back from the Y and to the Y was always to take a tiny back road between Columbus and Swan. So I know that tiny road by heart. And here it was right in front of me.

Yes a lot of booboos happened on the way. I was glad of so many stop signs for practicing stopping. But when engine went off, I couldn't get truck to start moving again after 5 tries.

But so what! By some crazy miracle I just sailed across Swan, disobeying everything Jim said to do, and was back on a tiny road behind my house.

I continued along it to first turn to Arcadia Street.

Turn on Arcadia and drove into my own driveway.

So I guess that's enuf excitement for today.

We got home at 7:30.

Hahaha Anne drove around Tucson for hour and half.

Monday evening   October 3

This morning's driving lesson was so sweet

Anne is happy

This morning's driving lesson was so sweet.

We are back to only once a week.

It means so little progress, but fits the rhythm of our lives right now better.

The era of sleepless nights seems to be winding down, but neither of us can count on having slept thru the night.

Either I am up all night and hope he cancels.

Or he is up all night and calls to cancel.

I guess this morning we both slept thru the night, because this morning a driving lesson happened.

He took me back to Corona Road so I could experience "vind" in my face.

The beauty of the morning was tremendous. The fat white clouds were all pearls. Every color of pearl was in them.

And they were dramatic too. Like living beings. So alive, so beautiful. So vivid!

The sky was lovely blue and the mountains off to the north as I was driving were gorgeous. The charcoal is now filled with purple.

It turns out I really do have to concentrate on the road while I am driving. I tried drinking in the beauty instead, but it doesn't work.

It was Monday morning, there was traffic, there were big trucks.

And Jim wanted me to keep up my speed because there were cars and trucks behind me. He didn't want my slowness to be a pain in the neck to them.

I was so relieved when we got to broken line so they could just pass me and I could drive at my own rate.

But the big difference between Monday morning,

today, and Sunday morning when we usually drive, there was almost always traffic behind me.

It was certainly not the relaxed driving I now do in Mervyns empty parking lot, where I know the route by heart and am the only one in it.

I have to pay attention every second.

I did get into trouble 3 times, all 3 times while doing U turns.

I didn't call the first two times "getting into trouble." On the ride home I said "I'm not sorry I got myself into hot water, it gave me a chance to practice what to do when I am in hot water."

"Yes" he said, "you did very well the 3 times you were in hot water.

"I was in hot water 3 times!" I exclaimed.

I was stunned.

I thought it only happened once.

I had been driving long, and there was a stop sign up ahead just before another road.

"What road is that?"

"Nogales Highway" he said.

"I don't want to drive on Nogales Highway."

"OK" he said, "do your U turn here."

It was just before the stop sign leading to Nogales Highway.

I pulled into the embankment to organize myself for the U turn.

I don't know what I did wrong but all of a sudden there I was in the middle of road with traffic in both directions, and huge trucks bearing down on me in both directions.

My foot was still on gas pedal but going very slowly.

I turned to Jim, "get me out of this!"

He reached over and steered the wheel for me out of it, so I was on the side of the road I wanted to be in the direction I wanted to be going.

As soon as I was driving again I said "I'm not mad at myself this happened. That is what you are here for.

"This is why I am not driving alone, I am driving with you sitting next to me.

"So if I need help you are here to help. If I get myself in trouble you are here to get me out of it."

Jim was impressed I did not panic at all but instead instantly said calmly "you do it!" and leaned back so he could reach across me to the driving wheel.

That is why on the way home I said "I think I did very well when I got into hot water."

And you can see why I was so surprised when Jim said "All 3 times you got in hot water you did very well."

I don't consider the other two times hot water. They were just two times I was doing a U turn and had trouble with it. Had to go thru 7 steps before I finally got it.

But neither of those times was I stretched across the road with trucks bearing down on me in both directions. I didn't have to have Jim get me out of it. I just patiently kept at it till I got it.

But it turns out all the times I had flounced out of the car, sat on curb and smoked cigarette, mostly in Mervyns parking lot but once on Corona Road, Jim had not realized I was just having a temper tantrum. He thought it was because I had panicked.

The result is he is constantly proud of me now for NOT panicking!!

I always hear how wonderful I am this time for *not* panicking.

Let the boy enjoy himself.

It gives him so much pleasure to remark on how much progress I made this time because I did not panic.

The Y was closed today so he took me to Fort Lowell pool.

I hadn't been back in a year.

It was wonderful to arrive and there were Aveya and Fred with their faces flooded with love for me.

When I said to the lifeguard "I don't have my card," she said "that's ok Annie go right in."

She was so happy to see me.

I had forgotten about the flooring beauty of that pool. High up by the mountains. With those stunning clouds in full view. And the mountains so gorgeous. And that huge pool with so much deep water.

It was paradise.

I swam in the deep water and then chatted with Aveya and Fred in the shallow water. It was so nice to be chatting with them again.

Jim picked me up when pool closed an hour later.

"Let's go to Paco's for tacos" I said, "my treat."

Paco's is around the corner from pool, it is take-out fast food Mexican.

I ordered two tacos, rice and beans, a side of guacamole. And a flan. Jim just got a burrito.

He did drive-in by the window.

He was chatting with the Mexican girl at the window, she was handing him the order and the change.

He said to her "she's a meshuginar."

The Mexican girl said "what?"

He said again referring to me "she's a meshuginar."

I cracked up all the way home. I couldn't stop laughing. I said "I can't believe you said meshuginar to the Mexican girl."

I had taught Jim 3 Yiddish words when we were driving around Mervyns few days ago. I taught him meshuginar, pupik, and schmacta.

"Hand me my schmacta" I said when I got first got in the drivers seat. I keep a scarf in the truck to tie around my head to keep the hair out of my eyes while I drive.

"What's a schmacta?" he said

"When I was in high school each time I bought a new dress my mom said *I can't believe you spent all that money for this schmacta!*"

I really don't know what pupik means. I said "I only heard it when my mother said *You're wearing your dress up to your pupik!*"

As I said to Jim "I hope it just means belly button but it sure sounds dirty."

I said to Jim "my father always called out *who wants the pupik* when my mother served roast chicken for supper."

But I realized as we were driving around Mervyns parking lot two days ago, I said to Jim "how can a chicken have a belly button?"

"That's right" Jim said, "they are born from eggs."

So we both agreed it must mean something dirty.

Instantly it became his favorite word. He has big smile when he says it, but he blends it with schmacta, the other word I had just taught him so it comes out schmookit.

He is so proud of himself when he says it, his eyes glitter, and he has huge smile.

He loves knowing his dirty word in Yiddish, but it takes me a while to figure out schmookit is how Jim is saying pupik.

On the other hand he is brilliant with meshuginar.

Absolutely he is as good as Bill was at it, and it was Bill's favorite word.

I think he is as good as me at it.

He really took to meshuginar like a duck to water. He was brilliant at it the first time he said it, and he never lost it.

He uses it all the time in conversation with me now.

I'm constantly being called a meshuginar.

But I tell you it blew my mind when he said it to the

Mexican girl at the drive-in counter at Paco's this morning. All I could think was "I hope Leon Geller (that is my dad) is watching this from Heaven."

When I learned meshuginar at his knee when I was 4 years old on Riverside Drive I'm sure he never imagined Jim would now be saying it to the Mexican girl at take out window at Paco's.

This is Jim's dream for me, he wants me to be the girl behind the wheel

Jim has a laugh

Last week's lesson was practicing how to reverse and turn in Mervyns parking lot. Jim tried to tell me how to do it.

"Don't tell me how to do it! I know how to do it!" I said.

After 12 tries and failing, I said "OK maybe I will try it your way."

"There's a thought," he said and burst out laughing

"Well your way worked," I said to Jim.

"Big surprise!" he said..

Anne tells Jim maybe I will try it your way

Friday October 14th 8 pm

My baffling experience

Email to a friend

I am baffled by this experience, so if you have any ideas please tell me.

My neighbor rents out rooms in her house.

One of her boarders was Bill's karate teacher when we went to the Club.

Odysseus, that is his name, is such a fine individual that when he showed up at my front door the other evening asking if I would like to rent him a room,

I said he could have Bill's room and I don't want any money.

I know so much about him because Bill told me all about him when he took karate from him.

But I guess he knows nothing about me, because when he came over to talk to me about it (before we went inside so he could see the house, when we were sitting in backyard so Beanie could get used to him.)

He asked me if I use hard drugs, if I use alcohol.

I told him I am a cigarette smoker, I don't drink or use drugs.

Then he asked me if I expected our relationship to be sexual as he would not want that.

I was completely taken aback. I would never have invited him to have Bill's room, if I wasn't absolutely sure the idea of sex would not cross his mind.

Because he doesn't know me at all, he thought it was in my mind.

I haven't cleared out Bill's room at all, plus I pulled everything out of his closet to find his rifles to give them to Jim.

And I never bothered putting all the stuff back in.

So it is a huge mess

Odysseus was appalled, understandably so.

He said he would want to pull out the carpet, he doesn't like carpet.

I said fine, but after he left when he said he will think about it, and how maybe we would try it out and see if it works,

I thought it is the only room which still has carpet in it, because that carpet was pristine, Bill vacuumed it and kept it immaculate and the room was not used too much.

Of course it looks like a mess now because I have not cleaned that room at all.

But all it would take for carpet to be pristine again, is good vacuuming, but Odysseus said he doesn't like carpet.

The next morning when I woke up I wasn't sure it was a good idea, I would not want the carpet pulled up if he is going to leave shortly.

Odysseus on his own had come up with the idea that he would do some of the work Bill had planned to do on the house to repay me for not having to spend a penny to live here.

He asked me what were Bill's plans for the house, and I told him.

But I didn't get a chance to say that no way do I expect him to do that, I had planned to pay someone to do that somewhere along the line.

I understand now that when I offered Bill's room to him, he wanted to know what I wanted in return.

It would have been better if he just asked me.

Since I wasn't expecting anything in return, except

that he would help me clear out Bill's room to get it ready for him.

But it all became too rushed at the end when we started to talk about practical things, he was late for work.

And said he wouldn't be able to return to talk to me about it for 2 days.

It's just not the way I operate, I would not have wanted to drag out this decision for a whole week.

I had made the offer in good faith because I knew he would be fine person for a roommate, and it seemed like a friendly thing to do on my part, I had a room I wasn't using at all.

And it seemed nice for me to have someone else living here again.

And I thought he could do little favors, like if I wasn't strong enuf to move something he could help me move it.

I never had in my mind he would do work.

It simply seemed like a friendly thing to do that would work out nice for both of us.

I found out from my neighbor today, that he wants to move out of her house, and they also want him to move out.

It has been happy for 3 years but it stopped working.

But when she decided to rent out all her rooms for boarders, she went all out to make all the rooms beautiful.

I guess Odysseus was expecting that.

Bill had just started renovating his bathroom, pulled out the linoleum tiles, and it is all ugly floor underneath.

Odysseus was appalled when he saw it, plus Bill's stuff was still in it.

Maybe nothing was thought thru properly.

When Odysseus came to door to ask if I wanted to rent a room in my house to him, I said "Bill's room is here, you can have it and he has his own bathroom, but I don't want any money."

I am perplexed at how badly it all went since it was my Higher Self's idea to me two months ago to invite Odysseus to live here.

My Higher Self said it would be friendly for him and friendly for me, and when I hear a noise in the middle of the night I wouldn't have to worry because a karate master is living here.

So when Odysseus came to the door few nights ago and asked if I would like to rent a room to him, I told him I had the same idea but I don't want money.

I am perplexed at how it turned out, that Odysseus is

so appalled that my house is in no condition for him to just move in happily right away.

I think he was also appalled that whole house was dusty and the huge back living room which Bill had started to renovate, was in bad shape.

Bill had pulled up the whole carpet, threw it out. But it's all in the middle of work being done. He had planned to paint the floor and paint the room and do other things to make it beautiful, meanwhile it looks like a mess...

Odysseus was here in the afternoon day before yesterday. He left in big hurry because of being late for work.

If he had said "we will continue to discuss it at the soonest possible moment," I would have agreed.

But because it sounded like it would not be for two days, when I woke up the next morning I wrote note "let's call it off."

I had to write a note because he sleeps till 11 am and then has to rush off for work.

I wrote "I am willing to reconsider and hear his ideas, but if he wants me to reconsider he has to leave me a note right away saying 'I would like you to reconsider.'

"Because I don't like decisions to take forever. I like

to decide and then move forward on them whichever decision it is."

I wrote "I am open to reconsidering if you have ideas, but you must leave a note in my door saying that is what you want."

Since there was no note all day yesterday I figure we both wanted to back out of it.

That we both realized it was an idea which would not work.

It's best for him to find a nice room and nice bathroom, and just pay rent.

I spent a month in Bill's room recently, and it has many lovely features, the west window, you can see the sunset, it is the only room in house that the beautiful sunset you can see.

And the tree outside it has birds singing all day and all evening.

And the southern window gets the sun, which makes it bright and warm in winter.

It is really so much nicer than the garage which my neighbor Caren had transformed into a room for boarders, altho she had put in expensive Mexican tile.

If Odysseus had been able to overlook the mess and

the carpet, and understood what those two windows faced, he could have known it was a little room in paradise.

But to him it was just awful.

I am sure he is as satisfied as I am that I called it off.

I am just so perplexed why my Higher Self pushed me into it to begin with.

My Higher Self had told me there's so much we could offer each other, and it was a great idea, which is why I was ready to commit to the idea before Odysseus even knocked on my door to ask for it.

But I think if my Higher Self had really wanted it to take place, it would have been worked out so it would happen.

Instead of it working out so it won't happen.

Altho the second I wrote Odysseus that note saying "I am calling it off," I sure did get to appreciate having the house to myself.

So maybe that was the purpose, so I would notice all the nice things about having the house to myself.

If you have any ideas about all this I sure would like to hear them. Since as you can understand, it is a baffling experience to me.

Love, Annie

October 18th

My Higher Self explains it to me

Communicated from my Higher Self

Anne had not planned to tell this experience in email. Instead the urge to tell it and hear feedback was so strong the first day after it all happened (after she had written the note to Odysseus that morning and received no response, so she knew it was all over, he was not going to move in).

That afternoon she tried to call her friend Helen on the phone. But when she received Helen's voice mail, she said "I had a strange experience I want to tell you about it but it will take 20 minutes, so wait until you have time to talk on phone before you call me."

She knew how busy Helen is and really didn't think she would call back for almost a week. So she put the urge to talk about it on the phone out of her mind.

So she clicked on the computer and there was an email from her friend Larry in Texas. He and his partners (his partners live in Georgia) own an apartment complex in

Austin which Larry manages.

His email to Anne said he did not have a good day, he is upset he had to do an eviction.

This is the second time he wrote Anne about having to do an eviction and how upset it makes him, but he has partners he is responsible to and when tenants don't pay their rent he has to do it.

The first time he wrote that to Anne several months ago, I went all out to compose an email for Anne to write back to him to take away his guilt and give him peace.

I explained how the soul of each individual is responsible for the experiences which come into their life, and their souls had arranged the circumstances so they would be evicted.

And Larry doesn't know the circumstances, they could be a husband or a wife who left their marriage pushing them into returning to it. It could be that the place they would move to when they were evicted had an opportunity for them.

The email made him feel better and I was glad and so was Anne.

But now we see 2 months later he had forgotten everything I had Anne put in that email and was upset all over again.

So I gave Anne the words to say it again but this time shorter. I simply had Anne write "you don't know their destiny, and you may be the instrument Heaven is using so they will move on with their destiny."

But because Larry is a landlord and has tenants, he has so much experience in this, I had Anne tell him the whole story.

I thought it would help him move his mind about being upset about doing an eviction that day, that it would interest him, and he may say something helpful to Anne. It is his department in life.

So I had Anne write it all out in email to him and send it.

After that I said to Anne "now that the whole story is already written in email, you can send it to your friend Helen, you don't have to wait till she calls you back to tell her the story."

And after she did that, I suggested a few other of Anne's friends who might have helpful input which would help Anne. Since she was totally baffled by the whole experience on every level.

And she received a few emails back about it and two phone calls, one from Jan, and from Helen last evening.

She got an email back right away from her friend Linda in New York City who said Odysseus had been too abrupt with Anne.

Which helped Anne immeasurably, since she had the experience, but didn't know how to describe it and didn't know there was a word for it. And Linda had the word for it.

All the emails helped Anne. As a result she understood her experience, she understood her feelings, she understood what happened.

And when Helen did call back yesterday evening, although by that time Anne was over it, it was still very helpful what Helen said about Odysseus. Helen's son lives at home plus his friend is now staying there too.

And Helen explained how easy the friend is to live with. And Odysseus would not be easy to live with.

And Larry's email from the point of landlord and tenant was very helpful too.

Altho Anne had not anticipated at all that Odysseus would carry out the renovation which Bill had intended, and cut out most of it when Odysseus asked to be shown what it was and planned to do it, Larry said in Austin a room in house with a bathroom goes for 850 a month,

Odysseus should do that work in return for getting it for free.

And Anne had also planned to let Odysseus use all her utilities for free too, she had not planned to charge one penny.

Electric, gas, cable tv, cable internet, telephone, plus she would not need the heat for herself in winter, it does not reach to her back room, but she said to me "how can Odysseus come home late at night to ice cold house!" she planned to heat that side of house so he would have heat to walk into house. And wake up in morning to warm house, and pay electric for his space heater.

Larry was right when he wrote Anne it is an incredibly generous offer.

Which made Anne feel better because even tho it was not something I had suggested at all to Anne, Odysseus had offered it on his own, but it was splendid offer on his part, sure Anne would have loved it!

And it is an idea which might have worked because Odysseus might have preferred doing something in return, instead of it all being a gift.

Altho when Odysseus first left after visiting the house.

When Anne was reeling from the experience, to help

Anne, because Odysseus had been so pushy and so dominating in so many ways, I said to Anne "he would be a guest/roommate."

I wanted to make it clear to Anne, Odysseus was a guest, he does not control what goes on in the house. It is her house, he is the guest. Because Anne sure didn't feel like that when he left.

He was way too take-charge for Anne. She felt like it was his house or they were co-partners in the house which was never what I intended.

Anne felt like it was no longer her home. So I said "guest/roommate" to help Anne understand his role.

What had appalled Anne although she did not write this in her email is when he looked at Bill's room and said "the thing for her to do is take all Bill's stuff to the dump."

Anne had pulled all the stuff out of Bill's closet to find all the rifles to give to Jim. Bill had a few rifles of his own but when his friend Mike left for Florida on the bus he had given Bill all his rifles.

And there was an ammo box in there too. It was a small closet, all of Bill's clothes had been on top of that. Anne had just pulled them all out, they were still sitting on floor by the bed by the closet in a clump.

But most of the clothes were brand new or only worn once because Bill lived in bermuda shorts and T shirts.

Anne said to Odysseus when he suggested she bring them all to the dump, "but I planned to give them to charity."

"But they are dirty," Odysseus said, "no one wants dirty clothes."

Anne was still very reluctant.

So finally he said "why don't you call and ask."

Anne was still reluctant.

"OK" he said, "I'll make the phone call."

"No" Anne said, "you'll call up and say 'do you want dirty clothes' and they will say no.

"I'll ask my Higher Self what to do about Bill's stuff, that is the best way."

Anne had started to right there, saying it all aloud, her question and my answers but Odysseus was late for work. He had to leave.

"This is a good beginning," he said.

"You don't have to decide right away," Anne told him at the door, "you have as much time as you want."

"Thank you," he said

It was still in middle of me relaying my answers to

Anne when Odysseus absolutely had to leave, he was late for work, "I have to go but you can continue talking to your Higher Self after I leave," he said.

Odysseus was trying to be kind and sensitive, as he had all along. His big problem was he didn't know what to be kind and sensitive about.

When he had first arrived, when they were sitting in the yard and he hadn't seen the house he asked Anne if he could do her chart so he could do compatibility chart to see if they are compatible.

He knocked himself out to be sensitive about this. "Maybe you don't believe in astrology or you have objections to astrology" etc etc etc.

Of course Anne was delighted, she is an astrologer, she loves astrology. Mary Anne at the club had told her both she and Odysseus are into astrology and the 3 of them should all bring their charts and do them together.

When Anne first discovered last year Odysseus was living next door to her she rushed over to ask if they can do astrology together. That was the only conversation they had ever had before he arrived in her yard and house the other day.

But Odysseus had not been responsive to the idea.

"Who is Mary Anne?" he asked. And obviously he had forgotten all about it if he was so circumspect about asking for Anne's birth date so he could do a compatibility chart.

On the other hand when sensitivity was called for, he should not have bluntly suggested she take all of Bill's stuff to the dump.

And sensitivity was also called for when Anne had said he could stay in that huge room in middle of house while they cleared out Bill's room for him.

Anne said "do you want this to be your room instead?"

Odysseus said "yes.'

"But you'd have no privacy," Anne said, "there are no doors."

"That's easy I will put up a curtain."

But Anne thought it over and said "I would not like to be denied access to half my house."

It upset Anne that Odysseus wanted it and would have accepted it if she had said yes. Because all of Anne's thought, she was thinking with me.

What I am trying to say is I was thinking for both Anne and Odysseus, what would work for both of them, being fair to both of them, making them both happy. This was the mind behind Anne's thinking.

But clearly it wasn't behind Odysseus' thinking if he would gladly take something which denied Anne access to half her house. It was a selfish thought, it did not take Anne into account at all.

This is why it disturbed Anne.

Actually it disqualified her trust in him.

And this was immediately followed by "take all of Bill's stuff to the dump."

The only thing he said when he first looked at the room was he would want to take up the carpet.

Anne had said OK. But when he had mentioned later on "we can try it out for a while and if it does not work out I'll leave."

Anne thought "then İ will have no carpet in here and I like having carpet."

Altho that didn't really hit Anne till the next morning.

What hit her when they were both in the house, is it felt wrong when Odysseus wanted to appropriate that huge living room which is 9/10s of the other wing of house.

Actually that other wing of house is just that huge living room, Bill's bathroom, and Anne's bedroom. All Anne would have left of whole other wing of house is her bedroom. The whole wing would be his territory except for her back bedroom.

It would turn into Anne having a bedroom in Odysseus' wing of the house. And that wing of house is as big as the original house. It really is giving Odysseus half of her house, minus one room in it for Anne.

Anne did not know why she turned off Odysseus at that point, she stopped being happy about the idea, she became unhappy about the idea. It is because she lost trust in him.

And never in one million years should he have said right after that "throw all of Bill's stuff in the dump."

And then to go on about how dirty all Bill's stuff is. Which is not true. Bill was always washing his clothes.

And then as he was leaving to say "I have to go but you can go right on talking to your higher self."

Anne understood he was late for work, he had wanted to leave before because of time for work, she had asked for few minutes to consult me about what to do with Bill's stuff. It was taking longer than she thought.

This is a big question. There is other stuff in Bill's closet, her mom had sent all her dad's cameras when her dad went to Heaven and sent her dad's old books. And Bill's fishing rods were in there too.

I had started to say what do with all the stuff. "Give

the cameras to Jim, he says he can get good money for those cameras from the 1940s, just give the books to charity."

That is when Odysseus said "I have to leave but you can go on talking to your higher self."

And at the door he said "we accomplished a lot, it was very good, I'll come back in 2 days and we will continue."

And Anne was completely upset and completely unhappy.

The idea of it being 2 whole days before conversation continued, so she would have to stay in this state of mind with no clarity at all was unbearable to her. The conversation should have continued as soon as possible. This had to be resolved. Nothing was resolved.

LOL it was all a big mess.

And Anne was stunned that Odysseus had given permission for her to continue talking to me without him being there. She talks with me 24/7.

He hadn't meant it to come out that way.

He didn't know what he was saying, he was late for work and wanted to leave on a considerate note.

Everything about it was wrong. It's not Odysseus' fault, he was too rushed. But bringing me into the conversation and the decision making was exactly the right thing to do. It should have been done much earlier before they tried to do it without me.

They both did a poor job without me. Anne was way too acquiescent and just said yes to everything he said. And he did not know how to take Anne into consideration at all.

LOL a Higher Mind was really called for, and I was right there eager to help.

But Odysseus is always rushed, always late for work. He teaches karate at many various clubs. And goes there on his bicycle, he does not like cars. He is always late for work.

It was handled all wrong. There should have been enough time and I should have been brought in right from the get-go when talk about decisions was made.

This is not something you undertake in a rush. And then don't get back to it for another 2 days, just keep it hanging on. That works for no one, it totally upsets Anne and is not good for Odysseus even if is the way he is used to doing things.

Bill had taken karate from Odysseus when he was at the club. All Bill did was sing Odysseus' praises. So before that conversation inside the house, Anne was 100 per cent for Odysseus, in her mind he was perfect. Anne's respect for Bill's mind is to the skies. If Bill esteemed Odysseus that highly, that settled it for Anne.

It was never open to question.

That boy will never know how gung ho Anne was for him when he first came over to talk about moving in.

She treated him like a prince.

The next morning Anne woke up so upset and disturbed, I communicated a letter for her to bring over. Since we both knew Odysseus doesn't wake up till 10:30 am and rushes off to work.

Anne didn't want to wait around that long, she gets up at dawn. And then he would have no time for her to even say two words.

So I communicated a lovely loving letter calling it off. Altho I had Anne write she has not shut her mind to the idea and if he has ideas all he has to do is write a one sentence note before he leaves for work, saying "please reconsider."

I was leaving the door open to Odysseus in case he woke up wanting to do it.

There was never a note, and Anne went out of her mind with relief that the house was just her, Beanie, Priscilla and Cupcake again.

OK now the $64,000 question. What about Odysseus,

what were his thoughts and feelings and decisions?

He was appalled at Bill's room. As Anne said in her email he didn't even see what those two windows offered him. That it is a little room in paradise. All he saw was the stuff, the mess, and the carpet.

All he saw was that he didn't want anything which was in the room to stay in the room.

Bill who worshipped Odysseus would have seen what Odysseus did not see.

Bill worshipped Odysseus, but did not realize his own mind is far more sensitive and higher. Also Bill is an artist. He would see that everything has to be taken out, he too would have liked the carpet to go, but he would have recognized it was a room in paradise.

Because of what that west window faced and what that southern window faced.

And of course Bill would never have acted like Odysseus. Odysseus' behavior is totally appropriate to a karate teacher, but not at all for someone invited to live for free in someone's home.

Bill is sensitive, considerate, and polite to a fault.

It never would have worked, Odysseus did not know how to tread lightly.

So Odysseus left not liking Bill's room one bit. And appalled by the bathroom. Bill had taken up the cracked linoleum and not had a chance to clean and paint the floor underneath. Which was stained black from the glue which had held the linoleum tiles.

It looked like a cave. It looked like small dark cave and Bill's stuff was still in it.

So from Odysseus' point of view the room which would be his was the last room in the world he would want, and that bathroom was just awful.

So if Anne was upset by Odysseus, Odysseus was upset by his room and by his bathroom.

Anne no longer wanted Odysseus as a roommate, and Odysseus no longer wanted his room and his bathroom.

And the mountain of work Odysseus had volunteered to take on for a room he didn't like and bathroom he didn't like, made him want out too.

So it was huge relief to Odysseus when Anne called it off. It would have been conflict for him, because the temptation of rent free is big temptation. But it was for something he didn't want.

So it was a favor to both of them when I called it off.

Now Anne's big question why did I suggest it if it

turned out not to be good idea for either of them?

And the answer to that is because at this point in their lives it clarified living conditions for both of them. Odysseus was leaving Caren's house because he wanted to, but Anne just found out from Jack (Caren's brother) that Odysseus was also going to get an eviction notice.

Odysseus could not change his mind about staying. He had to leave.

Odysseus will now look for just the room he wants and bathroom he wants and be so glad to pay rent for it.

Like Anne he feels he had a narrow escape.

And Anne had a big experience.

And there is nothing wrong with that either. Just because she did not enjoy her big experience and it rattled her day and night for few days, does not mean it did not offer Anne all the riches experience offers a being.

She is tremendously enriched by the experience as is Odysseus.

So I am satisfied I did everything right. Altho Anne may not see it that way.

And so all my darlings God bless you

All my love to all of you from Anne's Higher Self

October 29th

Ups and downs in learning how to drive in traffic

Friday early morning, I write email

Sent: Friday, October 28, 7 AM
Subject: I am having big hurdle trying to drive in traffic

I am still having my driving lessons. However I went back to formatting my book for publication and this book is giving me such a tough time because it is so much longer.

So driving lessons have been down to once a week on Sundays. Jim wants me to learn red lights and I want to learn to drive in town, so we have now had 3 lessons driving around town.

I drive on Columbus Road to my Y and back again. My Y is on Columbus Road so that is the route I would take.

So far it is not going well. If I don't start up immediately when light turns green the car behind me honks me. This flusters me, so motor goes off and it takes me 3 lights before I am organized to actually drive.

Plus I feel the pressure of the cars behind me who don't like it that I am going too slow to suit them. Columbus Road is two lane, they can't pass me.

Plus Jim wants me to change from first to second to third as I am driving. I don't understand why I have to do all these gear changes when next light is only a mile away and I have to be in First to start up when light is green again.

On Sunday I rebelled against changing gears but instead of calming me, that only made everything worse. I wound up completely unnerved by it all.

By the time I got home I lost all confidence and dread doing it again.

But there is no way to get out of driving in town, this is the purpose of learning to drive.

Love, Annie

Jim calls a few hours later

When Jim called soon after I had written my hopeless email, I exploded. I said everything I had kept bottled up for a whole week.

I said "I hate driving, I want to give up."

He said "I will pick you up right now, we will go back to Corona Road for *vind* in our face."

It was a brilliant solution. I am now in love with Corona Road and all the roads which branch off from it.

And I like being in the countryside. He did genius thing to have me drive straight to Swan Road so I would have no stress at all.

A long long empty road with no traffic because it ends in a dead end.

I was in heaven speeding along on it. Turns out I love speeding. It was the most beautiful day in the world.

There is no beauty to compare to our beauty when we are having the most beautiful day. Our flawless blue sky turns such a deep blue it is tinged with purple.

And the crystal clarity turns it into paradise.

All I cared about was driving and being happy driving again.

I had a rough week being demoralized about it.

But underneath the girl who really does want to learn how to drive, I am still me.

Which is why I was thrilled to see the 3 coyotes.

I was speeding along Swan for the second time when Jim said "look there are 3 coyotes!"

I instantly pulled over and stopped.

I am sure they are from the same litter because they were all so young, they looked about 6 months old. They were all climbing the high embankment and were too soon out of sight.

But the joy! The joy of 3 young coyotes out for fun together on a beautiful morning on the desert.

The next day Saturday

Good news

Email Saturday 11 AM
To Mary, Bill's sister in San Diego

Well good news

Last night (Friday night) at 10:40 pm, there was nothing on tv for me, it is all Halloween scary movies.

God said "Call Jim now, tell him you want to drive around town tomorrow morning."

"Do I have to drive around town tomorrow?"

"Yup, time to get back on the horse.

"You read those emails from your cousin Betty and from Harry.

"They all said the more you practice the easier it will get.

"So start tomorrow morning."

"But it is 10:30 at night won't Jim be asleep?"

"No he is watching zombie movies all night, he loves that."

So I called and said "I want to drive around town tomorrow."

"Great" he said. "We'll go early so there won't be much traffic."

First I had Jim drive me all the way out to Pima College East, because Jerry, the head lifeguard of all the pools said he taught his 3 daughters there, "the parking lot is perfect and then you can practice on that big road next to it" (I forget its name now.)

Jim drove us out there, but parking lot was filled, I guess Jerry took his daughters on early Sunday morning.

And the road next to it was filled with whizzing cars and only two lanes, nobody could pass me.

"Lets go back to town" I said, "we'll do Rosemont." Rosemont is small two lane road with lights.

Right near my house.

He drove to my house and parked across the street.

We changed seats.

I practiced the pedals. Yesterday he took me out to Corona Road so I could re-experience the joy of driving and get back my confidence.

But I mixed up the brake with the gas a few times. I kept going when I wanted to stop.

And it wouldn't go when I wanted it to go, because I was stepping on brake instead of gas.

So I ran thru all the gears and did pedals.

And then drove on my very own street to Rosemont.

* Turn onto Rosemont.

We came to the light on Speedway Boulevard.

Speedway red light is what kicked my ass the 3 previous times. That is when I got beeped at all 3 times for not starting up right away, got flustered and they had to wait 3 whole lights till I got it.

So naturally it was very suspenseful for me to arrive back at red light on Speedway.

But I was determined and I succeeded.

That sure built my confidence.

Then I turned on Pima Street, Jim said to do it.

It was great idea because Pima started off with extra lanes, if someone wanted to go faster than me they could pass me.

If they wanted to drive fast there was fast lane.

So naturally I was relaxed and confident.

And by the time it turned into two lanes, I was fine with that.

I was changing gears when Jim told me to, I was driving along fine.

No problemo!

I drove about 4 miles, the light was always green so Jim said step on it

And turned off before we reached Campbell Ave. which is huge major intersection

The neighborhood I turned into had stop sign every single tiny little block

Finally I just did "California stop," hahahaha.

And got back on Pima and drove home.

Beautifully!

Even into my own yard!!

Yes I did some booboo in my own neighborhood, truck was stretched across my own street and I couldn't start it up again.

But I knew there were so few cars and there was room to go around me, so no stress.

Jim popped it into first for me.

And I drove the extra block and into my yard.

"STOP!" he called out as I neared my house.

LOL I am sure I would have had the sense to hit the break myself once it was too close.

I am no longer the dumb dumb I was when I started all this.

Jim had not wanted me to stop driving when we

were back on Rosemont.

He said "let's do more."

But I figured I was so happy and had loved my lesson, let's stop before something stressful happens.

Tomorrow we will do it again.

So naturally I am the happiest girl in the world, and I now do believe if I keep practicing driving around town I will get it.

Jim is happy and pleased with me.

And it turned out he picked up another word in Yiddish from yesterday's lesson. When I was driving too fast in countryside on Corona Road and made my turn onto Swan and forgot to break for a turn

"Oy gevalt!" I kept saying "Oy gevalt! Oy gevalt," as I was whizzing into my turn and couldn't control the car.

I must have said it 8 times until I got sorted out.

"Oy gevalt" Jim said when he picked me up this morning.

I was so proud of him. Hahaha he is learning Yiddish the same way I did.

He even must have heard me say "Oy vey!" on occasion

"Oy vey" he said as we were first driving to Pima College East.

Because Jim speaks fluent Spanish I had been so looking forward to learning Spanish from him.

But the opposite has happened, because of my driving lessons, Jim is picking up Yiddish from me the same way that Bill did.

Altho Bill knew words in Yiddish I don't even remember using. When he was playing with our dog Happy, he would call Happy "my little knadela."

Knadela happens to mean matzah ball. When my grandmother made matzah ball soup, she put in the knadelas, the matzah balls.

Wherever did Bill pick that up and use it for an endearment for Happy.

It gave me so much joy to hear Bill calling Happy "my little knadela."

I love you

Annie

The end
Tucson Arizona
November 2, 2011

Thank you to my wonderful driving instructor
You did great!

So dear reader, Let life always come up roses for you and blues skies for you always.

I love you

Anne

Anne is off for new adventures....

Post script

I mail Jimmy's book of poems to my big cousin Carl in San Francisco here is the letter I wrote with it

Dear Carl and Betty,

Jimmy and I met walking our dogs in Tompkins Square Park on the Lower East Side. Because he was social worker for the Department of Social Services in NYC then (he did this whole life) mostly we weren't at the park at the same time. He walked Dandi before and after work. I was a writer and slept till noon.

I became close to Jimmy instantly. Mostly I got to talk to Jimmy on the weekends, when he would arrive when I was there and on the Jewish holidays and on holidays.

But because his clients are all in our neighborhood he had his lunch at B & H (the Jewish dairy luncheonette in our neighborhood). I would go there for breakfast and bump into him there.

And when I took my dog out in the evening, I would walk out of my apartment building on First Avenue, and there was Jimmy coming home with Dandi (his dog).

So me and Clio (my dog) would walk with him to Houston Street and I would chat my head off to him.

As his friend Stewart said about him (they were friends since 9 years old) "He was a quiet lad. And he still is."

My whole memory of my time talking with Jimmy back in NYC is me talking my head off to him.

But he is a very responsive listener. He only had one or two comments on the stuff I said but I remember them. He always understood and was on the same wavelength with me. I guess this is why I was always overjoyed to bump into Jimmy.

My life in Tucson is so quiet and so empty compared to my NYC life, that I have the time and quiet to notice and remember all kinds of things which got lost in the shuffle in NYC.

I remembered that once when I bumped into Jimmy at B & H when he was having his lunch, he mentioned when his father went to heaven he wrote a poem that he came back as a red geranium.

I mailed him my own books last year, that is when I discovered he is no longer on Ludlow Street and has moved to Margaretville in upstate NY.

After he wrote me back a letter snail mail, he is not on computer, I remembered the words "I wrote poem he came back as a red geranium." And it hit me "maybe Jimmy is a poet."

So when I wrote back to him snail mail I asked "Are you a poet, can you send me some of your poems."

And with his next snail mail letter was an envelope with 20 poems. The one on top was his long narrative about the Sixties (the one I put in my women's lib book) and instantly I went apeshit. I knew it was the greatest poem I ever read. And then the next one *Elsie talk,* again I jumped out of my skin, it is a great poem.

I instantly brought the whole sheaf of poems to Bill. I

said "my friend Jimmy from NYC sent me these, please do me the favor of reading them. I really like them. If you like them too please do me the favor and choose up to 10 and I will publish them in my next book."

And then I went in with my doggie to watch tv, and it fell out of my mind, till I looked up and there at the doorway was Bill. He looked excited. He had a big smile on his face and his eyes were lit up.

"I chose 11!" he said.

And I went crazy with joy. I was overjoyed he read them, overjoyed he loved them. Had liked them so much when I said "choose up to 10," he had chosen 11.

Instantly I called Jimmy on the phone, told him how much I loved his poems, how much Bill liked them, how Bill had chosen 11 when I said you can chose up to 10, and asked him if I could include them in my next book.

Jimmy was overjoyed. The poems were on typewritten sheets in his drawer all these years.

It is a long story of how it went from me planning to put 11 of his poems in my new book, to offering to do a whole book of his poems for him, to his friend Stewart (from childhood) taking over the mountain of labor which self publishing is.

Stewart finally accomplished it. I asked Jimmy for 20 copies so I could mail them to our mutual friends from Tompkins Square Park in NYC, and give copies to my cousins and friends.

He is so overjoyed to have his poems in a book out there in the world and no longer in a drawer in his desk, it was his joy to send me the 20 copies.

And he told me he put me and Bill on his thank you page. And sure enough it is there. Which does make me very happy.

The book was just published and my copies arrived. And so here is one for you.

Love and kisses,

Annie

Book is **Cracks in the Concrete** *by James Goldiner*

An open letter to anyone who wants to write or even dreams of doing it

Go for it!
Writing is easy and fun
Here is my experience

November is National Write a Novel in a Month and a month before November '08, my friend Lisa in Tucson told me about it, and suggested I do it. But I was used to writing short stories and posting them on my Blog (the stories are mostly about my yesterday)— I never wrote a novel and didn't know how.

So I just wrote polite thank you back to Lisa.

But thank God she pushed me. Because when November 3rd rolled around, I decided to give it a try. And to my big surprise, I loved doing it.

I just went to my machine when I woke up with cup of coffee and pack of cigarettes, and wrote for 45 minutes each morning for 3 straight weeks. I still spent my afternoons and evenings posting on current events forum.

I was doing it for a week when Lisa encouraged me to register at the site (NANO) (it is free) and then I received their pep-talk emails, which they sent out to everyone.

Lisa was doing it too, even tho she had never written in her life, she is a painter.

But this is a great way for anyone who has ever dreamed of being a writer to do it. Every November there is another one. I hope you consider doing it too. All you have to do is write for 45 minutes each day for month of November. No editing! No re-writing!

You can begin by telling about your yesterday too, but after you have done that several times, start to write a story which is long enough to hold your interest to keep telling it for a while.

(Telling a story means "and then" "and then" "and then." First this happened, then that happened, then that happened, then that happened.)

This will give you experience in narrative (telling a story) and there is very good chance that in the middle you will "find your own voice."

This means right in the middle of telling your story, suddenly you hear a voice in your head dictating a different story.

This one is about your earliest childhood, it is all things you have forgotten, and the voice is different, it is in the first person (even if you have been writing in 3rd person) and it is very personal. And you will love it!

If this happens, immediately stop writing what you were writing, and instead start writing everything you are hearing.

This is called "finding your own voice" as a writer, it makes writing so easy and fun, you just take down what it says— or as they say "you get out of the way, and the story writes itself."

That is the way I became a writer back in NYC. I was in my late 20s then and had just been fired from my job. Bill was working as Wall Street messenger then for $96/week. He said "why don't you become a writer, I will support you." I thought it was a great idea, I decided to do it.

So I wrote three tiny 2 page stories about my yesterday and then sat down to write long story, I wrote it in 3rd person and it was about a love affair before I met my husband. That topic interested me enough to keep telling the story.

But right in the middle of it, I was a few weeks into it, I heard that voice dictating a whole other story. It was my littlest little girl experiences.

It is the same as learning how to balance on a bicycle.

One day they are supporting you, and you are pedaling, and then suddenly out of nowhere, you balance. You can ride a bike.

You never thought it would happen to you, even tho you watched all your friends do it, because it looks like magic.

It is the same way with writing. You push yourself along telling a story, and then suddenly you balance. You hear that voice and simply take down what it says. The story writes itself, you get out of the way.

But you can only learn how to balance on a bike when you are on a bike, and you can only hear your own voice, while you are at the machine writing. But it is as natural and effortless as learning how to balance on a bike. It comes to all.

Guess what! CreateSpace owned by Amazon publishes any book written by anyone for free, but you have to do all the work yourself. No one even reads it.

You have to format it for a paperback book, all they do is press a button to print and bind it, and post it for sale on Amazon.

When I saw the technical work involved in formatting my novel into a paperback book I was terrified. I didn't even know what they were talking about or how to do any of it.

But I was too deep into it to quit. I wanted to publish my novel now, I didn't just want it lost on my computer.

It turns out CreateSpace has community boards. And there are angels on it (people who have published lots and lots of books, are completely experienced) and they walk us newbies thru everything. Ones even less experienced than me, they wrote their book and don't even know how to indent a paragraph or what a tab is or how to edit.

It turned out everything which seemed impossibly hard when I first heard about it, is not hard, you just press a button in your word processing program.

But of course I needed to learn from the community boards which button? where? things like that. They have the patience of saints there and love to help.

I tell you all this because it is God's gift to writers. That we can publish ourselves. CreateSpace also does videos, and music, photography books, art books, comic books.

Lulu does this too. It was first started by Lulu.com. Everyone at CreateSpace started there. Both places are wonderful and many publish at both places. Both Lulu and CreateSpace are free, they publish your book for free and post it on Amazon. A gift from Heaven to all artists.

I tell you all this to encourage you to go for it! If I could do it anyone can. Before I began writing I was convinced I didn't have a creative bone in my body.

I had always loved writing book reports and compositions for school, and always loved writing letters. But I was never artistic in anyway.

Because it turns out it is all there under the surface for everyone. But you have to be willing to give it a whirl for it to emerge. There is no such thing as talent. It is only when you are actually doing it, that interesting and surprising things happen.

Writing is a big treat you give yourself, because it is way to get to know yourself.

It is never too late to start. Whenever you do is the perfect time. And there is nothing to compare with the freshness of your early beginning.

So think of starting writing, as like the beginning of Spring. Later you will develop more skills, but there is nothing like the beginning. When all the miracles, freshness and inspiration happen.

I wish you luck on your enterprise!

I love you, Anne

Other books by Anne Wilensky

Haiku Helen Press

Novels

Ruthie Has a New Love, a novel

Girl Blog From Tucson, a novel of sorts

MORE Girl Blog From Tucson

History

Not what you'd expect
   How the women's liberation movement
   started
   My personal experience of it
Published June 26, 2011

Soon to be published
   A New Experience, a novel
